Radiant Lyre

Radiant Lyre

Essays on Lyric Poetry

Edited by

DAVID BAKER AND ANN TOWNSEND

Graywolf Press

SAINT PAUL, MINNESOTA

Publication of this volume is made possible in part by a grant provided by
the Minnesota State Arts Board, through an appropriation by the Minnesota State Legislature; a grant from the Wells Fargo Foundation Minnesota;
and a grant from the National Endowment for the Arts, which believes that
a great nation deserves great art. Significant support has also been provided
by the Bush Foundation; Target; the McKnight Foundation; and other
generous contributions from foundations, corporations, and individuals. To
these organizations and individuals we offer our heartfelt thanks.

MINNESOTA
STATE ARTS BOARD

NATIONAL
ENDOWMENT
FOR THE ARTS

TARGET.

Published by Graywolf Press
2402 University Avenue, Suite 203
Saint Paul, Minnesota 55114

www.graywolfpress.org

Published in the United States of America
Printed in Canada

ISBN-13: 978-1-55597-460-2
ISBN-10: 1-55597-460-0

2 4 6 8 9 7 5 3 1
First Graywolf Printing, 2007

Library of Congress Control Number: 2006929501

Cover art: Jeenee Lee Design
Photograph courtesy of Marjorie and David Davidson

Permission Acknowledgments

We gratefully acknowledge the cooperation of authors, translators, publishers, and agents for their permission to reprint works in *Radiant Lyre*. In some cases, all best efforts were made to obtain permission to reprint.

"Ode" by Elizabeth Alexander copyright © 1990 by the Rector and Visitors of the University of Virginia. Reprinted from *The Venus Hottentot* by Elizabeth Alexander, published by Graywolf Press, Saint Paul, Minnesota.

Dream Song #382 "At Henry's bier" from *The Dream Songs* by John Berryman. Copyright © 1969 by John Berryman. Copyright renewed 1997 by Kate Donahue Berryman. Reprinted by permission of Farrar, Straus and Giroux, LLC.

"Women" from *The Blue Estuaries* by Louise Bogan. Copyright © 1968 by Louise Bogan. Copyright renewed 1996 by Ruth Limmer. Reprinted by permission of Farrar, Straus and Giroux, LLC.

Sappho "fragment 31," translated by Anne Carson, from *If Not, Winter*, copyright © 2002 by Anne Carson. Used by permission of Alfred A. Knopf, a division of Random House, Inc.

Sappho ("Aphrodite dressed in an embroidery . . .") translated by Guy Davenport, from *7 Greeks*, copyright ©1995 by Guy Davenport. Reprinted by permission of New Directions Publishing Corp.

Ode III.13 "To the Bandusian Fountain" from *The Odes of Horace* translated by David Ferry. Translation copyright © 1997 by David Ferry. Reprinted by permission of Farrar, Straus and Giroux, LLC.

Brenda Hillman. "C ode" from *Loose Sugar*, copyright ©1997 by Brenda Hillman and reprinted by permission of Wesleyan University Press.

"Ode to the Maggot" from *Talking Dirty to the Gods* by Yusef Komunyakaa. Copyright © 2000 by Yusef Komunyakaa. Reprinted by permission of Farrar, Straus and Giroux, LLC.

yes! radiant lyre speak to me
become a voice

SAPPHO

Contents

Introduction   xi

I. Lyric Modes

1. The Elegy

David Baker, "Elegy and Eros: Configuring Grief"   5

Richard Jackson, "'One's Own Sad Stead':
    American Elegy as Self-Elegy"   20

Stanley Plumly, "Elegiac"   31

2. The Love Poem

Linda Gregerson, "Rhetorical Contract in the Erotic Poem"   39

Ann Townsend, "Meretricious Kisses"   56

Richard Jackson, "Eros and the Erotics of Writing"   66

3. The Ode

Carl Phillips, "The Ode"   89

Stanley Plumly, "Between Things: On the Ode"   113

Linda Gregerson, "Ode and Empire"   117

II. Lyric Means

1. *On the Pastoral: The Problem of Nature*

David Baker, "The Pastoral: First and Last Things"   133

Eric Pankey, "Meditative Spaces"   142

Stanley Plumly, "Pastoral Matters"   148

Ann Townsend, "Arcadia Redux"   155

2. *On the Sublime: The Problem of Beauty*

David Baker, "The Sublime: Origins and Definitions"   167

Linda Gregerson, "The Gay Sublime"   175

Stanley Plumly, "The Intimate Sublime"   183

Ann Townsend, "The Technological Sublime"   188

3. *On Meditation and Mediation: The Problem of People*

David Baker, "'I'm Nobody': Lyric Poetry and
the Problem of People"   197

Linda Gregerson, "Life among Others"   206

Stanley Plumly, "A Place for People in Lyric Poetry"   219

Ann Townsend, "A Mind for Metaphors"   225

4. *On Subject, Story, and Style: The Problem of Time*

David Baker, "To Think of Time"   235

Linda Gregerson, "Mortal Time"   247

Stanley Plumly, "Lyric Time"   264

Ann Townsend, "All the Instruments Agree:
Taking Time's Measure"   269

Introduction

The essays in *Radiant Lyre* are written by long-time practitioners of the art of poetry and form a comprehensive seminar on the lyric, poetry's most popular and enduring mode and means of expression. Lyric poetry's beauty stems in part from its interiority and its compression; it represents the mind at its most focused and direct. Yet lyric poetry is also highly connective, clarifying, and enlightening to audiences across the gulf of years.

Knowing the means and methods of lyric poetry is important for all poets and readers of poetry because the lyric genre is the rootstock from which so many subsequent hybrids emerge. A poem never merely takes on a single form. It exists always within a complex matrix. That is to say, every poem is a formal poem. Its linear and metrical form (is it iambic? syllabic? end-stopped?) operates in tandem and tension with its whole or inherited form (is it a sonnet?), which in turn operate alongside its stylistic form (is it in plain style? heavily conceited?), and these coexist with its syntactical form.

If a poem's linear and bodily forms provide its apparent exterior, then its rhetorical form—the structure of its story, the shape of its argument—provides its interior. Why, when we grieve, do we turn to particular landscapes for our setting? How does time underwrite every other subject in a lyric poem? How stories and songs proceed, through what kinds of evolutions—these are fundamental issues of form and identity. Ralph Waldo Emerson touches this point when he reminds us that "it is not meters, but a meter-making argument that makes a poem...." Such is our focus in *Radiant Lyre*.

One of the deepest pleasures for the artist is that of "free play" or discovery, that sense of adventure as we follow a process. Whether poetry arises from attention to technique and form, or from inspired guesswork, poems arrive at ends that may not be planned or bidden. We write poetry to find out what our poetry is like. And we cringe at the coercion of public rhetoric in so many of its forms, in advertising, political discourse, for instance, or military and corporate doublespeak. But we know poetry itself is not immune from rhetoric.

Indeed, poets have long been fascinated by this relationship. "We make out of the quarrel with others, rhetoric," W. B. Yeats wrote in 1918; "but of the quarrel with ourselves, poetry." Here Yeats identifies a focal divide between public and private utterance. To speak in public, to make rhetoric, feeds our need to persuade others of a position we have already staked out and hope to promulgate. To sing in private, to make poetry, requires more faith in discovery as we proceed. An even stricter dichotomy comes from Immanuel Kant in 1790 in *Critique of Judgment:* "The [separate] arts of speech are *rhetoric* and *poetry. Rhetoric* is the art of carrying on a serious business of the understanding as if it were a free play of imagination; *poetry*, the art of conducting a free play of the imagination as if it were a serious business of the understanding."

We hold here that, whatever its audience and purpose, lyric poetry is itself a kind of persuasion. Helen Vendler asserts in *Invisible Listeners:* "In its usual form, the lyric offers us the representation of a single voice, alone." But she further observes that even such lyric poems "offer us . . . tones of voice through which they represent, by analogy, various relations resembling those that we know in life." That is, our poems may hope to persuade us of something in our solitary minds. Or they may hope to convince a readership that something is beautiful, or necessary, or critically wrong, as in the rhetorical suppositions of John Keats's "Ode on a Grecian Urn," Robert Frost's "Mending Wall," and Allen Ginsberg's "Howl." Poetry is more than the sum of its facts, more than social or ideological vehicle, more than data or distilled information. Critic Daniel Tiffany makes the point powerfully: "Only a fool reads poetry for facts."

❧ ☙

In 2000 we assembled a group of poet-critics to present a panel on lyric poetry, moderated by Patricia Clark, for the Associated Writing Programs convention in Denver. In the years since, our group has explored further modes and issues of the lyric poem, beginning with the elegy, the erotic, and the ode, then moving to other shaping strategies essential to understanding the evolution of lyric poetry. We offer *Radiant Lyre* as a symposium on historical and contemporary versions of the lyric poem in the Western tradition. Each contributor to this book is a devoted poet, teacher, and critic;

each brings wide general experience as well as the special fields of his or her scholarly expertise to the conversation.

The lyric poem has evolved, over millennia, out of chants and charms, prayers and curses, ceremonies and songs. Part I of *Radiant Lyre* presents our study of three original or ur-forms of lyric poetry, a triad of modes from which most lyrics have subsequently developed. These are the elegy, the erotic or love poem, and the ode. We hold that these modes represent the soul, the heart, and the mind of the lyric impulse.

Of these three modes, the *elegy* has evolved the most dramatically from one function to another. We recognize the elegy as a poem of mourning and lamentation, a form of articulate, ritualized weeping over the loss of someone loved by or important to the poet. That has been its lyric purpose for millennia, and that is the focus of our present conversation. Still we note that in its original applications, in Greek and early Latin poetry, an elegy designated *not* a subject matter or occasion—the death of someone dear—but rather a technical requirement. An elegy was a poem composed in couplets of alternating lines of quantitative dactylic hexameter (the meter of epic) and dactylic pentameter; and its subjects might range from love to political advice to ceremonial celebration. Only slowly did the metrical form evolve into the rhetorical form we know now.

The modal qualities of the elegy offer essential lessons for writing and reading all poetry. A poem, language, even a single word, can never be the thing it represents. Thus the elegy recreates the loss inherent in all poetry, all language; it expresses the desire to replace what has been lost with a symbol, an image, a word for what is already bygone. As Robert Hass famously writes (in hexameter, no less), "a word is elegy to what it signifies." This is the mode of grief.

Like the elegy, the *love poem* or *erotic poem* is highly personal, intimate. This is the mode of rapture, of the heart—ecstasy, perhaps, rather than mourning. But like the elegy, the erotic love poem slips from one identity to another. In *Love, Sex & Tragedy*, Simon Goldhill points to this distinction between the love poem and the erotic: ". . . *eros* is not like 'love' in a Romantic or Christian sense. In a sexual context, it is most often described as a sickness, a burning and destructive fire." Yet the Western love poem is voiced in praise and self-control. Eros destroys while love builds. Sappho is an erotic poet; Elizabeth Barrett Browning is a love poet. These essays investigate the creative tension between desire and loss, between pleasure and pain.

If the elegy and love poem are intimate forms, if their dynamic typically involves the interplay between two people—the poet and the lost, or the poet and the beloved—then the *ode* represents lyric poetry in its social and elevated public mode. Pindar's early Greek odes feature a general speaker, hardly a person at all but rather the voice of the community who sings of ritual celebrations, races, festivals, and feats. Horace's odes, clearly more individual, still exploit the heightened drama of social discourse. The ode tends to be made of denser architecture than the love poem or elegy. The ode's triadic rhetorical structure—the strophe, antistrophe, and epode— provides a means for problem solving and for moral counsel. Its three-part logic leads not only to the Elizabethan sonnet, but perhaps more widely to the three stages within legal procedure, the Protestant hymn and sermon, perhaps even Freudian psychology. The ode serves both as the lyric poem's social face and its oldest mode for complex thinking.

Part II of *Radiant Lyre* investigates four further categories of lyric poetry. Here we consider not rhetorical modes but rather circumstances, land-scapes, and "problems": the *means* by which the lyric modes are achieved or addressed. Typically the lyric establishes an ideal, a wish, and then proceeds to critique or argue with its own untenable or unfulfillable desire. We ask why the lyric so often makes particular gestures, regardless of the mode at hand.

By focusing on the *pastoral* in this part's first section, we call up the oldest means of addressing nature in lyric poetry. Here we regard our shared home, the green world, and discuss a number of pastoral categories—the georgic, bucolic, eclogue among them. We trace the pastoral from its original Arcadian paradise to the contemporary field. Ironic, co-opted, limited, still the pastoral today continues to "remind us of its origins in ecstatic encounters."

Our next section intensifies the issue of nature. The *sublime* serves as a trope of nature heightened, elevated, in asking us to face the terror of beauty. We look at the origins of the sublime, consider how poets grasp or decline to grasp the sublime impulse, and identify the chaos and destruc-tion that the sublime stance impels. Here we probe the collision of the an-cient sublime with the contemporary environment of the "diminished" or belated vista.

A traditional definition of the lyric poem holds, at least in part, that it functions to identify and probe the perceptions of the self; that it is, liter-ally, a song of that self. Its audience of readers or auditors thereby operates as a field of bystanders, who may or may not identify with that self or that self's perceptions, but who—one way or the other—serve as viewers, as voyeurs, as unvoiced onlookers. So what is the place or problem of *people* in this highly intimate art form? Our sixth section, "On Meditation and Mediation," untangles some of the lyric poem's history as private song and suggests ways by which it has always been a vital social vehicle as well as a necessary voice for that imperiled persona of the self.

Our last section considers perhaps the most abiding subject of all lyric poetry: *time*. It is conventional to look to lyric poetry for immunity from the damages or corruptions of time, to "step out of time" into the lyric's still space. Once again we encounter the irony embedded in lyric poetry's desire. Just as the hope for solitude enables our social cohesion, so is our desire for timelessness articulated only through temporal gestures. Poetry is literally made of time, and so we discuss the tools we use when we attempt to track or keep time in poetry.

Each contributor to this book brings to these pages not only special area knowledge but also a distinct writerly personality. So a reader of David Baker's essays will find a voice that is confident and firm; Baker's essays are foundational, concerned with clarity of definition. He sets out the origins and terms for many of the discussions that follow, focusing often on the earliest of poetries. When you read his essays, you will know where to stand. Stanley Plumly's expertise lies in the Romantic poets. He reads Keats like a skilled lover reads the body of his beloved. Plumly's essays are meditative and empathetic, attentive to the grand and the small in equal measure. Just as he compels his own poems toward this sympathetic rigor, so do his essays render large ideas on a human scale. Linda Gregerson's knowledge of the Renaissance, its wit, its theater, and its political expediencies, informs both the tone and subject of her essays. She ranges widely in subject, from Isabella Whitney's social critiques to Mark Doty's contemporary "gay sublime." Quick, honed, and brilliant, Linda's prose dazzles like a prism held to the light. Ann Townsend's essays are intimate and playful, athletic in their maneuvers. She writes most often about contemporary poets, pondering how we writers stay connected to our sources even as we question and alter their original strategies. Carl Phillips, Eric Pankey, and Richard Jackson make significant contributions to the collection. Jackson's knowledge of Eastern European poetry and poetics enhances his reading of the American lyric, while Pankey's sympathetic intelligence opens a door into the pastoral;

Phillips's encyclopedic knowledge of the ode demonstrates the kind of lucid mastery each of these poets brings to their art and their criticism. The contributors of this collection come out of different literary traditions, but all of us have developed substantial knowledge both of poetry's history as well as of its changing face.

Radiant Lyre is a book about lyric poetry, meant to serve as a useful guide or goad in many venues, from public classroom to private desk. We hope this study will serve the various needs of teachers, students, scholars, poets, and the many others interested in the art and history of poetry. For us, awareness of lyric forms leads to a sense of mastery and pleasure, the pleasure of recognition. A poem holds meaning for us in its wording, its individual narrative, and also in the lineage of its design and rhetoric. The first line of *The Waste Land* ("April is the cruelest month") is deepened by our memory of Walt Whitman's prior April elegy, "When Lilacs Last in the Dooryard Bloom'd," which itself recalls Geoffrey Chaucer's opening to the *Canterbury Tales,* "Whan that Aprill...." As Harold Bloom formulates, "Literary thinking relies upon literary memory." A poem means something because of previous poems.

Poets can make more fruitful and complex decisions about their poems when they place their work within—and without—certain poetic conventions or gestures. Readers can savor the richness of lyric poetry more fully when they have a broad context for any single poem. Critics and scholars can examine the lineage of poetry's forms and a poet's inclinations, and students can trace the evolution of poetry through history into the present. We invite all of these readers to follow the passions of lyric poetry in *Radiant Lyre.*

David Baker and Ann Townsend

I. lyric means

1. The Elegy

> By duty bound and not by custom led
> To celebrate the praises of the dead ...
>
> ANNE BRADSTREET

Elegy and Eros: Configuring Grief

The issue is not just that we grieve, nor when we grieve. The issue is not just why we grieve in poetry, nor how the beautiful song of poetry capitulates to or conspires with the task of weeping. These and more. I like to think of the sound of weeping, along with the sound of laughing, as among the first thoughtful articulations a human being ever made. More than growls or grunts, more than snarls or barks or howls, weeping and laughter indicate passional responses to experience, to a perception of circumstances not only in the present but in the past and—even more fascinating—the future. Nothing else cries or laughs the way we do. These two primary forms of vocalization evolve further into song: ecstatic language, as it were, standing beside itself, speaking out of its head. It is no accident that the two fundamental modes of lyric poetry are precisely these, crying and laughing, the intonations of grief and pleasure. By this I mean, the elegy and the love poem.

I want to consider the configuration of the elegy, with two particular examples from the American nineteenth century. At hand is the problematic of Walt Whitman's great poem, "When Lilacs Last in the Dooryard Bloom'd." I want first to remind us of the complex narrative structure of Whitman's poem for his beloved deceased, and to unpack the poem's dense sets of images, stories, locations, and most important, its figures. As I intend the term, a figure is not just a body, a human figure; and not just a trope or metaphor, a figure of speech; but also a number, a mathematical figure. Next, I will relate this poem to another central nineteenth-century American elegy, Emily Dickinson's "Because I could not stop for Death." Finally I will propose a paradigm shift in our thinking, and reading, about the American elegy.

❧

Strange things are afoot. A foot in Whitman's poetry is a different body part than in other poets' work. Whose body is before us in Whitman's lilac elegy? The literal circumstance of Whitman's great poem is the funeral procession following Abraham Lincoln's assassination and death on April 14, 1865. Good Friday indeed. Whitman's poem accompanies the death-train that slowly bore Lincoln's body from Washington, D.C., all the way to burial in Illinois. At least in its beginning, the poem abides by a conventional, ritualized manner of mourning. Surely this poem is forefather of *The Waste Land*, commencing as it does in April, the cruel month, and proceeding in a series of aggrieved stages, through the city, into nature, into death, toward something sounding like prayerful redemption. As Peter Sacks argues in *The English Elegy*, the performance of ritual—the mournful, often staid formulation of grieving—is an elegy's primary rhetorical gesture.

Whitman's lilac elegy begins just so:

> 1.
>
> When lilacs last in the dooryard bloom'd,
> And the great star early droop'd in the western sky in the night,
> I mourn'd, and yet shall mourn with ever-returning spring.
>
> Ever-returning spring, trinity sure to me you bring,
> Lilac blooming perennial and drooping star in the west,
> And thought of him I love.
>
> 2.
>
> O powerful western fallen star!
> O shades of night—O moody, tearful night!
> O great star disappear'd—O the black murk that hides the star!
> O cruel hands that hold me powerless—O helpless soul of me!
> O harsh surrounding cloud that will not free my soul.

In these first sections we hear a sober, then almost quietly sobbing voice of the poem, in radical contrast to Whitman's usually hortatory and encouraging profusions. This is, remember, the ur-poet of exuberance, cheerleader for democracy, the electrically charged poet of erotic contact and corporal intelligence. But note in section 1 the restraint, the underspoken dignity, as well as the formalized introduction of the poem's primary tropes, the triple image-into-symbol or, as he says, the "trinity sure to me you bring" that accompanies the poet's imagination through the odyssey of this poem. This trinity will evolve, eventually becoming the western star, or the planet Venus, which serves as a figure for Lincoln; the fragrant, plentiful, natural emblem of lilac; and, as a stand-in for Whitman, that hermit thrush with its doleful song. The particular curse of spring's eternal rebirth here, its immeasurable irony, lies in its perpetuating *mementi mori*, its blooming reminders of death. That is T. S. Eliot's terror in *The Waste Land*, and Whitman's, who not only mourns, but *"yet shall mourn* with ever-returning spring [italics mine]." But why Venus, the goddess of love, in an elegy? Why lilac? Why, for that matter, Lincoln?

Section 2 sounds the poem's death knell and identifies the crisis at hand: how to face "the black murk that hides the star," how to accept that Death has taken the new democratic hero. Juxtaposed with the stasis of this seemingly insoluble problem is section 3, the "miracle" of the natural trope, a lilac growing by an old farmhouse with its human "heart-shaped" leaves and its perfume. In the odor of lilac—is there anything so sweet, so profuse?—lingers a touch of the poem's subversive power. Psychologists tell us the sense of smell is our most nostalgic sense, the one most capable of triggering memory. It is also our least articulable sense. That is, we have far fewer words to describe smell than any other sense. Another irony then: such bodily knowledge yet such intellectual stupor. But of course this is the romantic's ideal formulation.

Section 4 activates another sense, the sound of the solitary thrush's song calling from deep within nature's heart, from "the swamp," a place not quite water or land, or perhaps more meaningfully for Whitman a primordial place of *both* water and land. This solitary singer seems a strange figure for Whitman, usually so gregarious, hungry to situate himself among others and sing "over the roofs of the world," as he says in "Song of Myself." But again, so much about the lilac elegy is atypical. Whitman is not by any means an elegiac poet. Grief, sadness, pessimism are not the keys in which he typically plays. He is so energetically urban and hopeful, so enlivened by the prospect of crowds and bodily contact. But this will be one of the central trajectories of the poem: to move away from the city into the solitary, inhuman woods, in order to find his voice and regain his poetic vocation. The song he hears—always a necessary intonation in an elegy—is "death's outlet song," and the singer, the bird, is literally his "brother." Notice the increasing archaic formality at the end of this section. "If thou wast not granted to sing thou would'st surely die" takes its diction from Quaker idiom. Whitman's mother was a devout Quaker, we may remember.

Sections 5 and 6 find Whitman propelling his poem forward, making it move, as the train moves. Elegies rarely have momentum, preferring the mournful deportment of stasis, stillness. Here the natural images seem battle-scarred (the Civil War blue and gray of violets and debris, the "spears" of wheat and grain-"shrouds"), but also potentially healing as the world "springs back" to life. The gathered crowd of people in section 6 abide by Sacks's elegiac formula, becoming a country-wide funeral mass, listening to the poem's song, here still a "dirge." Notice at the end of this section how Whitman transplants the sprig of lilac that he broke off at the end of section 3 into the coffin of the president.

Section 7 continues the gestures of enlargement and forward motion: "With loaded arms I come, pouring for you." Echoing the dark confessions of "Crossing Brooklyn Ferry"—which he first published in the great 1860 edition of *Leaves of Grass* as "The Sun-Down Poem" (note the westward-facing gesture)—where Whitman's desire for intimacy and human-sameness finds him admitting that not "you alone" are weak or blank or susceptible to pain, here the figure of the dead hero first becomes a trope for all the dead of the war: a figure, in fact, for Death itself, "O sane and sacred death." The "you" of the poem evolves, swelling past them all, to the very thought of death: "For you and the coffins all of you O death." Then in a gesture of quiet but fertile abundance, he hastens to cover death all "over" with bouquets of roses, lilies, and as he says, "mostly" lilacs. He seeks not just to adorn the coffin but literally to bury death.

An aside about all these flowers. I mentioned earlier the immense, lush fragrance of the lilac. Why this flower, apart from its springtime significance? Imagine the body of Lincoln traveling, so slowly, for days and days across the country. Imagine the potential smell. We know that people heaped flowers on the railcar as it passed or as it stopped. They are paying tribute, but they are also covering the stench. Thus, for Whitman, the lilac provides a powerful aroma, not just a "scented . . . remembrancer" but a natural air freshener, making the very air new.

Whitman slows his momentum in section 8, at this point where he begins to discover his vision of transcendence. To be reborn, first he must die, or at least descend to an underworld. He calls it "the netherward black of the night." Thus Whitman's scheme for the elegy enlarges to include an epic trope. He himself walks into a dark wood, his Virgil the star, and commences his own journey to death. This is one of my central points: not just Lincoln, but also Whitman must die in this poem. His elegy, like his great song of himself, is ultimately a self-elegy. He asks for strength and direction in section 9, "lingering" in spiritual limbo in the swamp. He listens to the thrush; he begs for it to "Sing on." Like the bird, Whitman yearns to sing; it is his natural demeanor. But of course the second crisis of the poem is that the death of Lincoln has stifled or murdered Whitman's ability to sing and to praise. Such is the point of his awful doubts in section 10:

O how shall I warble myself for the dead one there I loved?
And how shall I deck my song for the large sweet soul that has gone?
And what shall my perfume be for the grave of him I love?

Sea-winds blown from east and west,
Blown from the Eastern sea and blown from the Western sea, till there on
    the prairies meeting,
These and with these and the breath of my chant,
I'll perfume the grave of him I love.

These first three questions serve to ask how Whitman himself might assume the qualities of the poem's eternal constants—the star, the lilac, the thrush. How, he asks, can he "warble," how can he shine, what shall be his perfume? Immediately nature answers. Carried on the world's winds, a breath of inspiration floats to him from around the globe. He breathes-in (*spiro* is Latin for "I breathe," we might recall) the breath of the world and knows now that his simple *expiration* will *be* his song. To expire exercises both of its meanings: to breathe out and to die.

Section 11 also proceeds by question and answer. That is, for a time he has suspended his impulse for literal propulsion—for movement, for change—in order to impel the poem by purely rhetorical means. Having found his breath, Whitman beseeches the subject for his song's exhalation:

O what shall I hang on the chamber walls?
And what shall the pictures be that I hang on the walls,
To adorn the burial-house of him I love?

Pictures of growing spring and farms and homes,
With the Fourth-month eve at sundown, and the gray smoke lucid
and bright,
With floods of the yellow gold of the gorgeous, indolent, sinking sun,
burning, expanding the air,
With the fresh sweet herbage under foot, and the pale green leaves
of the trees prolific . . .

He's preparing to reinvigorate the movement of his vision. But with what materials, he asks, can he refute death? The answer is: with life, with the body, the charged sensations of the natural, mundane, and eternal world. This world is—in both biological and writerly terms—prolific.

In this section and the next two, Whitman's tone changes, as though gathering new energy. He identifies and enacts his discovered subject, the "miracle" of daily life and the resulting new "song" borne "out of the cedars and pines." Whitman now can read the song of his brother, the dull "gray-brown" bird, for the song has become a "loud human" one. Has the bird become human, or has Whitman become something other-than-human? Rarely in traditional elegies do the speakers' identities themselves evolve.

So we arrive at the center of the poem, the critical section 14, wherein resides the song itself. This song seems like a force of nature, a powerful emanation. Here the cloud of death with its train-like "long black trail" has enveloped the whole world, and it is from this darkness that Whitman walks hand-in-hand with his two companions to listen to the thrush's "carol of death." Note, too, that the song is no longer a dirge:

Come lovely and soothing death,
Undulate round the world, serenely arriving, arriving,
In the day, in the night, to all, to each,
Sooner or later delicate death.

Prais'd be the fathomless universe,
For life and joy, and for objects and knowledge curious,
And for love, sweet love—but praise! praise! praise!
For the sure-enwinding arms of cool-enfolding death.

Just as this poem began, here the bird's song commences with Whitman's invocation and proceeds through his translation of natural sound into human ones. It is hard to characterize quickly the stunning power, the lyrical grace of these remarkable, formalized quatrains. The song of mourning has been transformed into a song of "praise! praise! praise!" His intensified diction, his incredible confidence, his giving-over to the "bliss of death" is Whitman at his most reverent and awestruck. It is this poet's greatest, most empowering paradox that at his most awestruck, he is at his most articulate and artful. As the cloud of death covers the world, now he spreads his song—once a dirge, now a carol, now a "serenade"—over treetops, oceans, prairies, and "teeming wharves."

It remains to exit. Section 15 is Whitman's summary explanation of the song. He looks back to the war-ravaged landscape to review the horrible sight of battle-corpses. His vision clarifies as well:

But I saw they were not as was thought,
They themselves were fully at rest, they suffer'd not,
The living remain'd and suffer'd, the mother suffer'd . . .

In war's paradox and elegy's consolation, the dead are free to rejoin the natural world while the living mourn and ache.

But Whitman's poem continues, hastening now, growing beyond the night and swamp, beyond the song of the bird. He insists to revivify the poem's procedure, its journey, its rhetorical evolution. For his song—in section 16—has evolved into a "psalm," its ultimate holy transfiguration. As the breath of the song floats away, "passing" as he says, so does Whitman, pausing only to return the lilac sprig to the farmhouse door (is it Lincoln's old homestead?). He bids farewell to the poem's assembled subjects—Lincoln, the war dead, the trinity of signifying tropes—but also he bids farewell to his old self. He has integrated all with all, death with life, and the despair of a country that tore itself in half with its continued, in fact rejuvenated, promise of continuity.

❦

Let me reiterate a few central observations about the lilac elegy.

1) The poem began as a schematic for funereal or elegiac ritual. Literary, even religious rituals must first have been natural. Certainly Whitman's

ritual is naturalistic, primitive—both pagan and holy. But quickly he abandons the static, inherited social ritual of the elegy in favor of a journey, a purposeful retreat from cultural engagement, and invents his own new transcendental, self-reliant elegy of praise.

2) The poem makes important use of trinities: three dominant symbols (lilac, star, thrush); three figures (Lincoln, the war dead, Whitman); and another group of three I want to come back to shortly. We recognize the Christian significance here, but the number reverberates with other possibilities as well. In writing about Book IV of *The Republic*, for instance, Susan Sontag sees how

> Plato has been developing a tripartite theory of mental function, consisting of reason, anger or indignation, and appetite or desire—anticipating the Freudian schema of superego, ego, and id (with the difference that Plato puts reason on top and conscience, represented by indignation, in the middle).

3) The lilac elegy resists the elegiac impulse for the static or suspended. It demands momentum, horizon, evolution. The figure of Lincoln turns into the assembled war dead, then into Death itself, even the figure of Democracy, and so becomes, ultimately, Whitman's figure of The Poet. The poem is driven by Whitman's desire to find a road back from isolate grief to the social realm and to locate a method and language to enable the restoration of the body and of the body politic, his democratic hope. Just so, the musical genre of the dirge transforms into the carol, then the serenade, and finally the psalm. That is, elegy becomes folk song becomes love song becomes testament.

This is one of Whitman's greatest achievements, given the severity of the poem's circumstance. For this is Whitman's particular horror: He saw the supreme figure for the democratic experiment in Abraham Lincoln, born out west, on the prairie, a self-invented, self-realized man, rough yet incredibly articulate. A hero-spokesman of the people. But this perfect natural man was killed—in an act Whitman saw as both heretical and self-loathing—by one of his fellow citizens. And this is the horror of the Civil War: How could the country Whitman loved, the world's greatest social and natural experiment, fail? How could it declare war on itself, killing its own beautiful son?

As I said before, the elegy for Whitman is highly atypical. He is a poet of social encouragement, and more so, a poet of erotic adventure. Whitman is a love poet, not a death poet. Even his early Civil War poems in *Drum-Taps* are generic and unbelievable, populated by faceless boy-soldiers whose bravery is unimpeachable and obvious and whose sacrifice seems negligible. These lines from "First O Songs for a Prelude" show Whitman's naïve sense of heroism as the war commenced:

> Arm'd regiments arrive every day, pass through the city, and embark
> from the wharves,
> (How good they look as they tramp down to the river, sweaty, with their
> guns on their shoulders!
> How I love them! how I could hug them, with their brown faces and their
> clothes and knapsacks cover'd with dust!)
> The blood of the city up—arm'd! arm'd! the cry everywhere . . .

Only after he spent months at a massive tent-city hospital outside Washington, D.C., did the war become real. In December 1862, Whitman traveled from Brooklyn to search for his brother George, a wounded Federal soldier. Amazingly, he found George and nursed his wounds. But after George healed and left (back to battle, in fact), Walt remained as a volunteer aide. Here he witnessed the nightmarish side of the democratic experiment, as he washed the bodies of maimed men and boys, brought them candies, bread, tobacco, gave them coins, wrote hundreds of letters to their families. In more than 600 trips to the hospital, Whitman became nurse, doctor, brother, mother, friend, and savior to tens of thousands. David Reynolds estimates that Whitman had contact with between 80,000 and 100,000 soldiers in the tents. This experience changed him utterly. It gave him the blood-coated horror that informs the lilac elegy.

⁂

I want to examine one more aspect of this poem, its most significant exchange, back in the swampy woods, with Walt and his two "companions." Therein lies the secret. But before I grapple with it, I want to pause, like Walt, suspended in the swamp. I need to listen to the song of another poem, from only two years earlier in 1863, by Emily Dickinson. This is another apparent elegy, a funeral poem, is in fact another strange American self-elegy:

Because I could not stop for Death—
He kindly stopped for me—
The Carriage held but just Ourselves—
And Immortality.

We slowly drove—He knew no haste
And I had put away
My labor and my leisure too,
For His Civility—

We passed the School, where Children strove
At Recess—in the Ring—
We passed the Fields of Gazing Grain—
We passed the Setting Sun—

Or rather—He passed Us—
The dews drew quivering and chill—
For only Gossamer, my Gown—
My Tippet—only Tulle—

We paused before a House that seemed
A Swelling of the Ground—
The Roof was scarcely visible—
The Cornice—in the Ground—

Since then—'tis Centuries—and yet
Feels shorter than the Day
I first surmised the Horses' Heads
Were toward Eternity—

If Whitman is not accustomed to the mode of the elegy, Emily Dickinson is gloriously at home with death, her weirdly familiar afterlife, and the language of that other world. How often does she sink through floorboards or grass into the grave? "And then a Plank in Reason, broke, / And I dropped down, and down—." How many times does she speak, as a corpse, to corpses?

I will not linger so long over this poem, her most renowned work, but I do want to walk through some important details. This is, to my thinking, the other great American elegy of the nineteenth century. How homely and comfortable is this ride in the hearse. How much fun! Dickinson's speaker seems hardly to have died at all, but merely to have gone on a little trip out of the village into the countryside and beyond. Does this sound familiar?

Whitman's ironies are situational while Dickinson's are both situational, or circumstantial, and tonal. How indeed is death "kind"?—yet he seems mannerly, genteel, even attractive. So another journey commences, with Dickinson, her companion Death, and the strange third figure, Immortality. Notice how small and meager Dickinson seems. Yet she clearly does not feel weakened or diminished by the presence of her powerful companions. In her rhymes, in fact, she seems purposely to point out to us the imbalance between "me"—two mere letters—and "Immortality," a dramatic, capitalized idea of such multisyllabic magnitude that it requires nearly a whole line. When we add the consideration of meter and stress, though, we see how delighted she seems to reverse the polarity of power between those two concepts. "[M]e" is smaller than "Immortality," and yet that little word commands a much heavier stress, even as "Immortality" fades away into lighter syllables and silence. "Me" is a very confident single pulse. "Immortality" staggers, wavering from its unwieldy size. We'll see a similar unbalancing irony in the last stanza's rhyme of "Day" and "Eternity," echoing off.

And that carriage: we know from Dickinson's own dictionary that a carriage is a heavy four-wheeled vehicle, suitable for cumbersome loads (like a hearse), compared to a buggy, used more likely for a spin taken by lovers. Like Whitman, Dickinson takes a trip, a more homely odyssey here, as we imagine the slow funeral procession out of town to the gravesite. The speaker has "put away [her] labor and [her] leisure too," her whole life, for the journey. In stanza three she retraces a life's progression, from childhood to maturity to death—in the figures of the schoolyard, the fertile fields, the sunset—and then in a touch of technical genius Dickinson decelerates yet continues her journey precisely at midpoint, in the radically enjambed third stanza (just as Whitman did at his poem's midpoint). We think the life is over when the sun sets, and yet, notice how it's all merely slowed down, how she continues the trip, as the sentence and the sun resume in stanza four. How deliberate, how halting, but how clearly continual: "We passed the setting sun— // Or rather—He passed Us—." Those brilliant dashes, and pauses, and enjambments—passing much as Whitman "passed" in section 16 of the lilac poem.

At this point Dickinson's body seems extremely vulnerable, exposed to time and the elements. Her burial clothes are dew and gossamer (a spiderweb-like material), her veil like a nun's, but of silky Tulle. And at just this point, arriving at the grave, the hearse ride surprisingly continues. They "paused" before the grave-swollen ground, glancing at the tomb, and then go on. Go on and on, for centuries. Eternity, for Dickinson, is not a place at which one arrives. It is rather the journey-toward, a continual evolving. That's the radical importance of the last little preposition of the poem. If we are going "toward" Eternity, then we are clearly not "at" it, nor ever will be.

I am taking pains to establish several narrative and figural details in both poems because I think we are in the presence of a radically new attitude toward the elegy, very different from the English tradition. How hopeful these Americans. Where *is* the promised land, heaven, the next life? Upward? No. Lincoln's train is moving westward, and Whitman's gaze is likewise to the west. Where is Venus? "Drooping early" in the Western sky. And in what direction is Dickinson traveling? If they pass the sun, or rather he passes them, then they too are going west. American Heaven is not upward, it is Westward ho. The promise is that the West will be forever a beckoning, enchanted horizon, a manifest destiny of perfection.

Peter Sacks asserts that the English elegy performs a ritual stillness of mourning and obedience, essentially a tribute to traditional forms of power. But consider the journey, the odyssey, these two poets undertake. They will not hold still nor bow down. In fact, the speakers insist on evolving. In many ways these poems reject conventional myths of mourning. Even Dickinson's apparently reverent meter—the common or anthem meter of her father's Protestant hymnal, after all (you can sing most of her poems to the tune of "Amazing Grace," or "The Battle Hymn of the Republic" for that matter)—even her meter is ironized by her blasphemous subject and radically idiosyncratic style and syntax. In these poems, the poets and their speakers are complicit in the narrative. They resist the static, the merely observant; they are not submissive; they do not seek the solace or council of a hierarchy of power-holders, whether religious, literary, or political. They are active participants in their own songs and become the subjects of their own elegiac impulses. Both of these are self-elegies.

If indeed they are elegies, or elegies only, at all. It's time to look hard at the most audacious element in both of these poems. Dickinson's work, with its more obvious configuration, will help us recover the very oblique but primary passage of the lilac elegy that I skipped over.

If Dickinson's poem is an elegy, the story of a funeral procession, it is also just as clearly a love poem, the story of a mild nineteenth-century date. She has a suitor, they have a chaperone, and off they go flirting, secretly aroused. Her arousal becomes obvious in the sensations of stanza four. Those garments are just as easily the apparel of a wedding party as a burial one, aren't they? *Today our bride is wearing a lovely, sheer white gown, a delicate shoulder-length veil*—she feels the innocent but clearly sensual excitement of her station. In fact, can't this whole poem be read as a wedding poem, the new couple on the way to, and *past*, their house? The very earth is pregnant, "swelling" with fertile possibility—a condition and a type of residence where, elsewhere, she says she likes to "dwell."

So what is the relationship of the elegiac to the erotic? And how does the eroticizing of her elegy permit Dickinson to subvert the elegiac tradition? Let's look back at her first stanza. If this is a love poem, then why are there *three* characters in the carriage? Thus we come to two more of my central arguments. Precisely this: the transcendental American elegy *requires an erotic component*. The planet-figure of Venus—originally a vegetation goddess, who becomes the Roman goddess of love and, paradoxically, lover of Mars, the war god—is therefore not merely circumstantial but thematically central to Whitman's elegy. But more: this elegiac-erotic component abides by a delicious observation made by Anne Carson in her *Eros the Bittersweet*. At issue again is the figuration of the poems, the math of the thing. In discussing the erotic lyrics of Sappho, Carson traces "the radical constitution of desire" in erotic discourse: "We see clearly what shape desire has there: a three-point circuit." That is, she continues, "where eros is lack, its activation calls for three structural components—lover, beloved, and that which comes between them." In other words, the geometry of lovers' discourse is not a line between two points: it is a triangle.

"That which comes between them" indeed. What comes between lovers? In the present poems, death seems to come between lovers. Families, villages, communities, language itself—words, art—come between them; perhaps faith, ritual, God; perhaps their own bodies come between lovers. Certainly the self, its needs, its sense of awareness, of separateness, can

"come between" them. Carson concurs: "It is not uncommon in love to experience this heightened sense of one's own personality." Who, I ask, has a
more charged, complex sense of personality than lover Walt?

So, let us go then—ah, that other great love poem to despair—let us go
back to the swamp, the primordial scene, where Whitman is listening to the
bird sing its song of grief-becoming-praise. I've returned to the middle of
section 14:

>   —lo, then and there,
> Falling upon them all and among them all, enveloping me with the rest,
> Appear'd the cloud, appear'd the long black trail,
> And I knew death, its thought, and the sacred knowledge of death.
>
> Then, with the knowledge of death as walking one side of me,
> And the thought of death close-walking the other side of me,
> And I in the middle as with companions, and as holding the hands
>   of companions,
> I fled forth to the hiding receiving night that talks not,
> Down to the shores of the water, the path by the swamp in the dimness,
> To the solemn shadowy cedars and ghostly pines so still.

At this magically archetypal point, with death at each hand, the poem and
Whitman's power shift into high gear. When that contact of hands is made,
as though an immense electrical circuit were completed, Whitman dies—
and is able to understand the song of the hermit thrush: "And the singer so
shy to the rest receiv'd me, / That gray-brown bird I know receiv'd us com-
rades three, / And he sang the carol of death, and a verse for him I love."

These are complex figures. Who is "the knowledge of death," and who is
"the thought of death," and how are they different? It's very hard to unpack
this figuration with much confidence. Is one the foreknowledge of dying,
while the other is the actual experience of dying? Are they two sides of the
same thing, in the middle of which is Walt? Let me propose that these two
figures serve the same functions as Death and Immortality in Dickinson's
poem. They are the human fact of dying, and the human hope of dying into
the next thing.

But let's not miss Carson's triangulation here, too, for I think it is precisely at this point where Whitman's elegy refocuses or is impelled into

Whitman's erotic poem. In "I Sing the Body Electric," Whitman longs for the contact of body for body, as a form of natural and democratic intelligence as well as a form of erotic exchange—erotic, autoerotic, homoerotic, all the same. To be electric is to be empowered: electrified, electrocuted, elected, one of the elect. Whitman persists to conflate the physical, intellectual, religious, and political. In "Song of Myself" he is "mad to be in contact" with the world's body. He sings with joy: "To touch my person to some one else's is about as much as I can stand." A touch, he tells us, "[quivers] me to a new identity." And in "Crossing Brooklyn Ferry," the contact of arms, the touch of the "negligent . . . flesh" of evening commuters, charges his vision. This contact "fuses" him with "generations" both before and after his, and this transformation generates—it engenders—the power to drive his poem.

My point is that this triangle of contact in the swamp is a figure for erotic empowerment. The touch of bodies—the exchange of electricity, of seminal power—is Whitman's revivifying solution; he is medium, conductor, receptor, lover. His lovers are Death, as Dickinson's are, and by marrying the figures of Death both poets subsume it. Let me be more precise. Here I think both poets make an original adjustment to Anne Carson's geometry. She identifies "lover, beloved, and that which comes between them." But in these two poems "that which comes between" the lovers may not be Death. In fact, Death already has two figures: Death and Immortality; or "the knowledge of death" and "the thought of death"—these are the lovers. "That which comes between" is, instead, the human poet. The *poet* is the irritant, the poet disrupts the fatal coherence of nature, the poet embodies a radical irony, and then the poet provides the necessary point of contact (or reconnection) between Death and the promised new world.

This is entirely a figure of the American transcendental imagination. Both Whitman and Dickinson purposely infuse a radical and personal erotic into the elegiac tradition. In these two poems, Death does not defeat the Self. It cannot stifle the song-of-the-Self. Death is being joined and thus defeated. It is being married and thus embraced. It is being enlisted and thus domesticated. It is being compelled—reborn—out of its stasis into a dynamic, erotic adventure. That is to say, in the American transcendental lyric, the journey continues on, in the direction of the sun.

"One's Own Sad Stead": American Elegy as Self-Elegy

When Marco Polo, on his travels, first saw a rhinoceros, he called it a unicorn, even though he had to radically redefine what a unicorn was in order to make the rhino fit his definition. I feel somewhat in the position of Marco Polo today, trying to pin down what is at best a chameleon form, and then trying to determine if there is a distinctly American version of it. "Elegy" in Western poetry began with the Greeks as a verse form of alternating five- and six- foot lines; but by the time of the Romans it meant basically any sad song, usually accompanied by a lute, as with, probably, Sappho's poems. Callimachus, Propertius, and Ovid, for example, in their love elegies, and John Donne and Rainer Maria Rilke much later, further expanded the idea of elegy. Later it metamorphosed with the ode, the pastoral, and other forms. Finally, if we look at what Larry Levis accomplished in his magnificent book, *Elegy*, we see a contemporary version of the form that has included narrative, comedy, pastoral, autobiography, history, politics—in fact, just about every form has been rounded up in the service of those poems to shape what might be truly the American elegy, a sort of melting-pot form. "A word is elegy to what it signifies," Robert Hass writes in one poem. Edward Hirsch knows what this amorphous form of elegy is; in a recent *Bloomsbury Review*, he says that too many of our poets, paradoxically, "seem to think elegy is the only correct form of poetry."

When W. S. Merwin writes his one-line poem entitled "Elegy" ("Who would I show it to"), he reveals a central paradox of elegy: if it is written for a dead person, then it is a failure; if it is written for some audience, it is a form of luxuriating in another's pain; but if it is written for the self, then that is another matter altogether. C. K. Williams suggests this sense of the elegy when he projects the possibility of his own death prompted by a vision of the atom bomb in "The Dream," and in his wanting the dead to speak to him in the orphic poem, "To Listen." Yet when we consider "Willow, Weep for Me" by William Matthews, we find an ironic understanding that "nobody gives a fig / for your parochial pain," (which, by the way, indicts a great deal of confession that passes for poetry), suggesting that all elegy is at least partly an elegy for the speaker. And so in the end the poem undercuts its own easy irony: "but to sing not as a subcontractor / but in one's own sad stead would set the whole / broken heart of nature to music."

So the phrase goes: "one's own sad stead." The dominance of the self in American poetry is a defining characteristic. Then indeed, why not think of the essential American elegy as "self-elegy," a kind of poem where the author projects his or her own death? This follows the traditional path of elegiac poets from Sappho to Elizabeth Bishop and, especially exemplified by John Milton's *Lycidas*, it also finds a way to surmount or locate some truce with the despair of that death. So I'm not suggesting that no other cultures write self-elegies, for certainly poems like John Keats's "When I have fears that I might cease to be"—with its consolation that the "love and fame" the self projects as losing is finally insignificant—is a self-elegy. But the American self-elegy tends to use, as the best American poetry seems to, a first-person "I" that serves, as Ralph Waldo Emerson suggests, as a "transparent eyeball," a self that observes, discovers its shortcomings, and attempts to transform and transcend what it sees in an empirical rather than philosophical way.

Richard Hugo follows a similar path as Matthews in "Death in the Aquarium," where the suicide becomes "that unidentified man in us all / and wants to die where we started." He then goes on to project not the sadness of a death but a death triumphant as he transforms death into a transcendent experience; he imagines dying "on the floor of the ocean" where his bones will turn to phosphorous, "And lovers, lovers would stop making love / and stand there, each suddenly alone / amazed at that gleam riding sand." The point, for Hugo, as for all of us, is to find some way for "making certain it goes on." Louise Bogan, in her last poem, unfinished, also projects a kind of transcendence as the poem's "dream shoots forward to a future / We shall never see," a future where "the living live / And the dead rise." What is at stake here is a transcendent vision of the cosmos, an almost religious view that there is an existence that thrives beyond the here and now of the "I."

We can turn to Merwin again for another example of this transcendence. Here is his "For the Anniversary of My Death":

Every year without knowing it I have passed the day
When the last fires will wave to me
And the silence will set out
Tireless traveler
Like the beam of a lightless star

Then I will no longer
Find myself in life as in a strange garment
Surprised at the earth
And the love of one woman
And the shamelessness of men
As today writing after three days of rain
Hearing the wren sing and the falling cease
And bowing not knowing to what

The poem quickly expands through the images of distant fires, the silence of death, the darkness of the universe, but it is at that very point where he seems most lost that he appreciates the small things around him, the sound of the rain and the wren, and starts actually to reverence whatever it is that death will bring: what started as potential lament for estrangement of the self ends as a prayer of communion.

Not every such act yields this sort of religious reverence. Philip Levine in "My Grave" describes a "little untended plot / of ground and weeds and a stone / that bears my name, misspelled." The poem itself is a sort of grave that contains beer-bottle caps from the speaker's son, a last will his sister hated, but more importantly, what is not there: his lost hopes, lost dreams, lost visions of love, that is, as the speaker says, "Nothing of me." And why?

> ... this is cheap,
> common, coarse, what you pass by
> every day in your car without a thought,
> this is an ordinary grave.

Levine's speaker passes his grave every day, not with Merwin's reverence but with an ironic understanding that the very commonality of this experience suggests a way of transcending it, an idea he poses in poems such as "Lost and Found," where emptiness and loss are made full and recoverable by the very act of remembering them. John Logan's "The Gift" is one of the more poignant elegies we have for its attempt to give back and revitalize possibility. After describing a series of gifts—love, tenderness, friendship—he concludes: "All that I will give back again. / This is my testament of love." The poem follows a long letter to his son, which is also an attempt to give back all he can in the form of final instructions written, as he says, when "My senses of taste and smell are made waste by disease."

Emily Dickinson's "I Heard a Fly Buzz When I Died" bears a similar ambiguity; she begins as the room around her echoes with the heaves of her last breaths and the breaths of the onlookers. As she waits for the "King" to arrive, she wills away her earthly possessions, suggesting her readiness for a spiritual, transcending experience. But the King never arrives, only the fly

> With Blue—uncertain—stumbling Buzz—
> Between the light—and me—
> And then the Windows failed—and then—
> I could not see to see—

This is one of the more complex and, as she says, "uncertain" moments in American poetry. The speaker's confusion between seeing as simple *physical sight* and seeing as *knowing* is reflected in the way the fly is both a physical fly and a demonic substitute for the "King" (God). However, even the spiritual aspect contains an ambiguity. While the synesthesia of the "Blue" to describe the buzz suggests the sky and the eternal, the buzz itself arises from a space between her and the "light." In the end, while she "sees" and does not understand, she at least seems to accept the fly, the everyday minute world that surrounds us, as a substitute, as a kind of salvation in itself. Even a little-known poem of hers such as "If I should die— / And you should live—" takes consolation in the fact that the world of commerce and trade goes on, even though it also satirizes the small concerns of that world.

Another self-elegy that uses the potent image of the fly is Larry Levis's "The Morning After My Death": "How little I have to say; / How little desire I have / To say it," he writes near the beginning and then finds a metaphor for this unsayable and almost unthinkable idea in the figure of a trumpet player who "looks around / A moment, before he spits and puts the horn / Into his mouth, counting slowly." It is that moment of delay and anticipation that contains the elegiac ambiguity Dickinson describes. But then Levis thinks of "the darkness inside the horn, / How no one's breath has been able / To push it out yet" even when the concert ends. It is "a note so high no one / Can play it." Thus the moment of delay turns into a moment

> like the dried blood inside
> A dead woman's throat, when the mourners
> Listen, and there is nothing left but these flies,
> Polished and swarming frankly in the sun.

The dark notes become the Dickinsonian flies that have always been there. What the mourners listen to is the unsaid, unplayed elegy, the elegy for ourselves, as well as for Levis himself, that is always just about to be played.

Mark Cox's strategy in "Talking Death to Death" is perhaps the ultimate and most ironic way of transcending one's encounter with death. Except here he discovers it was Death's "likeness quavering in the washbasin." We become Death, and the conversation with Death becomes a conversation with the self. All that's left for the poet is an ironic attempt to belittle Death:

> But redemption, Death,
> that's the straight pin
> I can't quite pick up.
> Houdini could do it with his eyelashes,
> but you don't see him performing much anymore.

The poem itself as it moves in time, as performance, as a way of talking against time like the Medieval chess player in Ingmar Bergman's film, is the poet's only hope here. "What shall I say, because talk I must?" William Carlos Williams begins "The Yellow Flower"; his "Asphodel" is a similar attempt to hold off death by talking time away.

Self-elegy, then, seems often to elicit an ironic tone: Even a poet as dark as Sylvia Plath can write a poem called "Last Words":

> I do not want a plain box, I want a sarcophagus
> With tigery stripes, and a face on it
> Round as the moon, to stare up.
> I want to be looking at them when they come . . .

As she continues to project, she imagines herself as an Egyptian queen and wonders what they will think of her, then reveals that she doesn't trust spirits and therefore wants to be surrounded by "things"—turquoise, pots, the things of her life. In the end, the tone becomes more serious as she says, "I shall hardly know myself." It may be that all self-elegies are really poems about knowing, or not knowing, oneself. So Edna St. Vincent Millay, echoing John Donne's "The Anniversary," writes a sonnet describing how those who now "wear the dust" will be discovered in the future and the memory they instill will be their way to surmount death. For Millay, as for Donne, this happens by having "lived and died believing love was true," though the language of the poem gives itself away as a plea, an uncertain hope that the poem's projection is itself true, and that the love is true.

Millay's poems are as much about the death of feeling, an entirely different type of elegy, as they are about Death. Frank O'Hara's "In Memory of My Feelings" depicts the speaker imagining himself as several selves in order to investigate what scientists today would call parallel lives. The hope is that a death in one would hardly affect the life of another. In the end, though, he realizes the attempt is all merely art, for he doesn't have the faith that others, like Mark Cox, might have in words themselves. Ultimately all the deaths of others are incorporated into the death of his self:

> and I have lost what is always and everywhere
> present, the scene of my selves, the occasion of these ruses,
> which I myself and singly must now kill
> > and save the serpent in their midst.

To kill the memory of death, to kill the self, is to overcome it in some sense. Of course, the other major originating force besides Dickinson in American poetry, Walt Whitman, also projects his own passing in "Good-bye my Fancy!" which is perhaps the origin in American poetry of this elegy for lost feelings. Such a tradition further includes poems like Robert Frost's great poem, "The Oven Bird," where he laments "what to make of a diminished thing." As Whitman says: "The slower fainter ticking of the clock is in me, / Exit, nightfall, and soon the heart-thud stopping." The way Whitman provides a consolation, in this farewell that is also about imagination (fancy), is to have the poem delay its own end: "Yet let me not be too hasty," and then continues for what becomes the whole second half of the poem. In the

end the good-bye also becomes a hello, a new beginning: "Good-bye—
and hail! my Fancy." The poem is a statement at least as major as William
Wordsworth's "Immortality Ode."

And this might be a subcategory of the self-elegy, though as soon as
I say that I begin to feel a bit more like Marco Polo. Still, we might recall
Frank O'Hara's "In Memory of My Feelings." The act of writing the poem
is where he feels the death of feelings, much like Samuel Taylor Coleridge
in "Dejection: An Ode," who exclaims "I see, not feel, how beautiful they are!"
The very fact that an emotive poem can be written about the loss of feelings
suggests that what is "lost [is what] is always and everywhere / present." A
similar movement motivates Marvin Bell's "The Self and the Mulberry,"
where the speaker tries but fails to blend into nature, and Edna St. Vincent
Millay's "And must I then, indeed, Pain, live with you / All through my life?"
Millay, in fact, has a number of sonnets where she projects her own death or
sees it manifested in the death of a love. Linda Gregg's "The Heart Flowing
Out" is another example: "All things we see are the shapes death makes. /
When we see straightly and hard we see / with the eyes of death," she says, and
then later—"When we enter death it gives way, / but not yet." Like O'Hara
and Whitman, the more she looks, the more she sees a world "shaking with its
own energy" and "making . . . meaning." In a similar vein, her poem "I Thought
on His Desire for Three Days" records a lost love and ends by quickly projecting ahead beyond her own death, in the last sentence, as a means of escaping
pain: "Summer rain. The liveliness of it keeps / me awake. I am happy to have
lived." These sorts of poems become what Wallace Stevens calls in "Waving
Adieu, Adieu, Adieu," a "practice" for heaven.

Perhaps the three most powerful recent self-elegies are by John Berryman, Paul Zweig, and James Wright. Berryman projected his own death
even more than Sylvia Plath did, and besides the poems read at his funeral,
the last throwaway poem he wrote, and a few other final lines, surely the
best example is "Dream Song #382":

At Henry's bier let some thing fall out well:
enter there none who somewhat has to sell,
the music ancient & gradual,
the voices solemn but the grief subdued,
no hairy jokes but everybody's mood
subdued, subdued,

until the Dancer comes, in a short short dress
hair black & long & loose, dark dark glasses,
uptilted face,
pallor & strangeness, the music changes
to "Give!" & "Ow!" and how! the music changes,
she kicks a backward limb

on tiptoe, pirouettes, & she is free
to the knocking music, sails, dips, & suddenly
returns to the terrible gay
occasion hopeless & mad, she weaves, it's hell,
she flings to her head a leg, bobs, all is well,
she dances Henry away.

How wonderfully the subdued, gradual, ancient music becomes the wild "knocking music," how the repetitions of the words "subdued," "dark," and even the phrase "the music changes" give way to the sudden bob where she sweeps Henry up and dances him away. In the midst of all this grief and solemnity the dancer's pirouetting shape turns a funereal vision into a vision of life. She becomes like Wallance Stevens's "necessary angel" in his poem "Angel Surrounded by Paysans," through which we hear not only earth's "tragic drone" but an apparition of "lightest look" that is quickly gone. It is as if, for Berryman, like Stevens, the elegiac transformation must take place quickly, impulsively, beyond logic and reason. It takes only one line in Berryman's poem, for example, one quick rhyme, to turn "it's hell" into "all is well," fulfilling the promise of the opening line—"At Henry's bier let some thing fall out well."

One of Paul Zweig's last poems is also one of the most moving elegies, for the self or otherwise. Written when he knew his cancer was overtaking him, the poem begins "I don't know if I can bear this suddenly / Speeded up time," and then goes on in lines that careen down the page, scooping up as many images from the world around him as he can and employing all five senses:

Cars grinding
Over the cobbles, the perishable mosaic of fruits
And vegetables in front of small stores.

. . . .
And girls dancing out of their clothes.

. . . .
        The car fumes, coffee, breath,
Old leather, urine, a young woman's perfume.
It smells of youth, death, sleepless nights.

And so the poem tries to cram as much life into itself as it can; yet in words like "perishable" (repeated in different contexts) we find we cannot evade death, and also realize that the poem itself has the power to be an "amazing story turning the fear of life / Into the love of life." That gesture allows the poem to rest in a kind of peace:

                a sweet smell
Comes from the fruit-stands, where cherries,
Apricots, peaches, plums soften and sag;
A cloying liquid wets the tilted boxes,
Darkening the sidewalk. Soon it will be evening.

There is a nearly Keatsian sense of the sensual richness of the earth here, so that it seems, in the space of the poem, a kind of relief, as at the end of Keats's "To Autumn"—that an end here euphemized as "evening" finally comes. The triumph is a return to the natural rhythm of a day as opposed to the speeded-up time of the opening.

    The last poem I want to take a look at is James Wright's "The Journey," also written when the poet realized his own approaching death. It raises a dramatic problem, how to create a self-elegy that not only allows the self to triumph but allows the speaker's friends to be consoled. Louise Bogan had done this in one of her poems that ends

Goodbye, goodbye!
There was so much to love, I could not love it all;
I could not love it enough.

Some things I overlooked, and some I could not find.
Let the crystal clasp them
When you drink your wine, in autumn.

Wright begins his poem with a description of a small windy Tuscan town, Anghiari, where "everything now was graying gold / With dust." Dust becomes the central image in the poem, really, for he leans down to rinse the dust from his face, and sees a spider web as he does so, itself coated "crazily with the dust, /Whole mounds and cemeteries of it." And yet when he sees the spider, it becomes an image like Dickinson's fly or Merwin's wren or Zweig's cloying fruits, an image of transcending death, for she is

> poised there,
> While ruins crumbled on every side of her.
> Free of the dust, as though a moment before
> She had stepped inside the earth, to bathe herself.

As with Hugo and Dickinson, as with all these poets, the way to transcend death and mortality is partly to immerse oneself in the earth and its sensual qualities, to immerse oneself in mortality, to overcome it by becoming a part of it. The self-elegy is a way in which the poet can imaginatively enter his or her own death in precisely this manner. For Wright, this is a consolation, not only for himself, but for those he leaves behind. And so, in many ways, this poem is the quintessential self-elegy:

> Many men
> Have searched all over Tuscany and never found
> What I found there, the heart of the light
> Itself shelled and leaved, balancing
> On filaments themselves falling. The secret
> Of this journey is to let the wind
> Blow its dust all over your body,
> To let it go on blowing, to step lightly, lightly
> All the way through your ruins, and not to lose
> Any sleep over the dead, who surely
> Will bury their own, don't worry.

Don't worry. In some ways a consolation, in some ways the most poignant of statements. The calmness of the voice provokes in the reader an outrage, an anger at death, at the idea that such a wonderful voice could end; but also a sense of peace for the way poem lets the speaker live on. "Surely the real fuel for elegy / is anger to be mortal," William Matthews writes in "An Elegy for Bob Marley." Perhaps in a way, then, all elegy must be self-elegy at some level. Matthews ends his poem:

> This is something else we can't
> control, another loss, which is, as someone
>
> said in hope of consolation,
> only temporary, though the same phrase
> could be used of our lives and bodies
> and all that we hope survives them.

Elegiac

The Purist

I give you now Professor Twist,
A conscientious scientist.
Trustees examined, "He never bungles!"
And sent him off to distant jungles.
Camped by a tropic riverside,
One day he missed his loving bride.
She had, the guide informed him later,
Been eaten by an alligator.
Professor Twist could not but smile.
"You mean," he said, "a crocodile."

This poem, by Ogden Nash, has almost everything that an elegy is supposed to have: that is, it has a death, and in this case, death of a close one, and a response to that death. What it doesn't have, of course, is grief; Nash is a witness, a reporter, a satirist, not a griever in this case. And what he is satirizing is Twist's attitude, about which he also has an attitude. On the other hand, grief, as the loss emotion, not only has attitude, it is probably the most straightforward of our emotions, however *twists* and ironies may bend it.

"All the new thinking is about loss. In this it resembles all the old thinking." These now familiar opening lines of Robert Hass's 1979 "Meditation at Lagunitas" pretty well set up the argument for the place of the elegy—or the elegiac—in the fairly short but crowded history of American poetry. It doesn't seem all that long ago that Ezra Pound said make it new, to which William Carlos Williams responded, make it newer. Make it whatever you want, says Hass, but make sure the issue of loss is understood: and the lamenting of loss.

Expressions of loss, the emotion that most underwrites the elegy, are certainly nothing new in English poetry, from "The Wife's Lament" to the fifteenth-century ballad "Edward" to John Donne's sequence called *First Anniversary*, in a poem entitled "A Funeral Elegy"—poems of losses all tied to local grief and particular individuals: familial, personal, parochial. Donne basically transformed the *elegie* of complaint into a poetry of lament, an emphasis further elevated by Milton in his pastoral elegy *Lycidas*. I draw a little line of history in order to emphasize that the elegy has been, traditionally, and especially in our forebearing English poetry, a poem of occasion, a reply to specific loss, specific longing, or someone's death, a love poem—if you will—of grief. In American poetry, however, the elegy has been less an issue of occasion than an expansive and inclusive way of processing emotion. It has been less of an occasion than it has been the condition under which the life of the poem comes into being.

The dominant feeling, the resonant tone in American poetry, right from the start, has been, it seems to me, elegiac, melancholic, meditative, aggressively expressive, and romantic, which is why truly early modernists like William Wordsworth and John Keats have become iconographic influences within our American canon. (Had Keats, in fact, followed his brother George to America instead of nursing their youngest brother, Tom, in Hampstead, Keats might have become our first great national poet—and a Southerner to boot.) It is not that American poetry is any more broody than other poetries, but rather that American poets, by internalizing poetic form to the extent they have, have further generalized the level of feeling generated by those new or invented forms.

By adopting as their premier mode the freer speech of what we carelessly call free verse or more carefully refer to as discovered form, American poets have created a greater dependency on and transparency before their various muses; they have consistently written in a way that more directly exposes the emotion; they have, over time, equated power in poetry with surrender or dissolution into the greater figure: They have, over time, equated power in poetry with that "which none else is more lasting"—because of that "which none else is perhaps more spiritual." In the process American poets have come to equate emotion with loss. The degree to which this equation has to do with the nature of the American experience within the American landscape and cityscape is another question. But our large, open, and dark spaces do map themselves on our hearts and self-consciousnesses; they do seem to demand an openness and exhaustive, sometimes an exhilarating, intensity in return. These large, open, and dark spaces do seem to break boundaries, rules, controlling circumstances; they do resist our need for village intimacy; our isolating spaces do break and heal hearts.

Whether we are watching Anne Bradstreet's house in the woods burn down or simply stopping to watch the woods fill up with snow on the darkest evening of the year; whether we are grieving the loss of a president and a whole generation of young men in Walt Whitman's lament for the Civil War or declaiming the loss of one of "the best minds of my generation destroyed by madness, starving hysterical naked"; whether we feel a funeral in the brain or the syncopated, drowsy, weary blues; whether we meditate on the fact that we shall not cease from exploration and the end of all our exploring will be to arrive where we started and know the place for the first time or address the "monsters of elegy" directly, "Of their own marvel made, of pity made." Whatever our posture or passion, American poets speak from an elemental, inherited sense of loss, whether that loss is Edenic, as some critics of American poetry have suggested, or organic to the character of the modern industrial age, beginning with the furnaces of Satan, as William Blake suggested. I think it has less to do with corruptions of our landscapes than the nature of our landscape itself; I think it has nothing directly to do with our exploitation of our resources and everything indirectly to do with the lure and promise of that green light across the water at the end of *The Great Gatsby.*

We are stuck with our idealism, our promises to ourselves. And we are equally stuck with the demands of our successes, with our pure products that go crazy, with our violence forever pioneering, with our line breaks that sometimes make no sense. Was it F. Scott Fitzgerald who said there are no second acts in America?—which suggests that our ambitions themselves are part of our tragedy, like our need to believe that from evil bloometh good. This must somehow be linked to our chronic individualism—our fantasy freedom to be, God forbid, ourselves; freedom from family, community, the past. Freedom from forms. I'm thinking of Whitman's freedom among the wounded and would-be dead in the Civil War hospitals in Washington; of his freedom in the Whitman household of his parents; his freedom within his own sexuality. I'm thinking of Emily Dickinson's freedom in tiny Amherst, Massachusetts, in her father's house. Freedom, yes, but to do what? freedom from what? I'm thinking of Meriwether Lewis returning from his great journey of discovery concerning the size and openness and darkness of this his country, returning to whatever fame and fortune Thomas Jefferson could bestow on him, yet finding too little in it all except a void in himself, a void not unlike his voyage. There is a strange elegiac closure to his complex circle of fulfillment and hunger, achievement and longing. Lewis, within three years of his return from his Northwest Passage, apparently kills himself. On his way back to Washington to rescue his political and moral reputation, he ends his days in the middle of nowhere on the old Natchez Trace, traveling alone on horseback, carrying all the copies he has of the red Morocco-bound journals of the Lewis and Clark expedition. Sixteen in all.

The condition of things, I believe, and not the circumstance, is what colors the American elegy. Oh, we celebrate, we honor, we grieve the individual, but we seem predisposed to do it, as if we expected it or loss confirmed our national neurosis, our characteristic depression. Abraham Lincoln's gloom is all over Whitman's elegy for him, like the smoke-cloud from the Springfield train obscuring the sun. Yet Whitman, who holds Lincoln's long, dark body in front of us, suspended in its coffin, cannot help but open his lament to include, classically, nature, and nationally, the Civil War itself. Whitman's "vigil strange" becomes almost anonymous. Perhaps it's our "forever pioneering" sense of our experience, our constant need to break new ground, that makes us extra alert to our vulnerability. We are ever a frontier culture; nature, American nature, seems "something . . . that doesn't love a wall," that destroys, erases our houses, farms, towns, as if directed to do so, which, in Robert Frost, it appears to be: nature either indifferent or endowed with dark purpose. We are children of such innocence.

Here's a moment from Robert Penn Warren's great visionary piece, *Audubon,* which becomes a sort of American weather report, with figure-in-landscape:

> Shank-end of day, spit of snow, the call,
> A crow, sweet in distance, then sudden
> The clearing: among stumps, ruined cornstalks
>   yet standing, the spot
> Like a wound rubbed raw in the vast pelt of
>   the forest. There
> Is the cabin, a huddle of logs with no calculation
>   or craft:
> The human filth, the human hope.

> Smoke,
> From the mud-and-stick chimney, in the air,
>> greasily
> Brims, cannot lift, bellies the ridgepole, ravels
> White, thin, down the shakes, like sputum.

This is American naturalism at its best, the kind of setting Meriwether Lewis must have found himself in at the end; the kind of place Sherwood Anderson builds, in atmosphere, again and again, in "A Death in the Woods." Primitive but potent, the lyric scene as survival, and as both a rendering and a projection. "How thin is the membrane between himself and the world," writes Warren.

Even the term "elegy" may be too specific for us: we are so elegiac it's as if we wear its tone as part of our national character. We live within and among so much emptiness, so much literal skyline space, so much horizon openness, or forgiving that, so much density of forest and the slum of the man-made. We project but we also internalize what someone once called "the emotive imagination." Here's a little, quiet poem, "Twilights," from James Wright's *The Branch Will Not Break:*

> The big stones of the cistern behind the barn
> Are soaked in whitewash.
> My grandmother's face is a small maple leaf
> Pressed in a secret box.
> Locusts are climbing down into dark green crevices
> Of my childhood. Latches click softly in the trees. Your hair is gray.
>
> The arbors of the cities are withered.
> Far off, the shopping centers empty and darken.
>
> A red shadow of steel mills.

We are all, I suppose, sunset poets, and, being American, we like the sun right at the edge, the bloodaxe edge behind winter trees. The woods are lovely, dark and deep, and, step by step, it's night. Whitman, in "Crossing Brooklyn Ferry," sees "the sun half an hour high" and holds it there for a hundred and thirty-two long lines, holds it forever into the infinite future.

Red and gold, light and leaf, we see the change even before it occurs. We live the mornings and afternoons, but feel the breath-like pressure of the sun fallen. This is our true, internal sense of time, autumnal, November especially, the month of the harvest moon, Edgar Allan Poe, Herman Melville, the last letting go of the leaves. It could be spring, but something in the light and wind would remind us that at the end of the day . . .

2. The Love Poem

A body wishes to be held, & held, & what
Can you do about that?

LARRY LEVIS

LINDA GREGERSON

Rhetorical Contract in the Erotic Poem

John Dryden once wittily described John Donne's love poetry as calculated to "[perplex] the minds of the fair sex." Part of the pleasure of the witticism, of course, lies in its cutting edge. Beneath the surface of impassioned court-ship, Dryden suggests, one finds a less than fully deferential attitude toward women: the overheated importunities of Donne's love poems—the most athletic love poems in the language—are assumed to be pitched quite be-yond the comprehension of the lady or ladies to whom they purport to be addressed. Does Dryden mean to suggest that Donne's method (the dizzy-ing virtuosity of his syntax and imagery) and his ostensible matter (sexual seduction) are intractably at odds? That Donne undermines himself by in-dulging in his own chronic propensity for showing off? Or are we rather to understand that perplexity is somehow conducive to sexual surrender? The one unambiguous link between Dryden's witty analysis and Donne's witty poetry, at least as Dryden would have us construe it, appears to be the rakish misogyny that serves as their common foundation: sexual games-manship is imagined to be a species of pleasure that takes place at the ex-pense of its "fairer" partner.

These playful entanglements of sex and condescension are conspicuous as well in the work of Donne's contemporary Andrew Marvell. Marvell does not favor so convoluted a syntax nor so fevered a display of philoso-phical speculation as those we associate with Donne, but, like Donne, he works at the boundaries of excess. His overwrought similes and outsized metaphors—conceits, as we call them—confess their own laboriousness and thus their insufficiency. Behind the busy surface of poetic figure there ap-pears a discomfiting gap, an inadequate "fit" between the material world, or the figurative imagination that draws upon it, and the "something else" that imagination tries to represent. When Dryden and Samuel Johnson sought to describe—and to disparage—this penchant in certain seventeenth-century poetry, they called it "metaphysical." Dr. Johnson in particular heartily disapproved of a poetry in which "the most heterogeneous ideas are yoked by violence together."

Modern readers have come to regard the Metaphysicals with a friendlier eye, but they have not disputed the violence of the metaphysical imagination, its willful enactment of discordance and disproportion, its preference for friction over smoothness. Our own sensibilities find sympathetic echo in these very dynamics. But we ought not to tame Dr. Johnson's insight overmuch: there *is* something dark, something dangerous behind the flamboyance and conspicuous exertion of the metaphysical imagination. We may see this darkness at work not only in the figurative yoking—the metaphysical conceit Dr. Johnson had in mind—but also in the sexual yoking so central to the metaphysical poem. Here, for example, is the first verse paragraph of Andrew Marvell's most frequently anthologized lyric, "To His Coy Mistress":

> Had we but world enough, and time,
> This coyness, Lady, were no crime.
> We would sit down, and think which way
> To walk, and pass our long love's day.
> Thou by the Indian Ganges' side
> Shouldst rubies find; I by the tide
> Of Humber would complain. I would
> Love you ten years before the flood,
> And you should, if you please, refuse
> Till the conversion of the Jews.
> My vegetable love should grow
> Vaster than empires and more slow;
> An hundred years should go to praise
> Thine eyes, and on thy forehead gaze;
> Two hundred to adore each breast,
> But thirty thousand to the rest;
> An age at least to every part,
> And the last age should show your heart.
> For, Lady, you deserve this state,
> Nor would I love at lower rate.

How shall we begin to parse this extravagant rhetoric? Exotic location: "Indian Ganges." Hyperbolic expanses of time: "an hundred years," "two hundred," "thirty thousand." Elevated language: rhymed couplets, stately tetrameter, refined grammatical mood (dominated by the future subjunctive). The poem is addressed to the speaker's "mistress," that is, a lady to whom courtesy and courtly convention and erotic longing attribute a superordinate status, a power to command. She is said to be "coy," that is, strategically withholding. She is thus imagined as capable of calculation and of extracting erotic compliment at a high "rate." The poet professes to be more than willing to provide what she would have, but surely it is less than complimentary to charge the lady with calculation. "Coyness" in Marvell's era might be used to connote mere reticence, but the less neutral connotation was already coming into ascendency; it would take a very innocent lady indeed to gaze into the mirror of Marvell's poem and see herself figured as unaffectedly "shy." We may note, while we're at it, the conspicuous third-person possessive in the title of the poem: to *his*, not *my*, coy mistress. That the title conforms to convention should not dull us to its strategic subtlety; convention is often the repository of strategic subtlety. The body of the poem is written in first- and second-persons; the lover addresses his lady directly. And yet in the title of the poem, he coolly acknowledges another audience. For whose amusement is this lady being wooed?

And then there is the extended subjunctive: hypothesis contrary to fact. *Had* we world enough and time . . . but we do not. Taking everything back before it is given, the poet inventories the lavish forms of courtship he "would," but will not, be happy to perform. The inventory itself, if truth be told, is rather perfunctory: ten years, a hundred, etc.; your eyes, your forehead, etc. "Vegetable love" is wonderful (though what exactly does it mean? Scholarly annotation about the ancient division of souls—vegetative, sensitive, and rational—falls flat somehow). "Till the conversion of the Jews" (i.e., till the eve of Apocalypse) is better yet. It is perhaps too good. The apocalyptic vista rhymes so neatly with the lady's scruple ("Jews," "refuse") that the poem's wide disproportions are made to seem preposterous. It is not chiefly lack of time and "world" that prevent the suitor from suing in the heightened manner dictated by poetic convention: it is aesthetic disdain. The suitor is burlesquing the very expansiveness with which he is expected to sue. Expected by whom? By the lady, or so her lover unchivalrously implies. It is as though a woman of our own day were charged with basing her fantasy life upon the daytime soaps. Marvell's coy mistress finds herself accused not only of manipulative affectation but also of frank bad taste. What kind of woman would be wooed like this?

The tone of insult deepens in the second section of the poem:

But at my back I always hear
Time's wingèd chariot hurrying near;
And yonder all before us lie
Deserts of vast eternity.
Thy beauty shall no more be found;
Nor, in thy marble vault, shall sound
My echoing song; then worms shall try
That long-preserved virginity,
And your quaint honour turn to dust,
And into ashes all my lust:
The grave's a fine and private place,
But none, I think, do there embrace.

Following the slightly acerbic stipulation with which he concluded the first section of his wooing speech (I think too highly of your deserts and of myself to love "at lower rate"), the lover puts forth his official explanation for refusing to woo by the book. And as if to show what he *could* do if he would, he "explains" in a flight of eloquence. Far from affording us dignified or delectable leisure, he says, time is a "wingèd chariot" hastening toward our end. The only vastness at our disposal is the vastness of the afterlife. That afterlife affords no vistas of erotic or moral "desért," but merely the emptiness of a désert. The logic of the lover's argument is the logic of *carpe diem*: "seize (or savor) the day." It was a well-worn logic in the Renaissance, as it had been since the time of Horace. "Gather ye rosebuds while ye may," wrote Marvell's contemporary Robert Herrick: "Old time is still a-flying; / And this same flower that smiles today / Tomorrow will be dying." Counseling a maiden to seize the day was also a well-worn stratagem of seducers, as the conclusion of Herrick's poem makes clear:

Then be not coy, but use your time,
  And, while ye may, go marry;
For, having lost but once your prime,
  You may forever tarry.

This poem is brazenly addressed "To the Virgins, to Make Much of Time."
  Like Herrick, Marvell is quite explicit about the unlovely threat his hurry-up implies. In neither poet do we find the faithful suitor's profession,

"To me you shall always be lovely." Nor even, "I shall love you forever despite the ravages of age." Not at all. Explicated for the benefit of virgins in general, or a coy mistress in particular, desire is found to be quite as ruthless as time. Desire has a short half-life; ladies must get while the getting is good. Lest the lewdness of the insult be lost on the lady, Marvell introduces a pair of genital insinuations. "You scruple to preserve your bodily intactness?" the lover taunts. "You haven't a prayer; it's either me or the worms." Nor is "quaint" honor half so fastidious as it at first appears to be: Chaucer used "queynte"—and Renaissance authors used it too—to denote the female pudendum.

Now that both mistress and lovemaking have been quite stripped of their pretensions, now that the lady knows just where she stands, both in the general marketplace and in her lover's particular regard, the lover unleashes his most fevered proposition:

> Now therefore, while the youthful hue
> Sits on thy skin like morning dew,
> And while thy willing soul transpires
> At every pore with instant fires,
> Now let us sport us while we may,
> And now, like amorous birds of prey,
> Rather at once our time devour
> Than languish in his slow-chapped power.
> Let us roll all our strength and all
> Our sweetness up into one ball,
> And tear our pleasures with rough strife
> Through the iron gates of life;
> Thus, though we cannot make our sun
> Stand still, yet we will make him run.

Note the driven enjambments: "all / Our sweetness," "sun / Stand still." This is forward motion with a vengeance. Not turtle doves, but "birds of prey." Not gilded portals, but "iron gates." The lover proposes a world in which the alternatives are not so much "eat or be eaten," but "eat and be eaten or be eaten alone." Not one creature is not caught in the mortal machinery; only with violence can the day (and the initiative) be seized.

The poet's bravado is undeniably exhilarating, and yet we may return to the question that Dryden implicitly asked of Donne: Can this poem really be after what it purports to be after? Can it, as a seduction poem, by even the wildest stretch of imagination be designed to *work*? What kind of woman would be successfully wooed like this? Either, I would suggest, she must be a very stupid one, one so dull to insult and so eager to be swept off her feet that she succumbs to her fate obliviously, or she must be a very clever one indeed, one willing to join the lover in his high-spirited contempt for convention, one capable of discerning the compliment behind the ostensible slur. This lady—the second one—would be a woman to whom the poet might signal above the head, as it were, of the foolish figure he playfully pretends to take her for. It is this second lady in whom I prefer to believe, and whom I believe the Marvellian poem proposes: a worthy and an active partner in intellect, in appetite, in irreverent conversation, and in bed.

⁂

To focus on rhetoric is to focus on the social premise that underlies all linguistic practice, to emphasize those aspects of language that constitute a series of tacit and explicit negotiations between speaker and audience. To focus on rhetoric in the lyric poem is willfully to ignore, or to take with a grain of salt, the historical and heuristic divisions between poetry and public speaking. For poetry, like public speaking, has a suasive agenda: the poem may affect the contours of solitary meditation or unfiltered mimesis, the recklessness of outburst or the abstraction of music, but it always also seeks to convince, or coerce, or seduce a reader; it is never disinterested, never pure; it has designs on the one who listens or reads.

And the one who listens or reads is never "one" in the literal sense. I have spoken as though Marvell's reader and his lady were in some sense equivalent, but of course there is a difference between the dramatic and textual "staging" of rhetoric. In "To His Coy Mistress," as in the vast preponderance of Petrarchan lyric, the poet's negotiation with his lady is dramatically staged. (In rhetorical terms, it makes no difference whether the lady is entirely fictive or not.) The poet's negotiation with his reader is, by contrast, textually staged, and harder to describe without falsification. We are used to construing this reader (every reader except the single imagined beloved, that is) as an outer audience, an audience who overhears or eavesdrops on the lyric conversation or complaint. Certainly this reader, this third party to seduction, is in many respects even further from the poet's reach than is the reluctant lady: belonging neither to a place, a sex, or a historical period within the author's control. But the helpful concept of "outer" is also misleading. The push and pull of pleasure and abatement, teasing and withdrawal, coyness and expectation are every bit as "inward" to the process of reading-in-time as to the process of dramatized seduction. The reader may ally herself now with the poet's virtuosity, now with the beloved's strategic silence, now with the momentums of genre and convention, now with their witty overturning; but in all these modulations the reader is an intimate too, one of the partners in utterance.

⁂

When the sonnet was imported into English from the Italian, early in the sixteenth century, it was understood to comprise a set of formal conventions (fourteen lines of eleven syllables, which became in English iambic pentameter; a fixed rhyme scheme) and, of equal importance, a set of thematic and rhetorical conventions. Sonnets came in groups, or sequences. They told a story; or rather, they refused to tell a story outright, but were built around a story that took place in the white space between individual lyrics. The story was of love: love unrequited, love requited but unfulfilled, love so fleetingly fulfilled as merely to make suffering keener, love thwarted by the beloved's absence, or aloofness, or prior possession by another. Impediment was as central to the sonnet as was love. Impediment produced the lyric voice. Without impediment, the lover would have no need to resort to poetry.

Argument had always been one of the common rhetorical modes of the sonnet, but it was the English who made argument supreme, subordinating every other rhetorical momentum. No longer was the sonnet exclusively dominated by the interior logic of meditation or the associative logic of image; no longer was the poet content to dwell upon fugitive sightings of the beloved (as had been the case in Petrarch, for example). The poet had a case to make and a primary audience of one: you, dear creature, should return my love for any number of excellent reasons that I could name; you should put aside this reticence; you should grant me a kiss; you should grant me more than a kiss; you should be faithful only to me; you should be as I imagine you to be. At a playful extreme, the poet/lover in Sir Philip Sidney's *Astrophel and Stella* pretends to catch his lady in a logical trap, applying the rules of grammar to force her erotic capitulation: "O Grammar rules," the lover expostulates, "o now your vertues show," for she, "Least once should not be heard, twice said No No." Since grammar says that a double negative produces an affirmative, the lady is now obliged by the rules of grammar to bestow her favors on her lover, or so her lover professes in his sonnet. This is speech act with a vengeance.

If the rhetoric of *Astrophel and Stella* is dominated by the stratagems and dalliance of foreplay, the rhetoric of Shakespeare's sonnet sequence is dominated by the postcoital: its "plot" and its rhetorical ingenuity are driven not by the beloved's resistance but by the beloved's inconstancy. In its roughest outlines, the argument of the Shakespearean sequence goes something like this: the poet begins by attempting to persuade the young man that he (the young man) should marry, or should in any case engender children. Women, the necessary vehicles of biological generation, soon drop out of the hortatory configuration altogether, however, to be replaced by the poet-lover and the posterity secured by his poems. Triangulation drops away, and the suit becomes direct: "Mate. Get children" becomes "Mate with me. Get poems." There are problems. There is a rival for the young man's affection. The young man is unfaithful. The poet appears to have been unfaithful. A dark lady enters, reintroducing the triangle. The poet is tormented. The poet adopts many rhetorical stratagems in his effort to extract stability from a radically unstable prospect. In "Sonnet 116," he resorts to lofty overview:

> Let me not to the marriage of true minds
> Admit impediments. Love is not love
> Which alters when it alteration finds,
> Or bends with the remover to remove.
> O no, it is an ever-fixéd mark
> That looks on tempests and is never shaken;
> It is the star to every wand'ring bark,
> Whose worth's unknown, although his height be taken.
> Love's not time's fool, though rosy lips and cheeks
> Within his bending sickle's compass come.
> Love alters not with his brief hours and weeks,
> But bears it out ev'n to the edge of doom.
>   If this be error and upon me proved,
>   I never writ, nor no man ever loved.

To whom is the sonnet addressed? Abstracted from its place in Shakespeare's sequence, the poem appears at first to be addressed to no one, to the ether, to the world in general. The speaker casts his argument as objective, not personal at all, not "interested" in the narrow sense of the term. But restored to its context, the poem is thick with vested interest and personal agenda. Its very efforts at objectivity assume the resonance of psychological portraiture: the speaker is trying very hard to keep his world from falling apart, to contain the psychic and ontological entropy occasioned by the beloved's faithlessness. The audience is threefold: behind the general audience the sonnet purports to address, it conjures an audience of one, the faithless young man who must be argued into a loftier conception of love and thus a loftier mode of behavior. Behind the second person, who will always be as he is now, elusive, unpossessable, the sonnet conjures a listening self, to whom the speaking self proposes a "love" (an informing passion and also a philosophy of passion) that will compensate for all that his other "love" (the young man) refuses to be.

"Let me not": the poem begins with an exhortation that, tellingly, makes the self the grammatical object, rather than the grammatical subject, of the verb. And yet the speaker seems both to envy and to emulate the declarative: delineating the allowable parameters of love, he aims for airtight definition. I will not grant, the poet asserts, that love includes impediments. If it falters, it is not love. The love I have in mind is a beacon (a seamark or navigational guide to sailors); it is the north star. Like that star, it exceeds all narrow comprehension (its "worth's unknown"); its height alone (the navigator's basis for calculation) is sufficient to guide us. The poem's ideal is unwavering faith, and it purports to perform its own ideal. Odd then, isn't it, how much of the argument proceeds by means of negation: "let me not," "love is not," "O no," and so forth.

These negatives are clues: the poem has been written to refute certain concepts (alteration, removal) that it relegates to the realm of abstraction. But in the third quatrain, abstraction begins to break down. Time, it seems, has something to do with change and threatened removal. The poet argues back: time is paltry compared to love. Time may alter loveliness, but love will not flinch. Time may be measured in petty hours and weeks; love's only proper measure begins where time leaves off ("the edge of doom"). Quite apart from the continued heaping up of negation (two more "not's"), this quatrain registers increasing strain. Line 10 (the ominous sickle) is all but unpronounceable: the consonants come fast and thick; the hissing alliterations deform the line as surely as time deforms the beauties of the flesh. "Doom" was capable of a neutral meaning in Shakespeare's day—it could refer to judgment of any sort, good or bad—but it was always a gloomy syllable, especially in the context of final judgment (again, "the edge of doom"). "Bears it out" rings with defiance, which ironically tends to direct the reader's attention to that which faith defies. That something else, that deliberately unnamed enemy to love has, in other words, begun to assume palpable presence. And what the poem has gained in forcefulness, it has lost in assurance. Quatrain by quatrain, line by line, despite, or rather by means of its brave resistance, the sonnet has been taken over by that which it has tried to write out of existence: by faithlessness.

The couplet represents a last, desperate attempt to regain control. It rests upon a sort of buried syllogism: I am obviously a writer (witness this poem!); I assert that love is constant; therefore love must be constant. As any logician could testify, however, these premises have no necessary relationship to their conclusion. The couplet is designed to shut down all opposition, to secure the thing (unchanging love) the poem has staked its heart on. It is sheer bravado and of course it fails. What fails as logical proof, however, succeeds quite brilliantly as poetry. The sonnet proposes and enacts a high-stakes rhetorical proposition: it aims to convince its layered audience, and thus to secure the metaphysical existence, of a love impervious to change. This rhetorical labor comes to constitute a portrait-in-action of the self under pressure, a self whose coherence depends upon the beloved's constancy, and whose erotic doubts threaten dispersal. The rhetorical proposition progressively reveals itself to be suspended in thin air: even as the poet's eloquence swells to a climax, his grounding in confirmable reality disintegrates. The poem stages its own rhetorical undoing and, doing so, traces a powerful portrait of human longing.

⁂

The Latin rhetoric handbooks Shakespeare's contemporaries adapted for their own offer counsel on what the rhetor must be, or seem to be, how the speaker must construct a self of words in order to suggest a presence behind the words, a presence that secures the efficacy of words. From the perspective of rhetoric, meaning is the measurable consequence of eloquence, an effect or manipulable impression, as when one spirit contrives to subdue another, as in, I *mean* to make you mine. Rhetoric emphasizes the transitive aspects of linguistic production, the conspiracy of words with power. The power to mold opinion is an emanation of the speaker's person, or so the classical rhetoricians frankly posit: a thing is so because I who say it is so am a reliable person. And you are willing to believe what I say, or to behave as if you do, because the self you see in the mirror of my words, the space I invite you to inhabit as interlocutor, is a self, or a space, you like. Rhetoric invents its audience, too.

The special innovation of lyricists in sixteenth-century England was to combine the flamboyant manipulations of rhetorical persuasion with the quasi-dramatic enactment of Petrarchan love-longing. In Wyatt, in Sidney, in Shakespeare, the speaker implicit behind the lyric is at once a technical virtuoso and a creature capable of linguistic self-betrayal. Idiosyncracies of phrasing, gaps in logic, ostensibly inadvertent lapses of proportion begin to be cultivated as symptoms of personality or clues to dissonant subtext. This turns the handbook premise against itself: rhetorical power is found to inhere not only in demonstrated mastery but also, paradoxically, in mastery's breakdown. The most compelling word is found to be the word that makes its own fallibility, and that of its speaker, most palpably felt.

⁂

Classical rhetoric is unashamedly *ad hominem*; it speaks "to the man" and "through the man" as well, constructing a self in language as an instrument of persuasion. The Petrarchan love lyric makes its address to the female beloved the occasion for masculine soul-making. But we are heirs to a powerful lineage of women who have raided and rebuilt what was once imagined to be a masculine preserve. Like Shakespeare's "Sonnet 116," the following lyric by Louise Bogan proceeds in the manner of a general argument, addressed to a general audience. Like Shakespeare's sonnet, "Women" derives much of its momentum from the imperfect sustaining of that rhetorical proposition:

Women have no wilderness in them,
They are provident instead,
Content in the tight hot cell of their hearts
To eat dusty bread.

They do not see cattle cropping red winter grass,
They do not hear
Snow water going down under culverts
Shallow and clear.

They wait, when they should turn to journeys,
They stiffen, when they should bend.
They use against themselves that benevolence
To which no man is friend.

They cannot think of so many crops to a field
Or of clean wood cleft by an axe.
Their love is an eager meaninglessness
Too tense, or too lax.

They hear in every whisper that speaks to them
A shout and a cry.
As like as not, when they take life over their door-sills
They should let it go by.

One of the immediate oddities of rhetorical contract in this poem, the who-is-speaking-to-whom part, is the use of "they." This poem written by a woman speaks of women in the third person throughout, and speaks with considerable acerbity. Are we meant to imagine that no one is speaking? That the speaker is transparent? On the contrary. The speaker is too opinionated to be transparent; her charges are too harsh to seem to come from nowhere in particular. The rhetorical action that establishes itself from the outset of the poem, the conspicuous vocal self-portraiture, is that of a speaker who is expending a considerable amount of energy to distance herself from her sex. The rhetorical premise is ironic: doubling or dissembling. The very plainness of the poem's assertions are part of its irony. "Content in the tight hot cell of their hearts / To eat dusty bread." Is anyone "content" to eat dusty bread? A person may be doomed, by fate or character or temperament or inaptitude, to eat dusty bread, but content? We may be skeptical.

"They do not see cattle cropping red winter grass," though this line, written by one of "them," would seem to embody the gift of seeing in abundance, and also to induce it in others. "They cannot think of so many crops to a field / Or of clean wood cleft by an axe." We begin to move into the territory of assertion-contrary-to-palpable-fact, of self-negating assertion, on the order of "there are no oranges in this poem." To write of a thing is to think of a thing, and clean words cleft by consonance are as close as poetry comes to clean wood cleft by an axe.

So we inhabit an unfolding field of dramatic irony, not the kind where the audience knows something the character does not, but the kind in which the speaker herself stands as flat contradiction to that which the speaker is saying. But this particular irony—the self-evident negation of self—is only the more obvious, and the lesser, of two contractual ironies that govern the poem. What is this poem about? Well, under the rubric of "women," it works to distinguish two modes of being. The mode commended is outward-looking, risk-taking, open to the invitation of wilderness, to the sound of snow water, to the logic of husbandry and the exhilaration of work. The discommended mode is based on inwardness, on hoarding, and on love. Love: it is the woman's subject and woman's profession (Bogan, writing during the ascendance of the novel, has willfully occluded those centuries in which love was the preserve of masculine lyric). And lo, another irony. The poem on women written by a woman to exorcize and excoriate the feminine obsession with love progressively reveals itself to be: a poem obsessed with love. The speaker's revulsion against kindness (against both nurture or tenderness and likeness or kinship) reflects the harshness of her own entrapment.

Thus far we seem to have a modern instance of the self-consuming rhetoric-machine we found in Shakespeare's sonnet. But the rhetorical transaction in Bogan's poem has a very different arc, a very different tenor than that in Shakespeare's poem. If the first contractual irony has to do with the relation of real to pretended speaker, the second contractual irony has to do with the relation of real to pretended audience. Both Shakespeare's sonnet and Bogan's five quatrains simultaneously enact and discredit a rhetorical proposition they appear to be invested in: love is by nature constant and true, women are by nature losers. But Shakespeare's poem stages the progressive disappearance of a second-party audience: rhetorical contract breaks down because the partner in discourse refuses to hold up his end of things (the young man proves faithless; the world in general refuses to endorse the lover's fervid hopefulness by affording plausible evidence). Conversely, Bogan's poem stages the progressive *appearance* of a second-party audience, an audience of one, which emerges from the shadowy universal and undifferentiated audience the poem pretends to address. Who is this one? He is one who has been taken in over the door-sill, much to the speaker's regret. He is one hereby sent packing, as he ought to have been "let go" in the first place. The general disdain that has seemed for the length of the poem to be directed exclusively to the female sex here narrows to disdain of a complementary and very particular sort. The general *you* unveils in its midst a singular *you* who had better by now be singularly discomfited.

❧ ❧

As in the poem by Louise Bogan, the space between the *I* and the *you* in William Meredith's sonnet "The Illiterate" is negotiated by means of the third person. But far from assuming the declamatory mode of demonstrative rhetoric, Meredith's speaker quietly introduces his third person within the structure of a simile. Except for its first six words, in fact, his poem is nothing *but* similitude, or metaphoric vehicle: the tail of a long-tailed simile:

> Touching your goodness, I am like a man
> Who turns a letter over in his hand
> And you might think this was because the hand
> Was unfamiliar but, truth is, the man
> Has never had a letter from anyone;
> And now he is both afraid of what it means
> And ashamed because he has no other means
> To find out what it says than to ask someone.
>
> His uncle could have left the farm to him,
> Or his parents died before he sent them word,
> Or the dark girl changed and want him for beloved.
> Afraid and letter-proud, he keeps it with him.
> What would you call his feeling for the words
> That keep him rich and orphaned and beloved?

Who speaks to whom here? A reticent *I* addresses one whose "goodness" he can only touch upon obliquely, being himself so unused to such goodness that its touch has come like a letter to the hand of one who cannot read. He professes himself inexpert, and yet he professes himself. Profession is indeed the primary business of his poem; it is the customary business of lyric poems and yet, for this persona, completely unaccustomed. The poem is a love poem; it performs the delicate ceremony of reciprocal acknowledgment; it is itself the epistolary response to an as-yet-unopened letter.

This sonnet was published in *The Open Sea and Other Poems* in 1958. Written in an era that was not so frank about homoerotic address as was

Shakespeare's era, "The Illiterate" takes cover in obliquity. The beloved described in the poem, if minimally described, as a "dark girl," is a figure of speech, an analogy only, a surrogate for the beloved who is addressed in the second person, and whose gender therefore needn't be specified. The metaphorical beloved—the dark girl—may also be a delicate allusion to Shakespeare's dark lady, and thus a coded key to the primary passion—the homoerotic passion—in which the poem is grounded.

The love poem is also an *ars poetica*, written with the apparent simplicity of a primer. Look at the end rhymes: man, man, hand, hand, one, one, means, means, etc. These are not simply the most frontal rhymes available in English (overwhelmingly monosyllabic, scored on the downbeat): they are also identical rhymes. Some of them further enact the form of sonic-repetition-with-semantic-difference that the French call *rime riche* ("hand" in line two has a different meaning that the "hand" in line 3). As the name suggests (*rime riche*), the rhyming deployment of homonyms has been admired as a kind of technical virtuosity in some literary cultures, but identical rhyme, especially in English, is generally looked down upon as a species of impoverishment, as though the poet were confessing, "I couldn't come up with anything else, so I've used the same word over again." The word always and only equal to itself: in the context of an *ars poetica*, these selfsame iterations insist upon the material, the iconic status of words, the status words must occupy for one to whom they do not habitually yield. The illiterate is a figure for the poet because he cannot or will not make words disappear into easy instrumentality, will not take them for granted. And thus, in his hands, words do not lose their aura but gather into themselves a remarkable conjunction of powers and possibilities.

"Or his parents died before he sent them word." Word of what? Of his happy inheritance, of course; we can find no other plausible antecedent on the page. But if the unopened letter contains the news of his uncle's legacy, it cannot also be the letter informing the recipient of his parents' tragic death; line 10 is a non sequitur. It is, in fact, a wholly deliberate non sequitur, as confirmed by the conjunctions in the last line of the poem: not "or" but "and." Rich *and* orphaned *and* beloved. Having left the letter sealed, the illiterate has preserved all its possibilities; they have not narrowed down to one. As a figure for the lover, the man clings to the ignorant beginning of love, orphaned, yes, cut loose from all prior experience that might ground or protect him, and yet protected by his very ignorance, by the still-sealed letter, from the treacheries and diminutions that love may hold. As a figure for the poet, the man is rich in reverence, orphaned or unsponsored by the common, disregardful pragmatism of language use, and beloved as only the last believer shall be beloved.

And see what the poet has gained rhetorically. The last lines of the poem are spoken in the form of a question. When we speak in casual conversation about a "rhetorical question," we too often mean a dead question, a placeholder, one whose answer is self-evident and whose purpose is at best to extract agreement from a silenced opposition. But that is to forget the full social contract that "rhetoric" always represents, the subtle play of power and consent, suggestion and reciprocity. I and successive generations of my students have spent many hours considering what the answer to the poet's question at the close of "The Illiterate" might be, and the only satisfactory answer we have ever been able to imagine is also the simplest: I call that feeling *love*. And see with what exquisite tact the poet has performed the ceremony of reciprocal declaration: speaking/not speaking the word himself, he has caused it to be spoken (if only silently) by the other, by the *you*, by the partner in feeling and discourse, by the one whose goodness has prompted the poem in the first place and now, in the act of reading, confirms it.

In an effort to speak with some specificity about rhetorical strategies within the erotic lyric, I've considered a scant four poems, two from the Renaissance and two from the twentieth century, all of them widely read and deservedly famous. That these poems share a common subject or occasion (erotic love) is surely no coincidence, but neither is it intended to be restrictive. Erotic address usefully aggravates the tensions between self-interest and persuasion, veiling and revealing, but it has been in the present instance chiefly a way of narrowing the field for discussion, providing some commonality within which we may observe a spectrum of local practices: the love poem is merely an example. The formal and semantic resources I've tried to adduce—rhyme and enjambment, syntax and grammatical mood, figures of speech—might be pertinent in any number of contexts, but my present interest has been in the way they serve and articulate the dynamic I call *rhetorical contract*: the negotiated push and pull between the partners in utterance, the one who speaks (truly or deceitfully, fiercely or playfully, with single or with multiple intent) and the one who hears or reads. What I've hoped to suggest by foregrounding the transitive action of the lyric poem—those performed rhetorical contracts that are part of the fiction of the poem, and those, too, that are prompted by the fiction of the poem—is how rhetoric can be as malleable and capacious an instrument, and one as worthy of our attention, as any of the other formal resources of poetry.

Meretricious Kisses

A connoisseur of kisses, Thomas Wyatt recognized a good kiss when he got one. He didn't like to stop at just one kiss. The poem "They flee from Me" tells us that and records one of the sexiest kisses in English literature. What makes a poem feel real enough that we "fall for it," read as if it happened, and in just this way? What compels a reader to make personal claims about this poem, this poet? The question should really be: What pulls us in? Even better: What makes such a poem erotic? The events in "They flee from Me" feel immediate despite their distance from us, despite how different Wyatt's life as a courtier in the service of King Henry VIII was from ours. Eros is eros is eros, across the centuries, and anyone is susceptible to its power. That's one answer. But to speak in a more nuanced way of poetry's power to convince us, we should consider the body of the poem itself. There we would find that Wyatt conjures an ongoing drama, in rhythmically intense language; he enacts his recollections as if they were still in progress. The kisses he describes continue to haunt him; they are, in equal measure, full of pleasure and pain. Although he mourns their loss, he can't forget them, nor the woman whose mouth he kissed:

> When her loose gown from her shoulders did fall,
>   And she me caught in her arms long and small;
> Therewithal sweetly did me kiss,
>   And softly said, *Dear heart, how like you this?*

Oh, he likes it. And continues to hear her mocking voice even after the event itself has passed. But throughout the poem "all is turned," their intimacy dissolved into painful memory, rejection, "a strange fashion of forsaking," and what remains are questions and no good answers. Good kisses, bad kisses, meretricious kisses: What are kisses for?

Erotic poetry makes its own strategic use of the emotional tactics that lovers have always employed on each other. Poetry enacts a simultaneously frustrating and engaging dance of intimacy: hurry and delay; contact and distance; love and hate; pleasure and pain. Poetry connects readers to the made and shaped lives of strangers. We encounter their inventions, their hopes, their passions. Not only is *erotic* poetry erotic, but so is *all* poetry erotic, whatever its supposed subject, intent, or device. It is a truism that poetic language is itself intrinsically erotic. "It is nothing new," as Anne Carson writes, "to say that all utterance is erotic in some sense, that all language shows the structure of desire at some level." Contact: we write when we need it, or when we lack it, when we are driven to speak. We intend to supply a missing thing—a body, a notion, an agreement, a delight. Words represent the material, tactile world, words help us find our way into imagined spaces, words are a conduit from a writer to a reader.

In the French troubadour poetic tradition, longing for the absent beloved provides the energy and momentum for hundreds of poems. Longing, always longing. The lovers never meet. Something (a husband, an ocean, a class divide) comes between them. Language sustains the romance. These components (lover, beloved, and what comes between them, in Anne Carson's formulation) derive from ancient poetry about eros, and were later developed and perfected by poets of the courtly love tradition. Such poetry assumes that attraction may only be sustained by placing obstacles between the lovers. The gap of longing must not be breached, the lovers must not meet. The common elements include the perpetually absent beloved, joy intermingled with anguish, and yearning as the governing state of mind. The ingredients are affecting in combination but limited in their forward motion. They prohibit consummation. The key emotional component of this poetics is thus erotic frustration. There's a difference between poems of longing or of seduction (as in the *carpe diem* tradition) and poems of contact, presence, or beholding. When nothing comes between the lover and the beloved, we enter another realm of erotic poetry. It's in their kiss.

How do poets kiss?

The early Greeks spoke of two souls mingling in a kiss. Roman grammarians categorized kisses into types: friendly kisses (*oscula*), loving kisses (*basia*), and passionate kisses (*suavia*). I am concerned not with *oscula* or *basia*, but with *suavia*, passionate kisses. For if poems of seduction want to hold off the moment of satisfaction or make a game of sexual persuasion, poems of contact seek to enact and replay the kiss itself. A kiss is an intimate greeting. When I kiss you, all my senses are in play; I taste and I touch; my skin encounters yours in an intimate, tactile exchange; I smell your skin, your hair, sense your excitement, hear the sounds you make, how you breathe. If I open my eyes, I see you, kissing me. We couldn't get much closer. That expression of contact in poetry is, for Wyatt, "no dream, I lay broad waking"; and similarly other poets of erotic verse seek to replicate and savor these intense sensory qualities.

Not only poets try to understand the mysteries of kissing. The motives for passionate kisses bewilder and bother Sigmund Freud, who writes: "A particular contact between the mucous membranes of the lips of two people concerned [is] held in high sexual esteem among many nations in spite of the fact that the parts of the body involved do not form part of the sexual apparatus but constitute the entrance to the digestive tract." Later, he notes that kissing is a version of the sexual act itself, both a prelude and an imitation. For Freud, an inescapable truth: kissing is a strange thing to do. E. E. Cummings recognizes that the first kiss is an encounter between strangers, lovers new to each other, and along with pleasure comes physical awkwardness. He describes

> a thing most new complete fragile intense,
> which wholly trembling memory undertakes
> —your kiss,the little pushings of flesh . . .

The narrator doesn't want this odd and pleasing experience to stop, and so the poem, made of a single extended sentence, unfolds in leisure, and even the landscape around them brightens with the power of the kiss. In the time it takes for the sentence to play out, we see how kissing alters perception, alters grammar, alters, even, the world. For when the second dash appears (after five intervening lines) to join the parts of Cummings's sonnet, we behold a changed world, a new space created by the breaching of the gap between them:

> —to feel how through the stopped entire day
> horribly and seriously thrills
> the moment of enthusiastic space

is a little wonderful,and say
Perhaps her body touched me;and to face

suddenly the lighted living hills

This turning point takes place at the volta of the sonnet, showing us how contact itself is a turning point. A good kiss, in a poem, has transformative power.

We read and write for contact; thus poetry seeks an audience, recipients who can be convinced to take our breath and touch for their very own. Poetry is a body. We speak of the basic element of poetic language as, rightly, a *figure* of speech. "The figure," Roland Barthes avers, "is the lover at work." The depiction of a kiss in a poem creates private space, face to face, in what Susan Stewart calls "the moment of beholding." But we guard our personal space in order to feel safe against incursions. A kiss is an intrusion, paradoxically making us feel both alive and endangered. Breaking the boundaries, the invisible bubble that surrounds each one of us, can imperil our sense of integrity. When we kiss, we open ourselves to another, and in turn enter into another body. So kisses nourish and feed even as they frighten by their strangeness.

Ouch

Alternately, kisses may wound. By their very nature they teach us to recognize our own insufficiency. In his wonderful book *On Kissing, Tickling, and Being Bored*, Adam Phillips reminds us that, for real kissing, we need other real people. We can never kiss our own mouths. Kissing the mirror is a poor substitute. And so, Phillips says, we become involved in "the dangerous allure and confusion ... of getting muddled up" with someone else." Kissing gives us access thereby to the strange, the otherness of a body besides one's own. I could eat you up, we say. Mouths are exploratory; they take in. Poems about erotic kissing dramatize this connection, play out what we gain and give. Poems of erotic contact often suggest not just a blurring of boundaries between two separate people, but something even more perilous. A kiss may wound, or imprint itself, it may leave a mark, as Cupid's arrow hits its target. These wounds can come not just from kisses but also from the lover's eyes, the gaze that is another sort of incursion, another kind of arrow. The sixteenth-century French poet Maurice Scève recognizes the doubled pain and pleasure in this erotic confusion:

> The less I see her, the more I hate her:
> The more I hate her, the less anger I feel.
> The more I adore her, the less it means:
> The more I flee her, the more I want her near.
> Love with hate, & pleasure with pain,
> The two arrows fall on me in a single rain.

Images of arrows are common in erotic poetry, but also frequent our daily discourse on love; in other clichés of erotic penetration, we say you are "getting your hooks in me," that you are "piercing me with your gaze," getting "under my skin."

In erotic poetry, metaphors of permeability are constantly in play. Edna St. Vincent Millay's narrator in "Sonnet 17," from her sequence *Fatal Interview*, cries "Sweet love, sweet thorn, when lightly to my heart / I took your thrust, whereby I since am slain, /And lie disheveled in the grass apart, /A sodden thing bedrenched by tears and rain." She blends the pleasures of physical love with the pain of postcoital rejection, first impaled, then overthrown, lying "apart," having become less than human, "a sodden thing."

So many varieties of penetration, so many similar tropes in erotic poems suggest that there is good contact and bad contact. Scève's contemporary, the French poet Louise Labé, writes of being harmed by a kiss, betrayed by a lover, saying "Every arrow makes a wound." Even so, she is greedy for more, as her adaptation of Catullus's poem #5 suggests. In "Sonnet 18" (translated by Edith R. Farrell), the lover vows to give back at least as many kisses as she receives:

> Kiss me. Again. More kisses I desire.
> Give me one your sweetness to express.
> Give me the most passionate you possess.
> Four I'll return, and hotter than the fire.
>
> There, did they burn? I'll change that hurt to pleasure
> By giving you ten others—all quite light.

Thus, as we mingle our kisses with delight,
Let us enjoy each other at our leisure.

This to teach one a double life shall give.
Each by himself and in his love shall live.
Allow my love this mad and foolish thought:

I'm always sad when living so discreetly,
And never find my happiness completely,
Unless a sally from my self I've sought.

The reciprocal kiss is Labé's subject. One kiss leads to the next, and the next. She argues for the pleasure of having it both ways, alone and connected, "a double life [...] / Each by himself and in his love," maintaining self-integrity while sallying forth into the strange appealing dissolution of a kiss. We have, she says, an insatiable appetite for kissing that reason will not recognize. Adam Phillips agrees, recognizing that kisses satisfy

the appetite for pleasure independent of the desire for nourishment or reproduction. When we kiss we devour the object by caressing it; we eat it, in a sense, but sustain its presence. Kissing on the mouth can have a mutuality that blurs the distinction between giving and taking ("In kissing do you render or receive?" Cressida asks in *Troilus and Cressida*).

The erotic kiss displays greed, a need for sustenance, a desire to absorb the other while still maintaining some control.

Lovers ask: Where do I stop, where do you begin? Maurice Scève poses this question in his series of *Délie* poems, which trace the obsessive nature of erotic love. For Scève, kisses create an erotic web:

You were, & are, and shall be DELIE,
So knotted by Love to my idle thoughts
That Death itself could never untie us.

In another poem, the Old Provençal "Car je te cele en ce surnom louable / Pource qu'en moy tu luys la nuict obscure" may be translated as "For I cloak you in this praiseworthy name / Because you light the pitchdark night in me." Richard Sieburth, editor and translator of Scève's poems, says

> The name "Délie" is thus a seal, a pseudonym, a troubadour senhal [or, in contemporary terms, a code name] whose function is not to refer but to hide—or, at most, to signify the vocative site of an address, of a place or clearing ... where the enigmatic Other might cast its ghostly, mirrored light back onto the obscurity of the subject's desire. ... the poet and his virtual Object are thus bound together as metaphors of each other, constantly exchanging places and genders, forever lost, like the name Délie itself, in translation.

The blurring of boundaries, as well as the potential loss of self, is always at the center of the kiss. Even the reader "taking in" the poem, "absorbing" what it says, is susceptible.

Poems about kisses take advantage of the special capacity of poetry to pay attention to a moment in time, to flood that moment with significance, and to apparently seal it off from other events. Erotic contact suggests not only a reciprocal action, boundary-breaking, but also an exchange, as in the Greek notion that souls may intermingle in the breath of a kiss. Xenophon and Socrates argue that it is wise to be cautious in the presence of Eros, that a mere kiss may be dangerous in more ways than one:

> "Good heavens," exclaimed Xenophon, "what a sinister effect you think a kiss has...." "You are *thick*," said Socrates, "do you think that beautiful people don't inject anything into you when they kiss, just because you can't see it? Don't you realize that the beast they call 'beauty and youth' is much more terrible than a poisonous spider..."

If we are too susceptible to "beauty and youth," we run the risk of being humiliated by our erotic need. The wound to our dignity is as sharp as any arrow. The clichés of erotic wounding—to be pierced, to be burned, to be dissolved or liquefied—all bespeak our essential fear of the edge of the known world. We give up our power when we display our hunger and need. The seam where the lips meet marks the border line between us.

"And thus it hapned, Death and *Cupid* met"

In *Eroticism*, George Bataille suggests that even as we treasure our existence as "discontinuous beings," we nonetheless "yearn for lost continuity . . . a total blending of two beings. . . ." The Platonic dream of being made whole, hermaphroditic, competes with the integrity of the solitary self, and our self-imaginings. Eros can disrupt our integrity and transport us into chaos. In erotic fusion, the good kiss and the dangerous kiss are the same kiss. A kiss is a conjugation. Even as *The Song of Songs* emphasizes the kiss's sweet nourishment ("Thy lips drip as the honeycomb, my spouse: Honey and milk are under thy tongue"), poet Richard Banfield's Renaissance sonnet sequence, *Cynthia*, spells out love and its discontents using nearly the same conceit. In sonnet 17, the lover's kisses carry a sting: "His mouth a hive, his tongue a honeycomb." Some three hundred years later, the pain of betrayal, of vulnerability, of being undone, is similarly exposed in Mina Loy's "Songs to Joannes." Published in 1917 and an early example of European Modernist fragmentation and narrative discontinuity, this poetic sequence is also an extended dance of intimacy, at first close, then distant; desiring, then ambivalent; open, then closed:

> Oh that's right
> Keep away from me Please give me a push
> Don't let me understand you Don't realise me
> Or we might tumble together
> Depersonalized
> Identical
> Into the terrific Nirvana
> Me you—you—me

(from "Song XIII")

"Songs to Joannes" displays the ambiguous status of a troubled relationship, and the pain that ambiguity causes. The loss of control that accompanies erotic fusion is felt in the discontinuity of the sequence itself. As Bataille reminds us in *The Accursed Share*, in embracing another we put ourselves at risk: "the totality of what is (the universe) swallows me. . . . In a sense it is unbearable and I seem to be dying. It is at this cost, no doubt, that I am no longer myself, but an infinity in which I am lost."

Sometimes all a writer has are kisses, and when the kisses go, so does the writing. After the death of her husband, Eugen Boissevain, in 1949, after her various lovers had drifted away into other arms, Edna St. Vincent Millay lived alone, increasingly dependent on morphine and alcohol. In the fall of 2004, I spent some days at the Library of Congress, reading her manuscripts, letters, drafts, working on my own poems, thinking about the nature of longing, of appetite. During that time I came across something unexpected: a series of grocery lists, written in Millay's hand, the lists themselves preserved amongst stacks of her literary papers and letters. I was struck by the repetitive nature of these lists, which, with few exceptions, contain the same four sad items, again and again. For at least the better part of a year (1950, the year she died), these lists suggest Millay subsisted on a diet of liverwurst, olives, Scotch, and cookies. As I handled and read each scrap of paper, I recognized someone whose appetite had narrowed to an extreme and impoverished state. She was alone, injecting herself with morphine, drinking heavily, and no longer writing. The passionate poems of her twenties and thirties, the passionate life she lived, must have seemed far away. If kissing is a kind of nourishment, how can we be—how should we be—reconciled to the fact that, some day, all kissing must end?

In *Don Juan*, Lord Byron tries to sustain the moment of pleasure, calling attention to the way that strong kisses last a long time:

> A long, long kiss, a kiss of Youth, and Love,
>   And Beauty, all concentrating like rays
> Into one focus, kindled from above;
>   Such kisses as belong to early days,
> When Heart, and Soul, and Sense, in concert move,
> And the blood's lava, and the pulse a blaze,
> Each kiss a heart-quake—for a kiss's strength,
> I think, it must be reckoned by its length.
>
> By length I mean duration . . .

A theory of kisses: Louise Labé's playful "Débat de Folie et d'Amour" asserts that "the greatest pleasure that there is, besides love, is talking about it." Indeed, talking about kisses makes them last, at least for the duration of a poem, in a memory, on the lips. This feels like paradox because a kiss itself is ephemeral. Despite this, we say: I know you by your kiss. It leaves its imprint on me. It burns me. I remember. That's what erotic poems seek—to burn, stay, to relive the moment of presence when my mouth first opened to yours, even though you have gone away. In E. E. Cummings's "in spite of everything," his speaker kisses a pillow in a memorializing gesture, linking love with the relentless passage of time:

> in spite of everything
> which breathes and moves,since Doom
> (with white longest hands
> neatening each crease)
> will smooth entirely our minds
>
> —before leaving my room
> turn,and(stooping
> through the morning)kiss
> this pillow,dear
> where our heads lived and were.

Poetry seeks to prolong contact, and the act of reading a poem replays that contact. In this way, both writer and reader delay the end of kissing, and maintain the possibility of keeping Eros alive.

Eros and the Erotics of Writing

In the last of his *Twenty Poems of Love*, Pablo Neruda writes: "I no longer love her, that's certain, but how I loved her." That contradiction, which lies at the heart of Western poetry from Sappho's denials through Petrarch's oxymorons to Edna St. Vincent Millay's apparent detachments, is a central form of the tension that generates lyric poetry. Throughout the poem Neruda attempts to keep a distance from a love he simply cannot resist:

> Tonight I can write the saddest lines.

> Write, for example, "The night is shattered
> and the stars are blue and shiver in the distance."

> The night wind revolves in the sky and sings.

> Tonight I can write the saddest lines.
> I loved her, and sometimes she loved me too.

As the poem progresses we understand that the self-consciousness of the first line is an attempt to mitigate the sadness, a strategy he continues with the casual "for example" in the next line. By the sixth line, he tries to diminish the love itself by ascribing the word "sometimes" to the beloved. Then the poet bursts in the next four lines into an emotional memory, only to use the word "sometimes" to describe his love, and subsequently offers a rationalization as again he pulls back, detaching himself:

> Through nights like this one I held her in my arms.
> I kissed her again and again under the endless sky.

She loved me, sometimes I loved her too.
How could one not have loved her great still eyes.

That this night is similar to the lovemaking nights only reminds him more strongly to recall those feelings of love and of hurt. The word "endless" suggests an ironic counterpoint to the loss, but also a sense of the intensity of their passion. The interplay is between an occasional or "sometime" love and a more permanent passion or memory or passion.

The poem continues like this, alternating and arguing with itself, and gradually expanding its references. The night is immense, there is the singing of someone "In the distance," and his soul searches for her through his sight and heart:

My soul is not satisfied that it has lost her.

My sight tries to find her as though to bring her closer.
My heart looks for her, and she is not with me.

But even as the stakes widen, the present emotion intensifies: the sight searches "as though" to approach her, the simile insuring a kind of safe distance for the emotions. Still, in the next line, the flat statement "she is not with me" brings the emotional hurt home again. The effect of all this is like a camera zooming in and out, panning across a landscape, changing perspectives. Finally Neruda arrives at the very conclusion he tried to avoid at the beginning, one that reveals the power of his opening restraint:

I no longer love her, that's certain, but maybe I love her.
Love is so short, forgetting is so long.

Because through nights like this one I held her in my arms
my soul is not satisfied that it has lost her.

Though this be the last pain that she makes me suffer
and these the last verses that I write for her.

The counterpointing of loving and not loving on the part of both lovers, of this one night and the endless sky, of change and constancy, passion and detachment, creates the poem's incredible power and tension. The repetition of certain lines and phrases, often with variants, adds to the insistence and intensity while at the same time suggesting an inevitable change. In the end the speaker admits what he was trying to eschew in order to avoid pain, as endless nights transform into the potential end of writing itself.

This poem reveals several essential aspects of the lyric: its dramatic unfolding, its quickly shifting perspectives, its attempt to deny the pain of what it knows. It further reveals the very pleasure of writing and of writing the saddest lines. After all, the poet "can" write the saddest lines this night, as the gradually uncovered love in the course of the poem creates a context for those lines. Perhaps this suggests that the last lines are posed, part of the inevitable progress of the meta-language of the poem. Nor is this to suggest a lack of dramatic or literal power, but on the contrary an intensification of that power. We understand there is a tension between the speaker and the poet: the speaker suffers the effects of the lost love, while the poet is able rationally to construct the poem about it. The poet's knowledge of the speaker's condition serves to deepen the emotion. This is an aspect of the lyric that often goes unnoticed or ignored, even denied by students who often see the effect of the poem in the theme per se, not in the artistry, who often see no veil between speaker and poet, between triggering event, as Richard Hugo calls it, and poem. Neruda becomes so enthralled by the language of the poem—seduced by it—that the writing itself becomes an erotic act.

A companion example might be Marvin Bell's "Trees as Standing for Something." The poem opens with a statement about trees ("More and more it seems I am happy with trees"), then reveals the speaker's circumstance as he observes them (waking, in bed, with a woman). Very quickly we see what the trees stand for:

> For my loves are like the leaves in summer.
> But oh!, when they fall, and I wake with a start,
> will I feel the sting of betrayal and ask, What is this
> love, if it has to end, even in death,
> or if one might lose it even during a life?

Better to die of it, or into it, or despite it now, he seems to answer. The second part of the poem commences with a description of cutting down trees—and loves—only to conclude by ending such speculation as his lover seduces him. The poem itself, what he will "say," is reduced to its essential erotic component, the repetition of the word "Oh" now transformed from the inquisitive "Oh" earlier in the poem:

> What was I to say then but Oh, Oh, Oh, Oh, Oh!
> Now you see a man at peace, happy and happier yet,
> With her breath on the back of his neck in the morning,
> And of course you assume it must always have been this way.
> But what was I to say, then and now, but Oh! And Oh! Oh!

The poem finishes ecstatically, having talked itself into a kind of orgasmic play with the language.

The erotics of writing, of language itself, the sheer "pleasure of the text," as Roland Barthes calls it, is often overlooked. But this is an essential concept that can help us understand what we do as writers, how we respond to our own poems as they evolve. By focusing on poems that deal explicitly with erotics, we can uncover some fundamental principles. In her *Eros the Bittersweet*, Anne Carson describes the void or absence which lies at the heart of much lyric poetry. At the poem's heart, Carson says, is the sort of tension and contradiction we saw in Neruda's poem. The Roman poet Catullus provides an epigrammatic motto for us here:

> I hate and I love. Why? you might ask.
> I don't know. But I feel it happening and I hurt.

Carson quotes from the *Greek Anthology* as further support:

> If you love me, you hate me. And if you hate me, you love me.
> Now if you don't hate me, beloved, don't love me.

She argues that the essence of the erotic is confusion—of emotions, of boundaries. The erotic poem becomes a gradual movement through these confusions, as in Neruda's poem, towards what Robert Frost calls the poem's final stance as a "momentary stay against confusion." Looking at the way these tensions are resolved, in other words, gives us a good idea of a poem's dramatic arc and also suggests something of the pleasure itself of writing, of the erotics of writing.

Sappho's fragment 31 enacts this dramatic movement:

He seems to me equal to gods that man
who opposite you
sits and listens close
to your sweet speaking

and lovely laughing—oh it
puts the heart in my chest on wings
for when I look at you, a moment, then no speaking
is left for me

no: tongue breaks, and thin
fire is racing under skin
and in eyes no sight and drumming
fills ears

and cold sweat holds me and shaking
grips me all, greener than grass
I am and dead—or almost
I seem to me

The poem begins as a description of her friend and her friend's lover, with a hint of erotic desire. By the fifth line with its exclamatory "oh," the speaker focuses only on the girl and herself. She moves from the metaphoric "heart on wings" to the more physical "tongue" and more insistent sense impressions of "fire" and "drumming" to the "cold sweat" and "shaking" of the last stanza. She is, in other words, overcome. Jealousy, as Carson and others point out, is the root cause here. But what sets the last three stanzas off is the quick move in stanza one from the man to "you" and her "sweet speaking," linking the girl to the sweet speaking of the narrator through her poem. The artistic situation is resolved poetically, by a sense of utter loss-as-death, while the dramatic or literal situation remains unresolved. We might see that Sappho adds a kind of fourth figure here, who understands what the speaker is going through and takes erotic pleasure in such "sweet speaking," just as Neruda finds erotic pleasure in the sad lines of his own poem. The author shares a vicarious pleasure in the speaker's situation: such an ironic context serves to heighten the tension.

Horace is certainly one of the most ironic poets we have. "Those wars,

Venus, are long over," an older Horace writes in Ode IV.1, hoping that all the trials of his past erotic life will not follow him into old age. As an alternative he describes how Venus and Eros should instead pick on Paulus, a younger man. But in writing the description Horace finds that his own words inflame him, as he addresses an old friend:

> ah Ligurinus, why
> does a tear now and then run trickling down my cheek?
> Why does my tongue, once eloquent,
> fall, as I'm talking, into ungracious silence?

As the poem ends, Horace has created in words the object of his erotic desire:

> At night I see you in my dreams,
> now caught, and I hold you, now I follow as you
> run away, over the grassy
> Field of Mars, over flowing streams, with your hard heart.

The very act of writing the poem has created the object of desire. Of course the poem itself can never finally contain this imagined other. The projection is always in the present, shown here in the repeated use of "now" as opposed to the poem's opening emphasis on the past, and shown as the love wars referred to in the beginning are replaced by the actual or metaphoric fields of Mars—suggesting a deeper, more mortal wound to the heart than the poet suspected at the opening. In short, the poem has created a more erotic situation than the one it set out to deny. This process of discovery, of uncovering an emotion we didn't know was there, is perhaps the central driving impulse of the process of making poems.

Ovid turns Horace's irony into his main subject and establishes the ironic basis for love poetry in the West. He begins the first book of his *Amores* with a parody of Virgil's *Aeneid*: "Arms, warfare, violence—I was winding up to produce a / Regular epic," but quickly reports that he taunted Cupid (Roman Eros) who then repaid him by making him change his heroic hexameters to elegiacs (alternating six- and five-beat lines), the form for love poetry. By the third elegy he is ironically making claims to a potential mistress that his erotic verse will make her immortal, and so establishes perhaps our first poetics of the erotic. He continues this in the *Metamorphoses*. In one story, Apollo, god of poetry, chases after Daphne because he, like Ovid, taunted Eros and was stricken with love, while Daphne was stricken with coldness. After being chased by poetry through proverbial hill and dale, she asks Zeus to be turned into a laurel tree, is granted that wish, and so escapes. However, Apollo still expresses his love, and in turn she tilts a branch to him; he vows that the laurel will be the poet's crown forever. For Ovid, who describes Apollo in bestial metaphors during the chase, emphasizing not only the external changes in appearance but internal changes in attitude, poetry itself thus becomes a continual metamorphosis, a continual progress toward something that is never achieved—what Carson calls one of the hallmarks of the erotic.

What is crucial is the ability of the poet to create the erotic from the text the speaker utters: the language of the poem is the source of the erotic. This motivates C. P. Cavafy's "Half an Hour" where "A few words . . . and nothing more" are enough because:

> Art's people, by intensity of mind,
> and then naturally for just a little while, sometimes create
> pleasure whose effects seem almost bodily, substantial.

"I had a perfectly erotic half an hour," he writes, as the poem recreates the scene in terms of an erotic flow of language. The erotic is enhanced by the fact that the other is about to leave, that the poem is about to end. The anaphora in the last lines suggests both the intensity of the desire and the attempt to sustain, repeat, the poem's moment:

> Because
> for all the imagination, for all the magic spirit of the wine,
> I needed to see your lips as well,
> I needed to have your body close to me.

Such repetition, any word "extravagantly repeated" or else surprising and therefore "unexpected, succulent in its newness," creates the erotic, according to Roland Barthes in *The Pleasure of the Text*. Once again, as in Horace, the repeated words fail to sustain the sense of presence that they create. The poem, the moment, the half hour all end. Goethe, who understands the erotics of language, places Eros in an elegiac format. In his "Roman Elegy VII," he describes the relationship between body and language as "seeing with vision that feels, feeling with fingers that see":

> Often I even compose poetry in her embraces,
>> Counting hexameter beats, tapping them out on her back
> Softly, with one hand's fingers.

For Walt Whitman, the beloved's body *is* the poem: "I believe the likes of you shall stand or fall with my poems, and that they are my poems," he writes in "I Sing the Body Electric"; a title that emphasizes not that he sings *of* the body, but that he sings *the* body itself. In "Spontaneous Me" even the poem is described in phallic terms:

> This poem drooping shy and unseen that I always carry, and that all
>> men carry,
> . . . .
> Love-thoughts, love-juice, love-odor, love-yielding, love-climbers, and
>> the climbing sap,
> Arms and hands of love, lips of love, phallic thumb of love . . .

"Words make love on the page like flies in the summer heat," Charles Simic writes in his memoir, *A Fly in the Soup.* Or here is Fernando Pessoa in a journal entry: "I enjoy wording. Words for me are tangible bodies, visible sirens, incarnate sensualities." Barthes describes this same erotics of language in *A Lover's Discourse:*

> Language is a skin: I rub my language against the other. It is as if I
> had words instead of fingers, or fingers at the tip of my words. My
> language trembles with desire. The emotion derives from a double
> contact: on the one hand, a whole activity of discourse discreetly,
> indirectly focuses upon a single signified, which is "I desire you," and
> releases, nourishes, ramifies it to the point of explosion (language
> experiences orgasm upon touching itself); on the other hand, I
> enwrap the other in my words, I caress, brush against, talk up this
> contact, I extend myself to make the commentary to which I submit
> the relation endure.

Language moves from the skin to all that is beyond it.

Gaston Bachelard says in *The Poetics of Space*: "the reader of poems is asked to consider an image not as an object and even less as the substitute for an object, but to seize its specific reality." That is, the reality of words themselves. For him, this is an area where the "margin" of unreality enters and perturbs us, wakens us. He says in *The Poetics of Reverie*: "I am a dreamer of words, of written words. I think I am reading; a word stops me. I leave the page." The erotics of language, in paying so much attention to the skin, the border between word and thing, poem and world, extends outwards and creates its own world as the poet does in *The Song of Songs*. In that text the body becomes fruit, tree, garden, hillside, forest, town and world.

One of Edna St. Vincent Millay's early sonnets demonstrates not only how the erotic can enter into the poem almost against the speaker's will, as in Horace, but also how much is at stake, how central the erotic vision can become in one's life. The poem begins in casual talk with a friend:

> We talk of taxes, and I call you friend;
> Well, such you are,—but well enough we know
> How thick about us root, how rankly grow
> Those subtle weeds no man has need to tend,
> That flourish through neglect, and soon must send
> Perfume too sweet upon us and overthrow
> Our steady senses: how such matters go
> We are aware, and how such matters end.
> Yet shall be told no meagre passion here;
> With lovers such as we forevermore
> Isolde drinks the draught, and Guinevere
> Receives the Table's ruin through her door,
> Francesca, with the loud surf at her ear,
> Lets fall the coloured book upon the floor.

The evenly balanced rhythm and rhetoric of the first two lines with their mid-point caesuras suggest an order and rational calm that is almost immediately threatened by the enjambed lines and the relatively long rush of lines from the middle of line 2 to line 8—a sequence of enjambed lines where the one line ending with a comma is followed by a relative clause that pulls the line over the comma nearly as if it were, in fact, enjambed. It is a masterful switch in tone. The "yet" at line 9 promises a solution, but the examples are all tragic and lead to upheavals in various states, ending with the reference to Dante's Francesca trapped in hell. The simple erotic situation becomes quickly complicated, suggesting a link to death, to dire consequences for the individuals, and to cosmic disruptions.

William Wordsworth's "Nutting" is one of the most famous examples of this relationship. The poet remembers how as a young boy he would set out from the "threshold" of his cottage into the woods. The great Italian Romantic, Giacomo Leopardi, describes this situation in his philosophical reflections when he says that the poet "stands in relation to nature more or less as an ardent and sincere lover, whose love is not returned, stands in relation to the loved one." Wordsworth continues by describing the woods in erotic terms:

> O'er pathless rocks,
> Through beds of matted fern, and tangled thickets,
> Forcing my way, I came to one dear nook
> Unvisited, where not a broken bough
> Drooped with its withered leaves, ungracious sign
> Of devastation; but the hazels rose
> Tall and erect, with tempting clusters hung,
> A virgin scene!—A little while I stood,
> Breathing with such suppression of the heart
> As joy delights in; and with wise restraint
> Voluptuous, fearless of a rival, eyed
> The banquet . . .

After he "luxuriates" in the scene awhile, playing among the flowers in this secret "bower," he suddenly rises up himself

> And dragged to earth both branch and bough, with crash
> And merciless ravage: and the shady nook
> Of hazels, and the green and mossy bower,
> Deformed and sullied, patiently gave up
> Their quiet being . . .

Oddly, only when this rape of the woods is enacted does the natural world get personified to the extent that it can "patiently" give up. The poet re-experiences the impulsive "rape" in one jagged monosyllabic line with its dangling phrase at the end ("And dragged to earth both branch and bough, with crash"). The line destroys the quiet, balanced syntax the poem has established. But then he quickly returns to the established syntax and abandons the woods as erotic object in order to address his sister, "dearest Maiden,"—though one could read it also as a direct address to the woods—in order to come to the conclusion that "there is a spirit in the woods." In this case the poet shies away from the erotics of the poem that he almost unconsciously has created, for it involves not only desire but destruction, not only Eros but Thanatos.

The erotic, then, poses a potential link to death: in Greek mythology Eros and Thanatos are always linked. The death can be physical, emotional, psychological or spiritual. It might be willed by the speaker, as Dante wills it in one of his so-called "Rime Petrose" where he hopes that his beloved's death will split her heart "per mezzo," down the middle. He calls her a "homicidal thieving gangster" a few lines later. By the end of the poem he wants the poem itself to travel to the beloved, but travel as an arrow that will strike her through the heart as a kind of lovely vengeance: "che bell'onor s'aquista in far vendetta." The arrow image is Cupid's, and the death is also love itself; so the end is both an expression of erotic desire for and a death wish for the beloved.

In his "October Ghosts" James Wright describes himself and Jenny as already dead, already ghosts: "Jenny cold, Jenny darkness," the poem begins. He associates their lives with the Greek poet Callimachus, with dead miners in Ohio, and then remembers his own family past, and especially a woman stricken with diphtheria when he was young who in turn allows him to describe Death as a lover who lives inside us:

> That time is gone when the young women died
> Astounded to hear black veins in their bodies
> Coil round one another all night.

He links his search for the beloved with all the times and places he has known; the endless search that marks Eros ends in the labyrinth of his own head:

Jenny, fat blossoming grandmother of the dead,
We were both young, and I nearly found you, young.
I could not find you. I prowled into my head,
The cold ghost of October that is my skull.
There is a god's plenty of lovers there,
The dead, the dying, and the beautiful.

What he finds inside himself is "That minor bird I hear from the great frost, / My robin's song, the ancient nothingness." But the puns, referring to Robert Frost's poem and then playing off of Edward Arlington Robinson's name and line, suggest a revitalization of the old, a new beginning yet a beginning based on utter humility and loss: "Now I know nothing, I can die alone," he concludes, describing the ultimate fate of the erotic lover.

The erotic link to death may involve more than physical or bodily death. In Dante's *Inferno* V Dante the pilgrim meets Paolo and Francesca and calls to them. Dante the poet sets us up for Dante the speaker's failure by having him first envision the sinners in this part of Hell as starlings, then as the more attractive cranes, then as doves (signs of love). Thinking Paolo and Francesca have answered the call of his poem, he stands flattered and amazed as they float over to him on literal flames of language. Francesa tells their story that includes a beautiful lyric—"Amor, ch'al cor gentil ratto s'apprende" ("Love which in gentle hearts is quickly born"), which is based on the repetition of the word "amor" in a pattern of similar constructions. Dante the pilgrim is so overcome by this language that he recreates it in his own phrase, repeating the word "quando" ("when") in a similar pattern, describing his own falling in love with love "when" he hears her words. Dante the epic poet, to be sure, is warning us against the immense power of language as a kind of Barthesian skin that his pilgrim succumbs to. The situation is not comic as in Ovid, or ironic as in Horace, or even melancholy as in Sappho, but potentially tragic, for the erotic has led Dante the speaker beyond the physical to the ethical, from the worldly to the cosmic. His being seduced by the lovers' language leads to his being seduced by sin.

If the stakes are so high, if the process is so endless, if the end brings such pain, why bother? As Sappho says to Britomart in Cesare Pavese's *Dialogues with Leuco*, we might question how a lyric poet like Dante the speaker can accept a force that "turns you into desire, into shuddering desire that struggles over a body . . . like the foam between the rocks? And this body rejects you and crushes you, and you fall and long to embrace the rocks. . . ." The answer lies in another of Pavese's dialogues where Eros and Thanatos argue over Apollo's killing of Hyacinth. For Apollo, Hyacinth is just a metaphor for beauty who simply dies when his function is over—when the poem is over. For Eros, it is all about "richness of feeling," for Hyacinth, he says, "knew perfect joy, he knew its rapid, bitter end." The erotic joy could not be had without a deep understanding that it must end. This explains why Hesiod makes Eros the son of Night and Death.

The erotics of poetry involves a seeking after what Charles Simic calls the evasive "marvelous prey," playing off the medieval idea of the hart/deer hunt. For the Slovene poet Tomaz Salamun the poem itself is a way to "seduce the reader." The poem as a "hunt" for the "inexpressible," which he describes in an interview as a "beast in the woods the hunter always knows only by its tracks (its words). The very fact that we can't describe it adequately now, searching as we do with various metaphors and similes, shows what a powerful thing it is, what attraction it has." He also describes the process of writing a poem as an attempt to "pry open" the

> sacred seed of everything, which is at the center of the fruit . . . then something strange can happen to you because you've gone so far, taken so many chances, you begin to rest, to come back down, and there's an indescribable joy at having lived in this orgasmic language. You feel like you've lost yourself.

In #656 (Franklin system) Emily Dickinson creates a lover through erotic metaphor. The poem begins as a simple trip to the shore, but the sea and a house quickly intertwine so as to dislocate place. We understand the poet is creating her own place in language, and more, she confuses her own identity with that of a house mouse itself dislocated and run aground:

I started early—Took my Dog—
And visited the Sea—
The Mermaids in the Basement
Came out to look at me—

And Frigates—in the Upper Floor
Extended Hempen Hands—

Presuming Me to be a Mouse—
Aground—opon the Sands—

Dickinson shifts the context again to reveal what has been operating here:
a confusion of place that leads to a confusion of roles and eventually to an
erotic desire. This desire takes over the poem as the imagined suitor in his
guise just as the sea begins metaphorically to fondle her:

But no Man moved Me—till the Tide
Went past my simple Shoe—
And past my Apron—and my Belt
And past my Boddice—too—

And made as He would eat me up—
As wholly as a Dew
Opon a Dandelion's Sleeve—
And then—I started—too

Now the poet is fully involved: taking a hint from her suitor, her own erotic
reaction leads the way, and the scene is consummated:

And he—he followed—close behind—
I felt His Silver Heel
Opon my Ancle—Then My Shoes
Would overflow with Pearl—

Until We met the Solid Town—
No One He seemed to know—
And bowing—with a Mighty look—
At me—The Sea withdrew—

As with Cavafy and Horace, the erotic scene ends suddenly. The poem
evolves from a seemingly innocent description of the natural world to an
erotic situation characterized by such phrases as "eat me up," "overflow with
Pearl," and "sea withdrew." The pauses and dashes themselves enact a hesi-
tating movement that emphasizes the tension between natural and imagined scene.

In Cesare Pavese's uncollected poem "Hard Labor" (not to be confused with the poem by that title in the book *Hard Labor*), the poet describes how a woman and a man playfully flirt on the grass:

> The two of them, stretched out on the grass, fully dressed, stare
> At each other through the tender stalks: the woman tastes her hair
> And then the grass. She smiles flirtatiously through the grass.
> The man takes her slender hand and tastes it, pressing
> His body against her. The woman rolls away from him.
> This is how half the meadow has been pressed flat.
> The girl, sitting up, teases her hair, and won't
> Look at the man, eyes open, stretched out beside her.

Later, at supper, they stare at each other, barely seeing the passersby who in turn hardly notice them. The source of the erotic for each of them is not in the actual other but in a created other. Her memory is of another kiss, another man—yet the syntax of the poem clearly does not distinguish between the imagined and actual other men:

> All day they chase each other and the woman flushes
> From the sun. In her heart she feels gratitude for the man.
> She remembers a furious kiss, exchanged in a forest,
> Interrupted by the sounds of passersby, which still burns.
> She clutches a bunch of grass—curled up over a stone
> In a grotto—like beautiful maidenhair, and turns seductively
> With eyes that could melt the man.

The man, for his part, dreams of the hidden, the edge, what cannot be seen or had in the actual woman:

>   The man looks at the tangle
> Of black stalks set among the tangle of green stalks,
> And turns seductively as if to look at another tangle,
> Which must be between her legs and under her bright dress,
> But the woman ignores this. Not even his anger
> Can move her, because the girl, who loves him, counters
> Each assault of his kisses by taking his hand.

His reaction is to return home and create another woman to replace what he could not obtain. The tone of the poem becomes more intimate:

> But later tonight, after leaving her, he knows where he'll go.
> He'll return alone to his house, broken, and dazed,
> But at least his satisfied body might be mended
> By the sweetness of sleep in his deserted bed.
> Only, and this is his revenge, he himself will imagine
> The body of a woman which will be something like hers,
> And will be, without shame, lustful, hers in fact.

Of course it is precisely after such an experience that Pavese returned home to commit suicide—Eros and Thanatos finally coming together in his life and art.

The Pavese poem raises a complicating issue in that the translator himself enters the mind of the poet: Linguistically the translator participates in the creation of the other when he chooses equivalent English words. The situation becomes even more complicated in the case of imitation or adaptation. An example from Petrarch illustrates the point:

> If I had stayed to strike the match ends of stars in poetry's cave
> instead of trying to break the worst dark night over my knees,
> you might have had your poet now, someone who'd weave
> a blanket against the cold, who'd bury every grave inside a grave.
> If I had stayed to echo each fist of smoke, to work the soul's lave
> and shape a world you already knew by rote, to breathe each ready breeze,
> I'd never know to cut the twisted vines from your heart's withered trees,
> to spread my wings above your fire, or pull the dagger from the milky way.
> Listen, the world beside this one cares little for us. It's an argument of stars.
> Some say these crippled words are the smoke that abandons us for sky.
> Don't listen. Even if it's only a light across the marsh, it can tell us we're
>   alive.
> I'll reap whatever I need from thistles and thorns with this broken scythe
> of a poem, and, one hand filled with dirt, the other clearing away false stars,
> I'll sow a world in every smile of yours that lately had become a scar.

This poem, "The Cave," is my adaptation of Petrarch's Rime CLXVI. It contains metaphors and similes not in the original and deletes Petrarch's references to Florence, Arezzo, and classical figures. For example, a reference to gardening in Petrarch's first quartrain is adapted later in this English version as a metaphor for combating misfortune: "I'll reap whatever I need from thistles and thorns with this broken scythe / of a poem." The author of the adaptation disappears into Petrrach's speaker, and Petrarch's speaker into the narrator's version. By implication, Petrarch's Laura is absorbed into the beloved of the English version. The whole process is a linguistic version of Wordsworth's possession of the bower in "Nutting."

All of these poets are using Roland Barthes's notion of the edge, the seam, a sense of a boundary that is threatened and is threatening. It is often a boundary between word and thing, imagination and actuality, physical and spiritual. Simic provides a comic view of this mode of transgression in his early poem, "Breasts," which begins with just the sort of simple, almost innocent edge that Barthes describes as essential to the understanding of erotics, a sense that the thing itself stays hidden, in poetry, by language:

> I love breasts, hard
> Full breasts, guarded
> By a button.

He continues by comparing them to "bestiaries of the ancients," to "Two ovens of the only / Philosopher's stone / Worth bothering about," all the while conscious that language itself is creating these mythic breasts, this erotic mythos, for these breasts are also "Vowels of delicious clarity / For the little red schoolhouse of our mouths." And the poem keeps radiating outward—a sort of modern and ironically comic *Song of Songs*—to create a world where breasts can be "Like two freshly poured beer mugs" and what gives "each finger / Its true shape." Towards the end he pronounces

> That old janitor on his deathbed
> Who demands to see the breasts of his wife
> For one last time
> Is the greatest poet who ever lived.

Simic's poem concludes with a description of how he "will tip each breast / Like a dark heavy grape" into his mouth, a Chaucerian act that comically proclaims the greatness of both the poet and his poem. If the erotics of poetry are to remain erotic there must be at least some sense of discovered self-consciousness, some boundary that is threatened. The erotic exists in the threat imagination poses for our reality, comic or not, and the threat reality has in turn on our imagination. It exists in the way words can disrupt our comfortable visions: Tomaz Salamun's poem, "Photograph with a Quote from Yazoo: Deep in Each Other's Dream," threatens to cross several honored boundaries. The poem begins:

> Christ is my sex object, therefore I am
> not an ethical problem. I lead him to the meadows.
> Like a little shepherd I force him to graze.
>
> I root him out and clean his glands. Shall we
> rinse ourselves under the tree?

The sudden shift to address the reader is at least as jarring as the statements that precede it. For a moment we are unsure whether he is addressing Christ or, as it turns out, the beloved. Later in the poem, it is clear that the beloved and Christ are metaphors for each other:

> I am a little stone
> falling into your flesh. I made you twitch
> and tied you up. We crucified you.

The erotics of writing aims at the negation of the self and the beloved, perhaps an extreme form of John Keats's "chameleon poet," who is always "filling some other body."

This potential death of the self, the Thanatos side of the erotic coin, can also be seen as a beginning, a creation of a new self after the negation of the old self. Keats understood this when he had his lovers on his Grecian Urn "For ever piping songs for ever new," though he also understood this was a static scene, a "Cold Pastoral." In his letter on the mansions of the mind, one passes, he says, from the "infant or thoughtless chamber" to the erotic "Chamber of Maiden Thought" where we explore "dark passages" (his erotic metaphor here gives him away) to a third chamber of love and friendship. For him, the language of the poem can substitute, by its intensity, for the absent beloved: "there is nothing to be intense upon; no women one feels mad to kiss; no face swelling into reality," he writes in a letter. The erotic for Keats goes beyond the physical. In his "The Eve of St. Agnes," one lover dissolves into the dream of another and they both metamorphose into a wholly spiritual existence. Dante's *La Vita Nuova* is an early model: the poet's attraction for Beatrice, which started as such a physical sensation, gradually becomes a spiritual one that extends "Beyond the sphere that makes the widest round."

The origin of this idea is probably in Sappho, who begins one poem with the phrase, "Here is success for your tongue, my children / the poems of the pear-breasted Muses"—with its obvious pun on tongue as a reference to language and to erotic touch—only to realize in the end that what she ultimately desires is "refinement, and beauty and light." In *Phaedrus*, Socrates describes how the Muses possess the poet to produce a sort of trance. Thus his soul can be led by Eros from physical to spiritual beauty:

> Once he has received the emanation of beauty through his eyes, he grows warm, and through the perspiration that ensues, he irrigates the sprouting of his wing. When he is quite warm, the outer layers of the seedling unfurl—parts which by reason of their close-drawn rigidity had for a long time prevented anything from blossoming. As nourishment streams upon it the stump of the wing begins to swell and grow from the root upward as a support for the entire structure of the soul, fully developing the wing which every soul possessed in the past.

The lover, in moving from the physical toward the spiritual, does not abandon the physical and sexual but rather enjoys a sensual existence enriched by the spiritual. This is also William Blake's idea in *The Marriage of Heaven and Hell*. The transcendent vision will come to pass "by an increase in sensual enjoyment," he says in his *Notebooks*. The essence of Eros is desire, what takes us from where we are to where we might be, from the present to the eternal, from ignorance to knowledge, self to other, community to cosmos. It is what moves the words from the beginning to the end of the line only to find a new beginning in the next line, the next poem. It is what moves us from the beginning to the end of the poem, from the external poem to what Yeats called "the deep heart's core." It is the power of language to transform and move us, to *transport* us. Miguel de Unamuno, the great Spanish poet and philosopher, writes that "Our own struggle to acquire, preserve, and increase our own consciousness makes us discover in the endeavors and movements and revolutions of all things a struggle to acquire, preserve and increase consciousness, to which everything tends." Ultimately, poetry is a search for the divine, the immortal. The great Mexican poet, Octavio Paz, writes in *The Double Flame:* "eroticism is first and foremost a *thirst for otherness*. And the supernatural is the supreme otherness." This is perhaps the most noble aim of poetry, to attach ourselves to the world around us, to turn desire into love, to embrace, finally, what always evades us, what is always beyond, but what is always there—the unspoken, the spirit, the soul.

3. The Ode

She fights, she wins, she triumphs with a song,
Devout, majestic, for the subject fit. . . .

ANNE FINCH, COUNTESS
OF WINCHILSEA

The Ode

There are as many ways of thinking about the ode as there are forms of poems. Thanks to the two most well-known Classical odists, Pindar and Horace, the prevailing views are that an ode is either occasional—and that occasion a public one, a victory, say, or a wedding, or praise in memory of the dead; or else the ode arises from private reflection that leads to an epigrammatic wisdom whose resonance goes beyond private experience. In either instance, form—stanzaic and metrical—is crucial to generating an effect either of a lofty stateliness appropriate to public celebration (Pindaric) or (in the case of the Horatian ode) of a more muted and honed grace whose clarity is that of composed reflection itself. The ode is of course more complex than that, and is in fact less a matter of form than is commonly thought. Yes, we have the Pindaric and Horatian forms of the ode in English, forms modeled on the formal regularity of the Classical odes. But even in the Classical period, the ode had less to do with form than with the sensibility of struggle—between private feeling and public expectation, mortality and divinity, the human impulse toward order and the disordered experience of being human.

⁂

From the start, the ode in Greek is choral (i.e., a song to be performed by a chorus to musical accompaniment). Given this relationship to music, we would expect an attention to rhythm; it's no surprise, therefore, that these odes are always in a fixed meter and often in a fixed stanza. The effect is the same as that of verses and refrains in any song. As well, the Classical ode is agonistic, from the Greek *agon*, a struggle that can be variously physical, emotional, psychological. But as early as the seventh century BC, with the odes of Sappho, it is clear that the ode is otherwise not easily categorized. At one moment, Sappho presents us with an epithalamion to be sung at a wedding, at the next she is intimate, self-reflective. But the agon is the point of commonality:

Leave your siege of her violet softness.
The night is long and we shall sing
Epithalamia outside your door.

Call to your bachelor friends to come.
All night long, like the nightingale,
We shall stay awake and sing.

(Guy Davenport, trans.)

So go the lines from what remains of a wedding song, lines that would have been sung by virgin girls. Hence, the speakers in a sense pitch their own virginity against the deflowering that would have consummated—established as fact—the wedding. They know that this is the "point" of the wedding night, even as they see that night as one of siege, from which their impulse is to protect one of their own. In only a handful of lines, Sappho presents the conundrum of marriage itself—the joining of two people as one, and the fact of difference, not just in terms of gender, but of individual sensibility, that means the two can never be entirely one. There's also the imaging here of sex as combative—at least, a matter of power, with its implications of victory and defeat.

A different kind of agon occurs in the opening stanza of another of Sappho's poems:

A company of horsemen or of infantry
Or a fleet of ships, some say,
Is the black earth's finest sight,
But to me it is what you love.

(Guy Davenport, trans.)

Although this, too, would have been sung—more likely in the more intimate setting of a private home, as entertainment, say, before or after a meal—we see here that the ode is not necessarily occasional. Or if occasional, then the occasion is that of a private resistance to the general view. Sappho pitches the traditions of epic against lyric in this poem; also, a martial sensibility against the pacificism of love; also, the artifice of regimented order against a reality that includes how love can triumph over notions of order, as she goes on to cite Helen of Troy as proof—Helen who, because of love, "left her husband,/The best of men,//And sailed to Troia, mindless of her daughter,/And of her parents whom she loved."

Somewhere between the public ode of the epithalamion and the private ode of self-reflection, there's the ode of intimate dialogue, known as prayer:

Aphródita dressed in an embroidery of flowers,
Never to die, the daughter of God,
Untangle from longing and perplexities,
O Lady, my heart.

But come down to me, as you came before,
For if ever I cried, and you heard and came,
Come now, of all times, leaving
Your father's golden house

In that chariot pulled by sparrows reined and bitted,
Swift in their flying, a quick blur aquiver,
Beautiful, high. They drew you across steep air
Down to the black earth;

Fast they came, and you behind them, O
Hilarious heart, your face all laughter,
Asking, What troubles you this time, why again
Do you call me down?

Asking, In your wild heart, who now
Must you have? Who is she that persuasion
Fetch her, enlist her, and put her into bounden love?
Sappho, who does you wrong?

If she balks, I promise, soon she'll chase,
If she's turned from gifts, now she'll give them.
And if she does not love you, she will love,
Helpless, she will love.

Come, then, loose me from cruelties.
Give my tethered heart its full desire.

Fulfill, and, come, lock your shield with mine
Throughout the siege.

(Guy Davenport, trans.)

Sappho's ode is a fairly characteristic example of how prayer is structured in the Classical period: the deity is invoked—first by name (often a variety of names, as the postulant asks the deity to come by whichever name is preferred), and then by attributes or items associated with the deity. Aphródita, once named, is described as "never to die," "dressed in an embroidery of flowers," and "the daughter of God"; and hence the lovely description of the goddess's sparrow-pulled chariot. Evidence is then cited to confirm the deity's power—the idea is that if the deity was once able to do X, will he or she do X again on behalf of the one praying? Sappho cites an earlier instance of how the goddess once rescued her in a similar crisis. The prayer concludes sometimes with praise for or acknowledgment of the deity's power, or—as is the case here—a repeated plea for help.

Behind any prayer, of course, is the ongoing agon between gods and humans, the imbalance of power that makes prayer necessary. But as well, prayer commonly springs from crisis, from a struggling to which there seems no earthly resolution. And it's this agon that these three very different odes of Sappho have in common. That, and—as is true of all Classical odes—a formal regularity, even as the odes speak of restlessness. We might see that as another instance of the agon—between the constantly-in-flux human psyche and the human impulse to *contain* flux. The poem as the occasion of temporary restraint, a restraint we at once want and *don't* want. The ode as but a form of that strange occasion.

In the choral odes of Greek tragedy (fifth century BC), we see a formal structuring that throws the agonistic nature of the ode into the foreground and also shows how concerned the ode is, as well, with the resolution of opposing forces. These choral odes consist of a strophe (a verse to be sung by one half of the chorus), an antistrophe (for the other half)—the combination suggestive both of struggle and of balance—and sometimes an epode, enacting the resolution of their argument or debate, or sometimes just bringing together two different but not uncomplementary points of view. (This notion of argument and resolution would have been apparent at the level of meter in the Greek original, the strophe and antistrophe always sharing the same number of lines in exactly the same metrical configuration—reflective of the balance and counterbalance of argument—while the epode would have been a stanza of fewer lines, in a meter that was different from the meter of the strophe and antistrophe, but not unrelated to it.) Here is a choral ode from Euripides' *Bacchae*:

[STROPHE]

To dance the long night!
Shall I ever set my white foot
so, to worship Bacchus?
Toss my neck to the dewy skies
as a young fawn frisks
in green delight of pasture?

She has run away now from a fearful
hunt, away from watchful eyes,
above tight-woven nets—
while the dogleader cheers
the running of his hounds.

She strains, she races, whirls and prances
on meadows by rivers, delighting
in absence of men
and under shadow-tresses
the tender shoots of the wildwood.

[REFRAIN]

What is wise? What is the finest gift
that gods can give to mortals?
A hand on the heads
of their enemies, pushing down?
[No.] What is fine is loved always.

[ANTISTROPHE]

Never hurried, never
failing, a god's

fist comes down on men
who love to be hard-hearted,
who hold back what is due to gods
in the madness of bad judgment.
Ingenious, how the gods
keep time's long foot a secret
while hunting down irreverent men.
No one should ever be above the law,
neither in thought nor action.

The cost of these beliefs is light:
power lies
with whatever thing should be divine,
with whatever law stands firm in time
by nature ever-natural.

[REFRAIN]

What is wise? What is the finest gift
that gods can give to mortals?
A hand on the heads
of their enemies, pushing down?
[No.] What is fine is loved always.

[EPODE]

Happy the man who has come away
safe on the beach from a storm at sea,
happy the man who has risen above
trouble and toil. Many are the ways
one man may surpass another
in wealth or power,
and beyond each hope there beckons another
hope without number.
Hope may lead a man to wealth,
hope may pass away;
but I admire a man when he
is happy in an ordinary life.

(*Paul Woodruff, trans.*)

This ode occurs at a point in the play when the citizens of Thebes have been forbidden to worship Bacchus. This is the catalyst for the opening strophe: the chorus, made of Bacchantes—women who are followers of Bacchus—long to be able to worship their god and thereby know the delight that a frisking fawn knows when she's escaped pursuit. The strophe presents a situation—a ban on worship—that runs directly counter to the reverence that, as the antistrophe details, the gods both deserve and demand. What is, versus what should be— this is a way of understanding the relationship here between strophe and antistrophe. That's one agon. The other one is between gods and humans, a violent relationship in which "a god's fist comes down on men" while people continue to fall into "the madness of bad judgment." The refrain that closes both strophe and antistrophe suggests that the chorus is ultimately united in their thinking; the epode confirms that, and gives the resolution to the crisis: humility, satisfaction with one's place as divine law has ordained it, and an avoidance of the type of ambition that can only lead to defying the gods.

The instructional tone of this chorus is not incidental, any more than the religious subject matter is. While the choral ode in some way addressed the plot of a tragedy—and sometimes furthered it—its concern was almost always religious, meditating on the gods, divine law, the need to obey that law, and a distinctly human propensity for disobedience. The plays were themselves part of a religious festival held regularly in honor of Dionysus (Bacchus). And, though to attend the plays was not an act of worship, the choral odes can be likened to scripture in that they present religious material for the purpose of instruction regarding moral conduct. The combination of sacred material being sung and the frequent address to the gods or to their manifestation in divine law is what gives to the choral ode a suggestion of prayer or of a hymn.

With the choral odes of Greek tragedy, the ode's sensibility becomes a fusion of lyric and didactic expression, while its form becomes predominantly rhetorical, the structure of argument being used first to present a situation, and then to consider it in the context of the evidence that comes sometimes from history, and very often from mythology. The history of their own experience is what the chorus turns to in the choral ode above; this is presumably what allows them to speak with such authority on the ingeniousness with which "the gods/keep time's long foot a secret/while hunting down irreverent men." It was mythology that Sappho turned to, remember, when she cited Helen's experience with love as proof that love outweighs everything else.

Here is another example of the choral ode as it appears in tragedy, from Sophocles' *Antigone*:

OLD MEN [STROPHE]

Happy are those whose lives are free
Of the taste of disaster:
For when a house is shaken by the gods
It lies cursed forever,
Generation to generation.
It is like the waves of the swollen sea,
Driven by winds from Thrace
Across the dark face of the waters,
Stirring black sand from the depths
As they hurl themselves on
To roar and crash on stubborn cliffs
Fronting the teeth of the storm.

[ANTISTROPHE]

The house of Labdacus is cursed,
The sorrows of the living heaped
On the sorrows of the dead. Generation
To generation, god punishes them:
There can be no escape.
The hope of the house flickered
In the last roots of the children
Of Oedipus, flickered and was gone,
Quenched by a layer of blood-stained dust
Offered to the gods of death,
Quenched by madness of speech
And frenzy in the heart.

[STROPHE]

O Zeus, what arrogance of man
Can ever check your power?
Even Sleep, who snares all things,

Is powerless against it;
The unwearying months of the gods
Cannot master it;
Old age cannot make it grey.
You are and always shall be
Lord of the dazzling halls
Of marble Olympus.
In the past and the future,
Near and far, this law
Is fixed and unchanging forever:
When greatness enters mortal life
It brings disaster, always.

[ANTISTROPHE]

Hope wanders the wide world,
Comforting many men;
But this same fond hope
Lures others to disaster
In the foolish longings of their hearts:
Innocent and ignorant
They blunder on
Till their feet are in the fire.
It was wisely said
That evil always seems good
To those whose minds the gods
Are drawing towards disaster:
Only for the briefest moment
Can they find a breathing-space
Untainted with disaster.

(Kenneth McLeish, trans.)

The first strophe introduces a general observation: once a house is cursed by the gods, it's cursed forever. The first antistrophe gives a specific and especially relevant example: the house of Labdacus, of which the doomed Antigone is a member. A slight shift occurs in the next strophe, as the chorus leaves behind the folly of those who defy divine law and addresses

Zeus directly, acknowledging his supremacy; this strophe becomes a hymn of praise, the chorus meanwhile distancing itself from the aforementioned folly. But the point of this strophe, in terms of the argument, is to introduce what leads to a house being cursed: arrogance and greatness. The second antistrophe in turn answers the implied question: How do these things come into a human life? Via hope and longing, a lack of satisfaction with one's place, which is presumably the place ordained by the gods. To long for more or for difference, then, is a form of arrogance toward the gods, i.e., blasphemy, which can only lead to the disaster with which the chorus first began, given the supremacy of gods to humans, as again the chorus has also made clear. The argument is at once subtle, highly structured, and airtight—the irrefutable evidence being Antigone herself. (Note, by the way, that although this choral ode includes no epode, the ode ends with the epode's effect, that of resolution to the dilemma of the ongoing agon between gods and humans.)

All poems, of course, can be said to concern themselves with argument, whether presenting one or enacting one, or serving as response to an argument-by-implication. But the choral ode gets its entire structure, its trajectory of thought, from rhetoric: that science of argument that the Greeks themselves established. Thesis, antithesis, synthesis. It's not coincidental, I think, that both rhetoric and the choral ode began as purely public—performative—expression.

✦

Pindar's odes—the ones that survive, anyway—are almost entirely *epinikia*, poems written for the occasion of a victory at the Olympian, Pythian, Isthmian, and Nemean athletic games. Like the choral odes of Greek tragedy, Pindar's are highly rhetorical in their structure, seeking to instruct even as they praise. As well, these odes often invoke a deity or group of them to assist the poet in making as perfect a song as possible, which is to say that they take on the nature of the hymn or prayer, appropriately enough: each of the games was considered sacred to a particular deity—was held in honor of that deity, just as the Greek tragedies were presented at festivals in honor of Dionysus. Rhetoric as the language of prayer; the evidence of history and of myth; didactic; hortatory; public as a celebration, but the celebration of a private individual—with Pindar, we see how complex the ode can be. Its complexity is that of the mind itself, it seems to me, the poems moving in a highly associative, highly allusive manner, divagatory, as if each poem were a thought gathering itself as we read it. We can get a sense of the range even by looking at one of the shorter odes, performed at the Pythian games. Here is the sixth Pythian ode of Pindar, commissioned to celebrate the victory of Xenokrates who, with his son Thrasyboulos, won the chariot race of 490 BC:

Listen! It is the field of Aphrodite
with the fluttering eyes or the Graces
we labor now. We approach the templed
centerstone of the thunderous earth.
There stands builded for the glory of Emmenos' children
and Akragas of the river, and for Xenokrates,
a treasure house of song
for victory at Pytho in Apollo's
glen, with its burden of gold.

Neither rain driven from afar on the storm,
not the merciless armies
of the crying cloud, no wind shall sweep it, caught
and stricken with the blown debris into the corners
of the sea. The front shines in the clear air,
Thrasyboulos, on your father announcing
for you and yours the pride
of a chariot victory in the folds of Krisa—
a tale to run on the lips of men.

You, keeping Victory erect beside your right hand,
bring home the meaning
of the things men say once on the mountain Chiron,
Philyra's son, urged on strong Peleiades
left in his care: *First of all gods, honor*
the deep-voiced lord of the lightning and thunderstroke,
Zeus Kronides;
next, through all their destiny never deprive
your parents of such reverence even as this.

In the old days mighty Antilochos proved one
who lived in that word.
He died for his father, standing up
to the murderous onset of the Aithiop champion,
Memnon; for Nestor's horse, smitten by the shaft of Paris,
had fouled the chariot, and Memnon attacked
with his tremendous spear.
And the old Messenian was shaken
at heart and cried aloud on his son's name.

And the word he flung faltered not to the ground; in that place
standing, the young man
in his splendor bought by his own death his father's rescue.
And of those who lived long ago men judged him
pre-eminent among the youth for devotion
to those who begot them, for that terrible deed.
All that is past.
Of men living now, Thrasyboulos
comes beyond others to the mark in his father's eyes,

and visits his father's brother, with fame complete.
He carries wealth with discretion.
The blossom of youth he gathers is nothing violent,
but wise in the devious ways of the Muses.
To you, Poseidon, shaker of the earth, lord
of the mastering of horses, he comes, with mind to please you.
Also his heart, that is gentle
in the mixing of friends,
passes for sweetness the riddled work of the bees.

(*Richmond Lattimore, trans.*)

We begin in apparent metaphor, with the erection of a treasure house of song for victory by which Pindar means more than a single chariot-race victory, since he says the edifice has been built for the children of Emmenos—the ruling family of Akragas—and for the glory of the city of Akragas, as well as for the victor being celebrated, Xenokrates, who is the brother of

Theron, current tyrant (dictator) of Akragas. This building is indestructible, we learn next, as the poem addresses the son of Xenokrates, Thrasyboulos, who possibly drove the chariot. Father and son won the race by working together, which leads Pindar to move on to the subject of filial devotion. His entryway is myth—the words of the centaur Chiron to Achilles (Peleiades), one of the heroes of the Trojan War. And the words themselves have the combination of instruction and of religious duty that brings to mind the choral odes of tragedy, with which Pindar was quite familiar. After Zeus, revere your parents, goes the advice.

We might expect Pindar now to discuss how Achilles followed the advice, but he leaps instead to Antilochos, another warrior at Troy, and relates the story of how he died while saving his father Nestor, and thus gained pre-eminence for his devotion. Thrasyboulos, in his devotion to his father in the chariot race, exemplifies the devotion Chiron urged Achilles to exemplify, the kind of devotion that was enacted by Antilochos who thereby attained the glory of reputation that, in the present day, is exemplified by the glory of victory accorded to Xenokrates, thanks to the devotion of his co-charioteer, his son Thrasyboulos. This is typical of how Pindar's mind works. And once he has brought us, in a manner that seems both random and—in retrospect—deliberate, controlled, back to Thrasyboulos (who is now cast in the third person, direct address reserved now for the god Poseidon at the poem's end), the ode closes with a celebration of the qualities, besides devotion, that mark the young man's character: discretion, youthfulness (perhaps youthful beauty), wisdom, a mindfulness of the gods, and a heart whose sweetness rivals that of bees. The image returns us to the ode's beginning, when the speaker—who is Pindar, of course—spoke of laboring the field. Is this a way for Pindar to, in a sense, praise himself, the poet as a bee, the resulting ode as "the riddled work of bees," that particular sweetness? Meanwhile, what of Xenokrates, all but forgotten, but whose ode this is?

To describe this, or any of Pindar's odes, as a victory ode is clearly reductive. Victory, rather, becomes the occasion for reflection on human achievement and character, for prescription with regard to moral conduct and religious duty, and for a kind of logical working out of the human condition by means of exempla drawn from myth, history, ancestry, and what the Greeks called *nomos*—correct behavior, correct thinking, as established by and agreed upon by a culture, a society, over time.

As for the agon element, well, the occasion of these odes was a literal agon and the celebration of the man who had triumphed. But Pindar's odes commonly refer to the agon between gods and mortals, between arrogance and humility. In this particular ode, the agon is understood by implication; the virtues being celebrated in Thrasyboulos aren't in everyone. Another possible agon is the one between earlier times—the age of heroes, that included Achilles and Antilochos—and the present day, where "heroes" like Thrasyboulos stand out for their rarity; the implied agon here is between right and wrong conduct, something that seems to have become more difficult over time, hence the note of mingled regret and nostalgia when Pindar concludes his discussion of Homeric devotion with the simple line "All that is past."

One element that recedes in Pindar's odes is a sense of intimacy, the kind that characterized so much of the work of Sappho, a sense of the private "I," as opposed to the very public one we see in Pindar, or the "I" of the choral odes of tragedy, where the speaker inevitably speaks for the collective "we" of the chorus and, by extension, for the "common person," the one who knows and accepts his or her place, rather than aspiring to the greatness that has led to the downfalls they routinely witness. That intimacy confined itself, for the most part, to the archaic lyric poets of whom Sappho is a chief example. So it makes sense that it would next occur most notably in Horace, the first-century BC Roman poet who acknowledged his indebtedness to the Greek lyric poets and took pride in having introduced into Latin the Greek meters of such models as Sappho and her compatriot Alcaeus. But while the majority of Horace's odes are cast in either Alcaic or Sapphic stanzas (i.e., in the quatrains of a particular meter in which Alcaeus and Sappho wrote their poems), and while the fact of intimacy is a point in common between Horace and his models, Horace's odes can finally only be termed Horatian.

A chief difference between Horace and his seventh-century BC models is that his odes were not written to be performed either publicly or to music—if there's an audience, it's an implied one, or else an individual addressed solely in the poet's imagination—and I think it's this that in particular accounts for a different kind of intimacy in Horace's odes. To be sure, Sappho's work is intimate, but hers is an intimacy about private feeling, we might say—the poems read as announcements of feeling, emotion itself given voice. Horace, on the other hand, tends to transform an often ordinary situation into an instance of intimacy that we don't just overhear or witness, we are invited into it. The tone is, more often than not, one of familiarity, camaraderie—a tone combined, though, with a meditative cast of mind that is ever aware of life's sobering realities, without losing a sense, too, of the comic. The mix is all the more resonant for the subtlety with which Horace moves from one tone into another. Ode I. 34 opens in comedic bombast, for example, but note how that changes:

Lazy in praising or praying to any god
and madly rational, a clever captain
cruising the open seas of human thought,

now I must bring my vessel full about,
tack into port and sail back out again
on the route from which I strayed. For the God of Gods,

who slices through the storm with flashes of fire,
this time in a clear sky came thundering
with his storied horses and his chariot,

whereby the dumb dull earth and its fluttering streams—
and the River Styx, and the dreaded mouth of the cave
at the end of the world—were shaken. So the god

does have sufficient power after all
to turn the tables on both high and low,
the mighty humbled and the meek raised up—

with a swift hiss of her wings, Fortune swoops down,
pleased to place the crown on this one's head,
as she was pleased to snatch it away from that one.

(*Ellen Bryant Voigt, trans.*)

In the extended metaphor with which the poem opens, Horace mocks his own previous confidence in rational thinking, a thinking that had made for a slackness of reverence. Now the clever captain makes a hangdog retreat, his cleverness shattered by the instance of an earthshaking thunderburst, despite clear skies. From the comic entrance of the captain and his sudden retreat, Horace moves to a meditation on the gods and their power—the thunder as evidence of this—and from there to the idea that divine power is not only a fact but an unpredictable one, as is evidenced by the varying degrees of fortune from one person to the next. The seamlessness of the tonal shift at first makes it possible to forget another element that we expect in the ode, the agon, but it is very much here in the tension between the human impulse to know and the refusal of divinity to be entirely knowable. Intimacy is also here. The poem may end on a note of authority about the nature of fortune, but the self-chiding of the speaker at the start, along with his stage-like self-caricature, invite us in as readers; we're invited to watch, to be amused, as an individual gets humbled, and to gradually learn why we ourselves should keep humility in mind.

This juxtapositioning of high and low, in terms of tone—by which the poem enacts the agon of human experience—is characteristic of Horace. Ode III. 13 is on one hand a straightforward enough vow, to sacrifice a baby goat to a favorite fountain, in gratitude:

O clearer than crystal, thou Bandusian fountain,
To whom it is fitting to bring libations of wine

And offerings also of flowers, tomorrow the chosen
First-born of the flock will be brought to you,

His new little horns foretelling warfare and love
In vain, for the warm blood of this child of the flock

Will stain with its color of red your clear cold waters.
The cruel heat of Canicula the Dog Star

Can find no way to penetrate the glade
To where you are. Gladly your shady coolness

Welcomes the oxen that come, weary of plowing,
And welcomes also the wandering pasturing flock.

You shall become famous among the fountains
Because of my song that praises the ilex tree

That leans above the rocks the babbling waters leap from.

(*David Ferry, trans.*)

But note the tenderness with which the kid is described—"His new little horns"—and then how this description, which highlights the innocence of the kid, segues straight into warfare, itself paired with love, what might seem an opposite to war; and just as the portrait is getting fleshed out, just as we've moved from infancy to the anticipation of an adulthood that will include sex and combat, we learn that all of it's been "in vain"—with a suddenness that the line break underscores (this line break occurs in exactly the same way in the original). Similarly, the blood of sacrifice of an innocent victim is juxtaposed with the holiness of the occasion. "[C]ruel heat of Canicula the Dog Star" beside the fountain's "shady coolness." And the lofty tone of vow, of prayer, with its implications of humility, beside what verges on boast—or confidence, at least—in the poet's assertion that, thanks to his abilities as odist, this fountain will forever be famous.

One of the effects of this juxtapositioning is a poignancy that seems particular to Horace's work. It's how a comic prayer to Venus (IV. 1)—in which the speaker begs to be left out of love's arena, claiming to be too old for that, having "no use for/tender girls, or boys either"—can suddenly turn heartbreaking, as the speaker abandons his prayer to Venus, distracted by the memory of someone else:

Then why, Ligurinus, why
do my eyes sometimes fill, even spill over?
    Why, sometimes, when I'm talking
do I suddenly have nothing to say? Why
    do I hold you in my arms
in certain dreams, certain nights, and in others
    chase you endlessly across
the Field of Mars, into the swirling Tiber?

(*Richard Howard, trans.*)

This effect even occurs in the less characteristic odes known as the Roman odes, which read more like commissioned pieces designed to extol Roman virtues by means of the exempla of history. Ode III. 5, for example, opens by acknowledging Jupiter as king, but Augustus as a god on earth. Horace goes on, however, to detail how the citizens have become more "immoral," yielding to foreigners rather than asserting their Roman identity. The story of Regulus is told at this point: a prisoner of Carthage, he was sent back to Rome to negotiate an exchange of prisoners. Instead, he persuaded the Senate not to negotiate an exchange or any ransom—these being signs of weakness, a lack of valor—and he decided to go back to his prison in Carthage, rather than stay in Rome:

> What tortures were awaiting him he knew
> Perfectly well; but hurried out as though,
> Finally free of tedious hours in court,
> Demanding clients, he were heading out
> To some secluded valley, cool and green,
> Some innocent and peaceful little town.

> (*Rachel Hadas, trans.*)

Horace has spent the entire poem loftily detailing the events of history. He includes a dignified speech of Regulus on the collapse of morals. But he renders an otherwise rather stiff, moralizing poem, distanced by history, into a quietly moving poem, by comparing the heroic Regulus to any man leaving court for the day, and comparing the tortures which are Regulus's destination to the very different destination of "some secluded valley, cool and green,/Some innocent and peaceful little town." In the concluding handful of lines, the poem finds its poignancy, as the distant hero of history becomes something of an individual for whom we can feel compassion, and as the poem that began at the heights of Olympus finds conclusion in the "peaceful little town" of imagination.

Sometimes a hymn. Sometimes a prayer. An implied audience, or one just hoped for. Often dedicatory, therefore—*to* someone or something—and yet not every dedicatory poem = an ode ... Didactic, but what poem doesn't at some level have something to teach us? An agon, but won't any examination of or instance taken from human experience yield an agon? The relationship of self to the world outside the self. The mind-body problem. Memory. What is *not* an ode?

Horace's word for what he wrote was *carmen*, the same word used by his fellow Roman poets Catullus, Virgil, Propertius, and Tibullus for *their* poems, which we refer to as poems, not odes. Why?

In any basic Latin dictionary, *carmen* gets defined as song. But *carmen* turns out to mean much more: a prophecy, an oracle's response, a charm, a magic formula, an incantation, a formula in religion and/or law. Also any poem, from epic to dramatic to lyric. What is a *carmen*? What isn't?

Even the classical ode resisted easy definition, except in terms purely of form: i.e., there were established metrical feet to be used in lines, and the lines in stanzas; but that being the case, each poet made use of these elements differently. There was the convention in the choral ode of strophe alternating with antistrophe, but an ode of Sophocles is not a Eurpidean ode, and the difference is one of sensibility. Sophocles and Euripides were two different, distinct people. Isn't this what makes any poem different from others? Horace's odes are finally Horatian because they are by Horace, not because they adhere to a particular form, which they do not.

I suspect that any successful poem should resist definition (by in some way revising earlier definitions) and will inevitably, insofar as it springs from the agon of human experience, either contain and/or enact its own agon, as well. So it's hard to say that these elements are what survives of the classical tradition in the contemporary ode, whatever that might be. Certainly there are plenty of poems that call themselves odes, but they are as various as the ode tradition itself. Yusef Komunyakaa's "Ode to the Maggot," for example, recalls Sappho's prayer to Aphrodite, in its naming of the deity and the listing of divine attributes:

Brother of the blowfly
& godhead, you work magic
Over battlefields,
In slabs of bad pork

& flophouses. Yes, you
Go to the root of all things.
You are sound & mathematical.
Jesus Christ, you're merciless

With the truth. Ontological & lustrous,
You cast spells on beggars & kings
Behind the stone door of Caesar's tomb
Or split trench in a field of ragweed.

No decree or creed can outlaw you
As you take every living thing apart. Little
Master of earth, no one gets to heaven
Without going through you first.

The poem also has something of the Pindaric element of tribute/praise. The agon of life and death is here. Also, a resistance to the tradition it recalls, by making a deity of the maggot—an unlikely candidate, at first, but by poem's end, the maggot's omnipresence ("Over battlefields,/In slabs of bad pork") and its omnipotence ("Little/Master of earth" and of beggars, kings, decrees, and creeds) seem to earn it a place in the pantheon. Also, a formal regularity—the four quatrains—we expect in a Classical ode.

A different attention to form governs Robert Pinsky's "Ode to Meaning." Here are the poem's first six stanzas:

Dire one and desired one,
Savior, sentencer—

In an old allegory you would carry
A chained alphabet of tokens:

Ankh Badge Cross.
Dragon,
Engraved figure guarding a hallowed intaglio,
Jasper kinema of legendary Mind,
Naked omphalos pierced
By quills of rhyme or sense, torah-like: unborn
Vein of will, xenophile
Yearning out of Zero.

Untrusting I court you. Wavering
I seek your face, I read

That Crusoe's knife
Reeked of you, that to defile you
The soldier makes the rabbi spit on the torah.
"I'll drown my book," says Shakespeare.

Drowned walker, revenant.
After my mother fell on her head, she became
More than ever your sworn enemy. She spoke
Sometimes like a poet or critic of forty years later.
Or she spoke of the world as Thersites spoke of the heroes,
"I think they have swallowed one another. I
Would laugh at that miracle."

You also in the laughter, warrior angel:
Your helmet the zodiac, rocket-plumed
Your spear the beggar's finger pointing to the mouth
Your heel planted on the serpent Formulation
Your face a vapor, the wreath of cigarette smoke crowning
Bogart as he winces through it.

While the stanzas are irregular in length (as are the lines), certain elements provide a structure to the poem. There's the periodic naming of the "deity," not just in stanza one (a stanza that will get repeated—only slightly varied—as the penultimate stanza of the poem), but in stanzas like the third one, which is itself abecedarian, so a highly structured manner of naming the god in nine different ways. The poem is punctuated with anecdotes that attest to meaning's presence and absence; stanza four, mentioning a mother's changed mental state after a fall, is but one of several examples. At stanza six, we encounter a series of lines that begin either with "you" or "your," continuing through ten lines, the anaphora incantatory in its effect.

As with Komunyakaa's ode, Pinsky's does indeed attend to form; it, too, falls into the category of hymn/prayer/praise and invests something unlikely—meaning—with divinity. That divinity and our relationship to it becomes the crux of the poem's agon. It's not difficult to trace these two odes back to a classical tradition. Here, though, is Elizabeth Alexander's "Ode":

The sky was a street map with stars for
house parties, where blue-lit basements
were fever-dreams of the closest a boy
could get to home after yucca fritters,
rice, pigeon peas, and infinite chicken
made by anyone's mother before the night's
charioteer arrived in his beat-up boat
to spirit the three, or the four, or the five, or
as many would fit in the car to the party.
Pennies and pennies bought one red bottle
of Mad Dog Double-Twenty or Boone's Farm.
"Que Pasa, y'all, que pasa," Mister James
Brown sweated, and the Chi-Lites whispered pink.
White Catholic school girls never would dance
or grind or neck or lift their skirts to these
black boys with mothers who spoke little
English and guarded their young with candles
for *los santos,* housework, triple-locked
doors, jars of tinted water, fierce arm-pinches.
Love is a platter of *platanos.*
"Did you hear? Did you hear?"—the young men whisper,
but church calls its altar boys Sunday noon—
"They danced Latin at the Mocambo Room!"
The tale has been told again and again
of boys growing old, going bad, making good,
leaving home while the neighborhood rises
or falls, and this story ends the same.
Now dreadlocked vendors sell mechanized monkeys
programmed to beat *guaguanco.*

A single-stanza poem of lines that range between seven and eleven syllables—
not quite the attention to form we associate with the classical ode. But the
choral ode—with its attention to rhetorical structure—*does* come to mind.
The first thirteen lines work as a strophe, detailing an Hispanic youth, dinners
of yucca fritters and infinite chicken—suggestive of lower income—and the
house parties that briefly allow for an escape from harsh realities. Lines 14–23
seem to counter that escape from reality by bringing us back to it: the moth-

ers who speak no English, the religious superstitions and, more soberingly, the fact of prejudice in the White Catholic school girls who'd never deign to dance with these boys. Which is to say, we have the strophe of escape from reality, the antistrophe of a reality of prejudice and—in the concluding six lines—an epode of sorts, where the imagined chorus comes together in summation: how the story's always the same one, some failed, some succeeded, but what seems to be left of a vibrant culture and of a youth of dreaming is the music—the *guaguanco*—not played by young men but by mechanized monkeys to which, Alexander implies, so many of these young men were reduced. Which is not to say that Alexander's poem is a choral ode, but it does contain a similar rhetorical structure, enacting an agon of cultural restlessness between Hispanics and Whites. At the same time, this also can be read as an ode of tribute, to a time gone by, to a past of dreaming.

It's unclear whether Brenda Hillman intends her poem as an ode or not, but she surely knows that by breaking up the word "code"—as she does in the poem's title, attention is drawn to the presence of the one word inside the other. Here is "C ode":

when it moves up the alder
only its red C moves

> the- the- the-
> feels sorry for it

> the red-headed woodpecker
in front of *ofness*, moved before the tree

As envy feels sorry
> for the thing envied, after

C for career of searching, for the solid thing

> As for the red on his head: the hydrant stuck in snow
> feels "sorry" for it

A sharp cry from the schoolboy in the snow
> pierced the slipping C!

And texture took the position the bird
moved against

(The dim cry of my love
in his fever)

The bird moved against, a universe unscaled

Patches of striving

(Where my love in his fever   lay down)

It's a poem that can seem random in its structure, though there are three tableaux that get revisited along the way: the woodpecker of stanzas 3, 8, 10, and possibly 1; the feverish lover of stanzas 9 and 12; and in stanzas 4, 5, 8, 10, 11, the notion of searching and striving, which can also include envy and moving against. The act of feeling sorry recurs. The sharp cry of the schoolboy is echoed in the lover's dim cry. And indeed, searching—the career of searching, which we might translate as "being alive"—is one possible theme for this poem, or we might say that searching is the thing to which this poem is a kind of ode—the kind of ode that doesn't so much praise as acknowledge, the way Horace's I. 34 acknowledged the gods he'd been "lazy in praising." Hillman's poem seems to wrestle with the idea of searching—is this the poem's agon?—to long for an end to that restlessness; the satisfaction that we arrive at by poem's end comes, I think, from how it ends at the *release* from restlessness, the submission of the body in lying down.

In the first four stanzas, there's an alternating between the bird (stanzas 1 and 3) and the act of feeling sorry (2 and 4)—strophe and antistrophe? The last three monostichs of the poem seem to bring the three recurring tableaus together, as if in a kind of resolution. An epode?

Hillman's poem comes from a tradition that seeks to destabilize our conventional notions of meaning and of how meaning gets expressed. We can read her poem through the lens of the classical tradition, but the poem both resists that tradition and seems in places to conform to it, though the conformity may well be purely accidental. Hillman's poem reminds us that genre itself, while useful, is artifice finally, and in many ways arbitrary—including that genre that we sometimes call "the ode."

Between Things: On the Ode

Whatever else an ode is, whether it praises or muses, we think of it as a lyric with size—whether in actual length or imaginative displacement. The tone of the ode may attach itself to either loss or celebration (or both), it may speculate or meditate, but it always wants to have reach and size. The sonnet concentrates its time and energy; the pastoral broods by the roadside and lives in the lyric moment. But the ode invites memory and crosses borders; it acquires a past—historical or mythical—while focusing its attention on the drama of the present tense, usually in the present tense. My heart aches, not ached; and it's the sad heart of Ruth matched with emperor and clown.

Attitude-wise, we may prefer the balanced tone of the Horatian ode, with its calm perspective and more colloquial engagement; or we may want something a little more Pindaric and passionate and close to the subject, even panegyric. After the English Romantics, however, both of these elevations seem distant to the personal address and the interior life, in which the subjective of the emotion is elevated to public hearing. But whether Classical or Romantic, the seriousness and size of the ode is intended to be beyond question. Its form, its length and breadth, is formalizing. It makes a ceremony of our feelings, in stanzas and sections of mass and contemplation. It may even have a political agenda, such as Andrew Marvell's "Horatian Ode upon Cromwell's Return from Ireland"; or an artistic agenda, such as Percy Bysshe Shelley's "Ode to the West Wind," written in terza rime in honor of Dante and his Florentine home: "This poem was conceived and chiefly written in a wood that skirts the Arno, near Florence," says Shelley.

The central occasion of the sonnet may be love; the central, and obvious, occasion of the elegy is death; but what is the occasion, central or peripheral, of the ode? All poems, at heart, *feel*; the ode, though, seems to want to think and think through its event as well. Odes, in their embodiment, want to involve as much of the whole body and brain as possible. They, in fact, build a collateral body, in a form that emulates the process of that building. Their implicit sense of size speaks to the complexity, the duality, or whatever, of the wholeness and the fullness of what odes long for. Samuel Taylor Coleridge's marvelous "Dejection" ode goes right to the issue of what the modern, self-reflexive ode is about: the shaping spirit of the imagination:

> I may not hope from outward forms to win
> The passion and the life, whose fountains are within.

He's not sure himself what his complaint is—nor will he ever be—but it's ontological, he knows that for sure, and may even have its practical side: a loveless marriage, which places it in a line leading to *The Waste Land* that contains, among other forms, several odes.

William Wordsworth's Immortality Ode, at almost twice the length and half the psychological mass of Coleridge's "Dejection," surpasses the dark completely in favor of "celestial light." Wordsworth's is a vision of wholeness, the child as father to the man—indeed, such wholeness as to include our pre-birth ("Our birth is but a sleep and a forgetting") and our afterlife, which is our life here and now with intimations of our immortality among "The clouds that gather round the setting sun." This is the poem that Larkin almost died for. He was driving along one of the A roads near Hull in an early spring rain—cold enough to fog the windshield—listening to poetry hour on the BBC, which on this particular day featured "Ode: Intimations of Immortality from Recollections of Early Childhood," and began to weep. His warm breath and tears only compounded the problem of fog, he says, and he drove into a ditch, at some speed. Larkin is not a weeper. So this must have been one of those odal moments when the size of the heart of a poem meets the sublime and thoughts that lie too deep for tears but don't. The "Soul's immensity" is what Wordsworth is after, and the parabola of being he builds is like a rainbow over middle and old age, beginning in childhood and ending in lasting tenderness.

John Keats perfects the instrument of the ode and in doing so creates the modern lyric, the poem that both acts out and contemplates itself—"the form of lyric debate that moves actively toward drama," as Walter Jackson Bate puts it in his great critical biography of Keats. By drama I think Bate means literally a form of theater—a soliloquy perhaps, but more likely an internal dialogue with self involving a third thing: a bird, a goddess, a Grecian urn—a distracting object. You have to ask yourself: Why, in the space of a little over a month—mid-April through mid-May—does Keats pursue the discovered form of his odes—which amounts to an abbreviated combination of the English and Italian sonnet forms, varied sometimes with the Spenserian—through so many changes, beginning with the most irregular, "Ode to Psyche," and ending five odes later with the least—by comparison—successful, "Ode on Indolence"? The middle three, "Ode to a Nightingale," "Ode on a Grecian Urn," and "Ode on Melancholy," are almost beyond praise. "To Autumn," a reprising of the form four months later, *is* beyond praise. None of Keats's odes meets the test of length proposed by Wordsworth and Coleridge; only one, the "Nightingale" ode, at eighty lines, comes close. The so-called triadic dance of the classic ode—strophe, antistrophe, and epode—hardly has the opportunity to get going. As if Keats had intended such scaffolding.

What happens in Keats is that he takes the assumed energy and capacity of the mind and heart of the classic ode and refocuses its appeal to structure, balance, and gesture toward something more like texture, compression, reiteration. Keats fills out—or fills in—density; he transcends structure through the senses. As if structure were invisible, "form transparent before its subject," as Bate puts it. The length of the ode in Keats is in its depth, its richness, its thickness, its concentration. Keats, in his way, invents the vertical reading of poetry, its interiority of music and meditation. His odes teach us the importance of the byplay of assonance and consonance to the rhythm and memory-making of a line, the way the s's punctuate the pain in the first line of "Nightingale"—"My heart aches, and a drowsy numbness pains / My sense . . ."—and the way the open vowels keep the voice from closure and anger. They teach us to stay in the moment of the experience, to stay with the experience, to return and return, the way the Grecian urn itself turns in the circular space of the mind with more and more intensity. They teach us that the modern lyric has no announced beginning or ending, only the long contemplative moment in between, the way "Ode to Melancholy" gives up a whole starting stanza in order to achieve its vital sense of interruption at just the right instant. They teach us that the sublime is inherent in the most common of experience, such as an autumn day "o'er-brimm'd" with "ripeness to the core," a day that is like an allegory of human life, but without the least labeling, a day of harvest and store and twilight.

Whatever the occasion or emotion generating the modern lyric—love or loss or both—the mind of the poem owes its heart to the ode, the pensive part of us, the imagination standing before a small fire, looking into it. In the letter Keats writes to Richard Woodhouse in which he encloses the first draft of "To Autumn," September 21, 1819, the first day of autumn, he comments that "I should like a bit of fire to night—one likes a bit of fire— How glorious the Blacksmiths' shops look now—I stood to night before one till I was very near listing for one. Yes I should like a bit of fire—at a distance about 4 feet." I cannot help but think that some of the stuff behind the composition of "To Autumn" has to do with those fires Keats must have stood before many times during his stay in Winchester. Especially the fact that they were working fires, blacksmiths' fires, since so much of what Keats's great lyric is saying is about work, the human hand, the purpose of the harvest. Fires in the night, against the dark, like a sunset, like that odal moment of suspension, within time, between things.

Ode and Empire

In 41 BC, having defeated his enemies in the civil wars that followed upon the assassination of his great-uncle and adoptive father Julius Caesar, Octavius declared a general amnesty. Among those who took advantage of this amnesty to return to Rome and pick up the pieces of their lives again was one Quintus Horatius Flaccus, aged twenty-four. He had been a student in Athens when Julius Caesar was killed and had, in the general fervor of republican reform, joined Brutus's army and served as military tribune until the disastrous defeat at Philippi in 42 BC. Horace was penniless when he returned to Rome, his father having died and his father's estates having been confiscated as a result of his own ill-starred career as a patriot in rebellion. What was left of his inheritance he wore on his back, or in his head, for his father—himself a freedman—had made considerable sacrifices to provide Horace with the most fungible and disaster-proof sort of wealth he could imagine, a superb education. Horace became a scribe, or quaester's clerk, upon his return to Rome, but his real advancement came about through the friendship of poets. It was Virgil and Varius who introduced the young Horace, momentously, to Maecenas, senior advisor to Octavius and patron of the arts. It was Maecenas who bestowed upon Horace the Sabine farm that became not only a source of stable income for the rest of the poet's life, but also a touchstone of spiritual sustenance and renewal.

Maecenas is abundantly present in Horace's written works. He is recurrently addressed, he is praised, he is thanked. His name is the first word in the first poem of the first of Horace's books of *Odes:* "Maecenas, you, descended from many kings, / O you who are my stay and my delight. . . ." This poem proceeds to inventory the varieties of human calling or estate—athlete, statesman, lord of vast acreage, humble farmer, merchant, idler, soldier, hunter—and to conclude with the poet's own vocation:

What links *me* to the gods is that I study
To wear the ivy wreath that poets wear.
The cool sequestered grove in which I play
For nymphs and satyrs dancing to my music

Is where I am set apart from other men—
Unless the muse Euterpe takes back the flute
Or Polyhymnia untunes the lyre.
But if *you* say I am truly among the poets,

Then my exalted head will knock against the stars.

(*David Ferry, trans.*)

So the poet's place—not merely his means of sustenance and *habitus*, his villa in the Sabine Hills, nor even his claim to honor and attention, but his very "link to the gods"—is the abounding gift of patronage. The encomium so central to ode acknowledges tribute paid in varying coin: in acreage, in money, in public virtue, in eloquence and fame. The poet looks to his patron for recognition in material terms and also in judgment; he gives in exchange the ode. I name you *Maecenas*, and you name me *poet*.

※ ※

The history of the ode is governed by two rhetorical poles: large-scale public address and intimate meditation. The thread I wish chiefly to examine here is that which links the ode, throughout its rhetorical spectrum, to the seats of public power. In its origin, the ode is linked to those most public of public events, the civic drama and festivals of ancient Greece. Pindar (522–442 BC), who is generally credited with devising the form, wrote his odes to celebrate athletic victories, the three-part structure of the poem corresponding to three movements of the chorus by whom it was sung: a strophe, in which the chorus moved from left to right, an antistrophe, in which the chorus moved from right to left, and an epode, in which the chorus stood still. In subsequent centuries, the Pindaric ode came to be associated with other large-scale public observances: the unveiling of monuments, the formal accession of an emperor, the ceremony of state funerals. The Horatian ode is simpler in structure and often more modest in subject, a single repeated stanza form that may function as a drinking song, an invitation to dinner, or a celebration of fleshly dalliance. In the course of two and a half millennia, the ode has assumed many formal incarnations—tripartite, homostrophic, and, in later periods, much looser and more irregular. Its most enduring feature has been not form but occasion. The ode offers praise to a ruler, a patron, an athlete, a friend, to drink or childhood or a Grecian urn. It casts itself as the lyricist speaking-in-public. Coupling with occasion, it marks the boundaries of the self and the social.

And even in its earliest manifestations, the ode has accommodated tonalities and apprehensions that complicate the tautological circuits of patronage and praise. In the third ode of the first book, Horace calls down blessings upon the journey of his friend Virgil to Greece:

> May Venus goddess of Cyprus and may the brothers
> Castor and Pollux, the shining stars, the calmers,
> Guard you, O ship, and be the light of guidance;
> May the father of the winds restrain all winds
> Except the gentle one that favors this journey.
> Bring Virgil, your charge, the other half of my heart,
> Safely to the place where he is going.
>
> *(David Ferry, trans.)*

But even as he praises the history of human navigation and the courage of men who venture upon the seas, the poet finds himself in darker, more ambivalent territory. He considers those who brave the elements and venture into forbidden realms—the "impious" sailor, "Guileful Prometheus," "Audacious Daedalus"—as tempting the gods. He modulates from benison to warning: "Is it any wonder, then, that Jupiter rages, / Hurling down lightning, shaking the sky with thunder?" It becomes the business of ode, even as it plays the chords of well-wishing and affiliation, to contemplate the limits of human ambition and to issue implicit counsel.

Moving further in this direction, odes may offer frank instruction to figures conspicuous in the public eye. Ben Jonson's "Ode to Sir William Sidney on His Birthday," written to celebrate the latter's twenty-first birthday in the year 1611, is an example in kind. William was son to Robert Sidney, Lord Lisle, grandson to Henry Sidney, sometime Lord Lieutenant of Ireland, and nephew to Sir Philip Sidney, who was still remembered, in the disillusioned second decade of Jacobean England, as the flower, the consummate poet-courtier-military hero, of the Elizabethan age. Twenty-five years after Philip Sidney's death, his family was still important as a wellspring of literary patronage. But William, having inherited this luminous mantle and having recently attained his own majority, had to date led a conspicuously lackluster career.

Jonson raises a congratulatory toast ("Give me my cup . . . from the Thespian well"), but quickly turns to cautionary advice:

> This day says, then, the number of glad years
> 　　Are justly summed, that make you man;
> 　　　　　Your vow
> 　　　　　Must now
> 　　Strive all right ways it can
> To outstrip your peers:
> 　　　Since he doth lack
> 　　　Of going back
> 　　　　　Little, whose will
> 　　　　　Doth urge him to run wrong, or to stand still.
> . . . .
> 'Twill be exacted of your name, whose son,
> 　　Whose nephew, whose grandchild you are;
> 　　　　　And men
> 　　　　　Will then
> 　　Say you have followed far,
> When well begun;
> 　　　Which must be now:
> 　　　They teach you how.
> 　　　　　And he that stays
> 　　　　　To live until tomorrow hath lost two days.

(*from* The Forest 14; *published as part of the 1616 Folio of Jonson's* Works)

Jonson was a master of the ruthless compliment. He had a keen sense of his own worth and of his dependence upon sources of sustenance—the public stage, the private masquing halls, the circuits of aristocratic praise—toward which he felt decidedly mixed emotions. He expected public stricture to be recognized as value-for-money.

American poets have generally been wary of "forcing the Muse" in the service of public occasion. We do not commemorate the queen's birthday; the patronage systems to which we subscribe (foundation grants and universities rather than private purses) earn thanks on the acknowledgments page rather than in the body of our poems. However beset or driven by public intersections, the American lyric has largely grounded its authority in inwardness. Ralph Waldo Emerson's "Ode (Inscribed to W. H. Channing)" voices the national (and personal) ambivalence explicitly. First published in 1847, Emerson's "Ode" was dedicated to a clergyman and fellow abolitionist who had urged Emerson to become more active in the anti-slavery movement. The "Ode" begins with an ostensible demurral and apology:

> Though loath to grieve
> The evil time's sole patriot,
> I cannot leave
> My honied thought
> For the priest's cant,
> Or statesman's rant.
>
> If I refuse
> My study for their politique,
> Which at the best is trick,
> The angry Muse
> Puts confusion in my brain.

Emerson felt as keenly as did Channing that the times were evil, that slaveholding was the work of "jackals" and the current war with Mexico a naked act of aggression, that both slavery and the war were stains upon the country, its ideals, and its future:

> Virtue palters; Right is hence;
> Freedom praised, but hid;
> Funeral eloquence
> Rattles the coffin-lid.

But he differed with his friend on the deeper diagnosis and thus on the prospects of cure:

What boots thy zeal,
O glowing friend,
That would indignant rend
The northland from the south?
Wherefore? to what good end?
Boston Bay and Bunker Hill
Would serve things still;—

. . . .

Things are in the saddle,
And ride mankind.

In a world enslaved by "things," Emerson seems to argue, the poet has a more important role to play than that of political activist, however worthy the cause; his function as exemplar and public conscience exceeds the mere exigencies of topical engagement. "Every one to his chosen work," writes the poet: the "shopman," the "senator," and the servant of the Muse pursue distinct imperatives. But where does this leave the disposition of public affairs? And where does it leave historical perspective? Such transcendence as seems to be at work (the "over-god") "marries Right to Might ... exterminates/ Races by stronger races, / Black by white faces. . . ." This does not bode well. And the Muse, who has seemed to scorn the public forum and its noisy methods, finds herself at the climax of Emerson's ode "astonished" by the force of collective uprising in a distant land:

The Cossack eats Poland,
Like stolen fruit;
Her last noble is ruined,
Her last poet mute:
Straight, into double band
The victors divide;
Half for freedom strike and stand;—
The astonished Muse finds thousands at her side.

Emerson's sympathies are clear: he bitterly reproaches the nation, his nation, for failing to live up to its promise; he condemns the predations of private greed and expanding empire. But his critique is fraught with ironies and ever in motion: he writes a polemical poem that begins with the renunciation of public polemic; he adapts a public mode (the ode) to reconfigure skeptically the very foundations of public sphere.

※ ※

Poets love to construe themselves as oppositional, at odds with public decorums and public affairs. But recent decades suggest that American poets are no longer convinced that civic scale and private consciousness, philosophical reach and local idiom, historical imagination and lyric authenticity are inherently inimical to one another. Nor that public speaking must suppress an active and critical mind. Robert Hass's ode to the English language is keenly aware of the vested heritage in which it works: the teeth and vocal cords, the goose quills and printers' templates, the consciousness and material embodiments through which each word has passed to be here, in our heads and our hearts, the gorgeous, resilient, capacious, bullying, agent-of-capitalist-expansion global tongue it is our privilege and our burden to inherit. "English: An Ode" appears in *Sun Under Wood* (1996) and is composed in eleven sections. It begins rather slyly:

1.
   ¿De quien son las piedras del rio
   que ven tus ojos, habitante?

Tiene un espejo la mañana.

"The lines in Spanish," we are told in an endnote, "come from a poem by the Mexican poet Pura López Colomé in her book *Un Cristal en Otro,* Ediciones Toledo, Mexico City, 1989." Which is all very well, but the reader who does not happen to understand Spanish may wish the note had gone a little further. That reader, however, is required to wait: a gentle reminder of the waiting that immigrants everywhere are likely to encounter.

2.
Jodhpurs: from a state in northeast India,
   for the riding breeches of the polo-playing English.

English at last, as promised by the title. But what sort of English? English based on tributary languages: the English of empire. We begin to sense some sort of lesson. And indeed, the format of the poem has begun to assume the format of a common instructional tool, of a primer or a dictionary.

> *Dhoti*: once the dress of the despised,
> it is practically a symbol of folk India.
> One thinks of blood flowering in Gandhi's
> after the zealot shot him.

The dhoti was not Gandhi's native garb, but a garment deliberately recuperated from indigenous India, a garment Gandhi assumed and encouraged others to assume, indeed to produce, by hand and domestically, as part of the resistance to British occupation and British commerce. The dhoti was the centerpiece of economic boycott, national aspiration, and symbolic solidarity across caste lines in mid-twentieth-century India. But the alternately championed and exploited poor are scarcely unique to India. Rather than using the old term, "untouchables," or the official term, "dalits," to identify the traditional wearers of the dhoti, Hass calls them by a name that travels across otherwise-disparate cultures all too well: "despised."

> Were one, therefore, to come across a child's primer

Note the use of the subjunctive; note the unspecified subject "one." Note the naming, inside the posited hypothetical, of the object—"primer"—whose existence has been implied by the format of the preceding lines.

> Were one, therefore, to come across a child's primer
> a rainy late winter afternoon in a used bookshop
> in Hyde Park

Note the burnished, English-sounding name, and note, or fail to note until a little later, the slightly cloudy crossed signal, because Hyde Park in London is not a site for used bookshops.

> . . . and notice, in fine script,
> fading, on the title page,
> "Susanna Mansergh, The Lodge, Little Shelford, Cmbs."
> and underneath it, a fairly recent ball-point
> in an adult hand: *Anna Sepulveda Garcia—sua libra*

and flip through pages with asseverate,
in captions enhanced by lively illustrations,
that *Jane wears jodhpurs*, while *Derek wears a dhoti*,

And note how the hypothetical primer in the hypothetical bookshop has
begun to assume material weight:

it wouldn't be unreasonable to assume a political implication,

lost, perhaps, on the children of Salvadoran refugees
studying English in a housing project in Chicago.

Chicago! *That* Hyde Park! Some of us will have suspected as much,
and will be pleased, in our little way, to have our suspicion confirmed, to
have recognized the neighborhood or even the bookstore itself. We find it
reassuring (political implications here as well) to find ourselves possessed
of local knowledge. One was not wrong, of course, to detect the aura of
Englishness: a neighborhood in Chicago named for a park in London bespeaks the complex nostalgias and braveries of colonial emulation. Old imperium: the English in India. Older imperium: the English in North America.
Newer imperium: America in El Salvador, and refugees in America. The
movement of populations, and of language, follows the trajectories laid down
by money and force.

The poem's next hypothetical is a "high school math teacher" imagined
as a way of filling in the outline of Anna Sepulveda Garcia, second owner
of the primer.

> ... a former high school math teacher
> from San Salvador whose sister, a secretary in the diocesan office
> of the Christian Labor Movement, was found
> in an alley with her neck broken, and who therefore
> followed her elder brother to Chicago and, perhaps,

Note the "perhaps," the announced continuation of hypothesis.

> ... perhaps
> bought a child's alphabet book in a used bookstore
> near the lake where it had languished for thirty years

since the wife, perhaps, of an Irish professor of Commonwealth
    History
at the university had sold it in 1959

Irish: Mansergh. A yet earlier colonialism, which is why the Irish speak
English today, and why an Irishman might find himself earning a living
teaching Commonwealth History in a distinguished American university.
The reader who does a little searching online may discover traces of the
late Nicholas Mansergh, born in Tipperary to a family of Anglo-Irish (i.e.,
Cromwellian) origins, honored denizen of Oxford and Cambridge, author
of scholarly studies on *The Commonwealth Experience, The Irish Question*,
and *Constitutional Relations between Britain and India*. (One may also read
the political speeches of his son Martin Mansergh, Irish civil servant and
diplomat, still very much alive today.) Empire leaves a convoluted aftermath.

—*Math*, as it turned out,
when she looked up the etymology
comes from an Anglo-Saxon word for mowing.

How shall the poet imagine an interlocking fate for Susannah Mansergh,
first owner of the alphabet book, child of privilege from Little Shelford,
Cambridgeshire, and Anna Sepulveda Garcia, who bought it secondhand?
Privilege only extends so far: "maybe the child died / of some childhood
cancer—maybe she outgrew the primer" and her mother sold it and was
later depressed. "Probably she hated Chicago anyway," the mother, that is,
who hailed from Ireland or England or both,

And, browsing, embittered, among the volumes on American history
she somehow felt she should be reading,
thought *Wisconsin, Chicago*: they killed them
and took their language and then they used it
to name the places that they've taken.

"There are those who think," writes the poet, "it's in fairly bad taste / to
make habitual reference to social and political problems / in poems." In such
an intellectual climate, the author of an ode must stay several steps ahead of
earnestness. He may couch his observations in resourceful hypotheticals.
He may work a witty hybrid of fact and fabrication. He may distribute

point of view: it is Anna who flees for safety; it is Susannah's mother who notes the ironies of New World naming. He may pull a narrative coup: observing "far less objection" when imaginative literature stages an "accidental death" than when it succumbs to "moral nagging," he may unceremoniously kill off a central character: "'Helen Mansergh was thinking about Rilke's pronouns / which may be why she never saw the taxi.'"

Etymology is a river, whose tributaries bind us to farflung daily habits and patterns of observation, all of them local, all of them borne from one locality, of time or place or affection, to another:

> In one of Hardy's poems, a man named "Drummer Hodge,"
> born in Lincolnshire where the country word
> for twilight was *dimpsy* two centuries ago,
> was a soldier buried in Afghanistan.

How is it that a boy from Lincolnshire (or Moscow or New Jersey) finds himself transplanted to Afghanistan?

Some war that had nothing to do with him.

Empire requires it. And the fallen were not, in earlier eras, brought home, as witness the roadside epitaphs of ancient Rome. As witness the humbler grave of a British drummer boy:

> Face up according to the custom of his people
> so that Hardy could imagine him gazing forever
> into foreign constellations. *Cyn* was the Danish word
> for farm. Hence Hodge's *cyn*.

And country people in Scandinavia tended to take their names from local holdings.

> And someone of that stock studied medicine.
> Hence Hodgkin's lymphoma. *Lymph* from the Latin
> meant once "a pure clear spring of water."
> Hence *limpid*. But it came to mean
> the white cells of the blood.

Because the blood is a river, too.

In Hardy's poem, the fallen drummer is in fact a native of "Wessex" rather than Lincolnshire, a casualty of the Boer War rather than the Anglo-Afghan War; his body lies in the veldt of South Africa rather than the steppes of Afghanistan. But poets take liberties; "spheres of influence" and the wars that sustain them tend to run together. A poet may be ruthless in his liberties: in the meandering path of etymology (Hodge's *cyn*), he hears a ghostly confirmation of the childhood cancer he "chose to imagine" as the vehicle for cutting off the childhood he chose to imagine behind the inscription on a title page. "She has (strong beat) / a Hodg (strong beat) kin's lym-phom (strong beat)-a": in the rhythms of a diagnosis, he hears the rhythms of a popular song that "the woman in Chicago / might have sung to her children as they fell asleep." This is the other woman, the one from San Salvador; the poet has let her children live. "Yo soy un hombre sincero," she sings. The words were written by the Cuban nationalist José Marti. The song, "Guantanamera," became very popular for a time in the United States. People were protesting another war.

> ¿De quien son las piedras del rio
> que ven tus ojos, habitante?
>
> . . . .
>
> So—what are the river stones
> that come swimming to your eyes, *habitante?*

A more literal translation of the question with which the ode began would hinge on a possessive: *whose* (not what) are the stones. But the present poet, troubled by empire, has chosen to forgo the possessive and, in one key term, to forgo translation altogether. The world belongs to those who dwell there: *habitante.* The language belongs to everyone through whom it has passed.

II. lyric means

1. On the Pastoral:
The Problem of Nature

I came here for the view, and what is there to see?
The place is still a place in progress . . .

JOHN KOETHE

The Pastoral: First and Last Things

I want to be specific here in defining pastoral. I intend my references to be directed to pastoral as a noun rather than an adjective. The Pastoral. For indeed, there are also pastoral elegies, pastoral odes, pastoral dramas, pastoral satires, and so on. Especially in the Renaissance these modes were widely employed, and they overlapped, they leaked, one into the other. There are types of odes, for example, that operate by referencing the conventions of the pastoral, and it's fruitful to examine those as such.

Further, by pastoral, I do not mean simply anything with nature in it, though that seems largely what our contemporary poets regard the pastoral to be. Even Mark Strand and Eavan Boland, in their excellent guidebook, *The Making of the Poem*, include such pastoral examples as Louise Glück's "Mock Orange" (well, there's a tree in it), Thylias Moss's "Tornados" (bad weather), and Philip Levine's "Smoke" (where we find a baby crow and the titular smolder). But Strand and Boland really stretch things when they assert that Galway Kinnell's "The Bear" is a pastoral. Certainly it's got blood and bear turds, geese and "bauchy ice," and the action takes place outside— so it must be pastoral. But if the term means all of this, then it means nothing more precise than "nature poetry," nor does it attend to twenty-five hundred years of poetic convention. The thing I do like about Strand and Boland's definition of pastoral stems from their understandable perplexity about contemporary pastoral. Are there pastures where simple shepherds sing songs? Is there innocence-in-nature, as one Renaissance critic coined it? Does language *ever* directly correlate to what it seems to signify? They write that the pastoral is now "the almost invisible distance in the nature poem." I do love that. Or, as they suppose, it is the nature poem in which the dream becomes a nightmare.

But let's start back at the dream.

Strictly and generically speaking, the pastoral tradition grew out of bucolic poetry. Pastoral poems have, or had, pastures in them, and thus herds (usually of sheep, but sometimes cows—or *kine*, as poets once liked to say), and people to watch over those herds. The first collections of Theocritus's poems of which we know were called "Bucolics," though we now usually refer to this work as the *Idylls of Theocritus*. And Theocritus's work gave rise to his great Latin imitator, Virgil, whose bucolic and pastoral poetry is called *The Eclogues*—lately translated, brilliantly so, by David Ferry.

I think it's important to recall the actual meaning of some of these terms. An *idyll* is, according to the Princeton Encyclopedia, a short poem that deals "charmingly" with rustic life. This is a generic term, denoting no particular form or style. Mostly you just need a rural scene and some leisure time.

Bucolic is more interesting. It derives from the Greek word "bukolos," which means a "neatherd." We know, of course, a shepherd is someone, usually a young man, who herds sheep—as a goatherd herds goats. But a neatherd herds cows, oxen, the bovine. (That's where neat's-foot oil comes from, by the way. It is oil obtained from the boiled feet and shinbones of cattle, used as a dressing for leather.) Thus, in the purest form of the word, bucolics are the songs of cow herders. Of course, even to Theocritus, a bucolic tends to blur with a pastoral, since both his Idylls V and VII involve goatherders, not neatherds; this slippage moved the critic Thomas Rosenmeyer to lament: "It is best to acknowledge that at this point we do not know why Theocritus' poems about herdsmen came to be called bucolics."

An *eclogue* is a variety of pastoral or bucolic poem, but it specifies a kind of dramatic lyric. That is, eclogue is a speech or song constructed as a dialogue between two shepherds or neatherds. Often this dialogue is in the form of an argument or contest.

And finally, a *georgic* is a poem dealing again with rural life, but this time not with herding but rather with farming, the husbanding of crops. More particularly, a georgic is about manual labor, where a pastoral may be about ease, entertainment, love, even goofing off. Another way to say it: a pastoral's ultimate virtue is song, but a georgic's virtue is work. Hesiod's *Works and Days* is a georgic examplar.

Here's an even stranger but potentially very important distinction among these issues. It is likely that the wealthier Greeks were keepers of cattle, not keepers of sheep or, worse, of goats. So we might say, in the ethos and economics of the lyric tradition, a bucolic is a slightly more privileged subgenre than a mere pastoral, and clearly more elevated than a callus-handed georgic. It's no accident that the most practical, therefore, and undoubtedly the most pious or self-righteous of them all, is the georgic.

Back to the *pastoral*. Here I am largely distilling from Frank Kermode's analysis of the mode. Pastoral, Kermode writes, depends upon an opposition between the simple, or natural, and the urbane or cultivated. And thus, immediately, we see how pastoral and georgic can be set against each other, since "cultivation" implies not only farming and work but also refinement.

> Although this opposition can be complex, the bulk of pastoral poetry treats it quite simply and assumes that natural men are purer and less vicious than cultivated men, and that there exists between them and Nature a special sympathy. The natural man is also wise and gifted in a different way from the cultivated man. By reason of his simplicity he is a useful subject for cultivated study, since his emotions and virtues are not complicated by deterioration and artificiality. The themes of the cultivated poet may be connected with those of the primitive poet, much as the garden is related to the open countryside, but the cultivated poet sophisticates them and endows them with learned allusions.

Thus the pastoral can become a vehicle for poetic speculation on religious mysteries, Kermode concludes, and also on poetry itself.

※ ※

Theocritus and his pastoral lyrics are a slightly more recent development than the three ur-forms of the lyric. We might date the erotic poem back to Sappho, on Lesbos, around 600 BC. We can take the written elegy back at least to Simonides of Keos, in the early 500s BC, although we can trace the choral elegy back to Archilochos in the latter half of the eighth century BC, on Paros. And Pindar formed his great odes in the late 400s BC.

Theocritus was born in about 300 BC. He was, as he tells us, a native of Syracuse in Sicily, but his poems were not written for his countrymen, the Arcadians. Rather, Theocritus intended his poems for the audience of Greeks who lived in the highly sophisticated and urbanized city of Alexandria. Thus the cultivated audience observes the simple shepherd at work, or more likely at ease. This double life of the pastoral is extremely important, and basic. Pastoral is about one kind of life, one kind of person, but is intended for an audience of a very different kind. In fact, part of Theocritus's rhetorical success is due to his audience's nostalgia for this earlier way of life, countrified and easy, pure and plain. It's not hard to see how immediately the pastoral landscape then becomes idealized, even a figment of allegory. This art (and business) of cultivation seems interestingly ironic to me. The cultivated audience—at the Library of Alexandria—receives their instruction, in part, thanks to the rubes in Sicily, the Arcadians, who are clearly uncultivated but who, by their literal vocation, are cultivators:

> Sweet music, goatherd, the pine by the spring yonder
> makes with its whispering: sweet, too, your fluting,
> and worthy to win second prize after Pan.
> If his prize is the horned goat, you'll take the nanny;
> if the nanny's for him, the kid falls to you;
> kid's flesh is good eating, till the time you must milk her.

These are the opening lines of Idyll 1, where the shepherd Thyrsis invokes the songs of nature and also, gently and perhaps teasingly, urges a goatherd to join in with his own song. To which the goatherd replies:

> Sweeter, shepherd, your song than the gushing
> water that pours from the high rock yonder.
> If the Muses bear off the ewe as their guerdon,
> you'll take the lamb that's bred within doors;
> if their choice is the lamb, you'll take the ewe after.

And Thyrsis completes the introduction, situating the two in their restful pose, and setting up the contest to follow:

> I pray by the nymphs, goatherd, will you sit
> on the slope of the hillock, there by the tamarisks,
> and play on your pipe, while I mind your goats?

As to style: Theocritus wrote his poems in dactylic hexameter; but his was a meter shaped by quantities and durations (perhaps also pitch), rather than by stressed and unstressed syllables. His language is full of Homeric allusion and shows a sophisticated botanical sense, but still manages a kind of rhetorical purity, at least as much as his fairly heavy use of dialect permits. This dialect, by the way, derives from his Doric and Syrcusan background and would sound to us (most critics presume) roughly like the accented idioms of country folk.

Critics cite Theocritus as the father of the pastoral, but Virgil as its perfecter, its enlarger. David Ferry says "There's nothing in those Idylls of Theocritus that corresponds to the way Virgil makes us aware of the world of politics, economics, and war, whose pressures are felt within and upon his pastoral world." Virgil's *Bucolica*, which we know as *The Eclogues*, are his earliest authenticated work, dating from the mid-30s BC. He then wrote his *Georgics*, first read in 29 BC, and shortly after that started his decade-long task of composing the *Aeneid*, his epic on the founding of Rome. Satyrs and gods, nymphs and shepherds, show up in these eclogues, these gentle competitions between Menalcas and Damoetas. They riddle, they sing love songs and work songs, and finally their neighbor, Palaemon, declares their contest a tie. These ten eclogues are such fine poetry that they seem to have helped to invent the later Renaissance and modern lyric.

The following lines from Eclogue X show Virgil's narrative skill but also the richness and particularity of his metaphoric sense:

The shepherds came, and after them the swineherds,
And Menalcas from his task of getting ready
The fodder for the beasts for the next winter.
They asked, "What is it you are sorrowing for?"
Apollo came, and said, "What is this madness?"
Gallus, Lycoris your love has left you to follow
Another lover among the rough mountain camps
And among the freezing snows." Sylvanus came,
Adorned with fennel flowers and with lilies,
And Pan, Arcadia's god, his face and body
Stained with the juice of berries as if with blood.
—We saw him painted like that, with our own eyes.—
"Ever the same," he said. "Love cares for no one.
The bees never seem to have enough of clover,
The goats never seem to have enough of leaves,
The meadows never enough of freshening water;
Love never seems to have enough of tears."

Note as well, in the last lines, how able and moving Virgil is as he converts the story into a more general issuance of wisdom, and how lovely is his song.

By the Renaissance, the form is exploded, as so many Classical lyric forms exploded. I won't dally here over details, but I should point out some of the primary pastoral texts of the time. There are the major works like Edmund Spenser's *The Shepheardes Calendar*, and many passages from *The Faerie Queene*, many of Sir Philip Sidney's Arcadian poems, Michael Drayton's eclogues from *The Shepherd's Garland*, John Fletcher's pastoral sequences, early and strange things like Barnaby Googe's *Eclogues*, as well as lots of individual lyrics by Thomas Campion, William Shakespeare (especially in "Venus and Adonis"), William Browne, Robert Herrick and Andrew Marvell, and later, John Milton's great pastoral elegy *Lycidas*. As they did with other modes like the ode and the elegy, the sixteenth- and seventeenth-century poets reinvented the pastoral to their own purposes and rhetorical sensibilities. Its conventional playfulness, present from the beginning, takes on further wit and richness, and more complex metaphoric density. It woos, it romances, it argues. It is plainly and highly proud of its obvious skill. Christopher Marlowe's great pastoral invitation, "The Passionate Shepherd to His Love," exemplifies all of these traits:

> Come live with me and be my love,
> And we will all the pleasures prove
> That valleys, groves, hills, and fields,
> Woods, or steepy mountain yields.
>
> And we will sit upon the rocks,
> Seeing the shepherds feed their flocks,
> By shallow rivers to whose falls
> Melodious birds sing madrigals.

As he proposes marriage (or more likely lovemaking, sex), Marlowe's shepherd here finds himself in need of something to tempt and attain his lover. He must increase the quality of that temptation, upping the ante as his rhetoric unfolds. At first he promises her a good view, the spectacle of working shepherds, then pledges to provide goods—clothing, a rustic bed—and then even more, wealth and jewels. Finally, as his ultimate temptation, he guarantees to exchange immortality for lovemaking. It will always be a delightful "May morning," he says, if only she were his. The poem's whole scheme plays richly on the subjective condition established by the important "if" of his promise: "And if these pleasures may thee move, / Come live with me, and be my love."

When the pastoral arrives at the Romantic era, it assumes another set of qualities, considerably less playful or enchanted. Its strangeness, its distance—perhaps its growing alienness—is emphasized in William Collins's *The Persian Eclogues* and Thomas Chatterton's *African Eclogues,* and its heavy symbolism informs William Blake's songs. The pastoral of William Wordsworth's "Michael" or his misty Tintern Abbey becomes highly serious and sublime, melancholy, even stricken, for its powerful nostalgias. Here, in Percy Bysshe Shelley's *Adonais,* in John Keats's *Endymion,* in Matthew Arnold's grand *Thyrsis,* and in Thomas Gray's great elegy, the pastoral shivers with seriousness and grief. I think it is notable, too, that the Romantic pastoral features far fewer characters, focusing instead on a self, and a self-creation: a Self within Nature, a self made "out of" nature. Thus, at the birth of the city, at the inception of the smoky Industrial Revolution, nature—the pastoral—had never been more appropriate or necessary: as a haven, a refuge, a place to grieve, perhaps to heal (as in Whitman's pastoral lilac elegy), a place to think, to meditate, and (if we are Ralph Waldo Emerson or Henry David Thoreau) a place to be de-educated and retaught.

⁂

No other lyric mode depends on—indeed, requires—such complex webs of irony to complete it. This is in itself ironic, since the presiding tone and stance of the pastoral is typically extremely sincere, its aspiration pure, its promise ideal.

First, the pastoral is identified by its location—the quiet, serene pasture. But it also locates or situates itself, very knowingly, *by what it is opposed to,* what is erased or ignored. The point is that what is ignored is what is inevitable, the real world. Although Thyrsis seems to have no awareness of the outside world, as he sings in Theocritus's pastoral, of course the audience of the poem *is* that other world. The pastoral is thus knowingly fictive, and in a Classical sense deeply ironic. I say Classical because sometimes we presume irony merely to be tone of voice, the hip sarcasm of the literary teeny-bopper sneering "as if." But irony is more interesting as a situational trope. I mean irony as Harold Bloom describes it: "What happens to representation when altogether incommensurate realities juxtapose and clash." Oedipus at the crossroad. Or, of course, the Arcadian shepherd among the Alexandrian scholars.

Further, though the pasture appears as a place where shepherds work, they typically do anything but. They sing, mourn, rest, meditate, woo. This reminds me of a snippy but apt remark by Dr. Johnson in his critique of *Lycidas*. Johnson was entirely unimpressed by Milton's claim that he and King "drove afield" and battened their "flocks with the fresh dews of night." "We know," snaps the Doctor, "that they never drove afield" and never *had* "flocks to batten." His dismissal extends beyond Milton's *Lycidas* to the mode of the pastoral itself: "Its form is that of a pastoral, easy, vulgar, and therefore disgusting." To Johnson the pastoral was useful only to give young poets something to cut their teeth on: "It seems natural for a young poet to initiate himself by Pastorals, which, not professing to imitate real life, require no experience."

It's this very distance that I am most interested in locating: the distance described by ironic circumstances, the distance between the ideal and the actual. Remember the distance between Theocritus's fields of neatherds in Arcadia and his highly cultivated audience in Alexandria. He knew it; the Alexandrians knew it. The formula was part of the rhetoric. To pursue this even further, I think the mode most similar to the radical irony of the pastoral is, of all things, the satire. In both, the illusion of the real is nowhere claimed, as it often is in the love poem, the elegy, or ode. The allegorical figurations in both satire and the pastoral are stretched to extremes.

Another important aspect of pastoral irony also dates back to Theocritus. Although the shepherd may be an unhappy or unfulfilled lover, he is a successful poet. This is fundamental. In fact, the shepherd constantly tells us, the *only* remedy for unrequited love *is* song, is poetry, which in the end may be more satisfactory—because more sustained, even eternal—than sex or even love.

Okay, sex. In pastoral, the closer the shepherd gets—the closer *we* get—to the physical, the animal, the closer we get to the divine. As poet Daryl Hine says about this ironic aspect of pastoral poetry, "It is the animal, indeed the bestial, that informs even the sublimest poetic flights." This may be the archetypal link between physical desire and the holy, between sex and god. And this, I think, is another profound borrowing of the Classical pastoral poets by the Renaissance.

Here is the greatest irony of all. The pastoral sings of the ideal, the green world perfected, of paradise not-yet-lost. It is the Edenic garden world not yet spoiled by thinking and feeling. But thinking and feeling are the very things that happen in pastorals. Certainly work doesn't happen. Love doesn't occur. But it's this suspended ideal moment that lingers in the shepherd's song. Wordsworth, in the final stanza of "The Solitary Reaper," anticipated the subject of my final irony:

> Whate'er the theme, the Maiden sang
> As if her song could have no ending;
> I saw her singing at her work,
> And o'er the sickle bending—
> I listened, motionless and still,
> And, as I mounted up the hill,
> The music in my heart I bore,
> Long after it was heard no more.

Here Wordsworth's "as if" pierces with anything but sarcasm. His is the irony of solemn fatalism, for he knows what the Maiden doesn't know. Already unable to hear her, he can only see her singing, and he knows that soon she will vanish entirely.

We know, in our further belated state, even more than Wordsworth. It is not simply that the song, subject, or life of the shepherd is now inaccessible. Nature itself, that green world, is no longer accessible. Wordsworth's reaper fades, farther, until she is gone. The pastoral is not our dream. It is our nightmare.

Meditative Spaces

In his book *Pastoral*, Terry Gifford argues that in the contemporary moment, the pastoral can be attributed to anything "ranging from [the] rural, to any form of retreat, to any form of simplification or idealisation," citing examples of recent usages: the Freudian pastoral, the pastoral of childhood, the urban pastoral—anything, really, that celebrates the ethos of nature over the ethos of city. As a way of focusing, rather than blurring, the idea of the pastoral, I would like to explore "Meditative Spaces" and the relation of such pastoral "spaces" to the lyric's sub-genre, the meditation.

In the meditative mode, a poet can undermine the lyric's drive toward, and love of, closure, without ever giving up on the moment of lyric insight, what William Wordsworth calls "spots of time," James Joyce calls "epiphanies," and Virginia Woolf calls "moments of being." Lyric insight within the lyric moment. Since the English Romantics, the clear presence of the pastoral has asserted itself as the time and space of the meditative utterance much more than as the bucolic landscape. The mode and method of Wordsworth's lapsed pastoral, "Lines Composed a Few Miles Above Tintern Abbey on Revisiting the Banks of the Wye During a Tour July 13, 1798," becomes the model for Wallace Stevens's "The Idea of Order at Key West," a poem that has nothing to do with sheep or the usual pastoral stage props. Both poems show the vestigial trace of the eclogue, with Wordsworth turning to and questioning his sister Dorothy, and with Stevens turning to and questioning his companion, Ramon Fernandez. The world before each of the poets is a world of their making.

"To live *in* the world of creation—" Henry James argues, "to get into it and stay in it—to frequent it and haunt it—to *think* intently and fruitfully—to woo combinations and inspirations into being by a depth and continuity of attention and meditation—this is the only thing. . . ." By staying, as James suggests, "*in*" the moment, by continuing to turn away from the conventions of closure through reflection, refraction, concentration, continuation, and

involution, by troubling the terms of an argument, by digressing, by spiral-
ing or orbiting around the lyric moment, pearling the grit of that moment,
one makes mutable the temporality of the meditative space, as in "Tintern
Abbey":

> Once again I see
> These hedgerows, hardly hedgetows, little lines
> Of sportive wood run wild; these pastoral farms,
> Green to the very door; and wreaths of smoke
> Sent up, in silence, from among the trees!
> With some uncertain notice, as might seem
> Of vagrant dwellers in the houseless woods,
> Or of some Hermit's cave, where by his fire
> The Hermit sits alone.

> These beauteous forms,
> Through a long absence, have not been to me
> As is a landscape to a blind man's eye:
> But oft, in lonely rooms, and 'mid the din
> Of towns and cities, I have owed to them,
> In hours of weariness, sensations sweet,
> Felt in the blood, and felt along the heart;
> And passing even into my purer mind,
> With tranquil restoration . . .

Here the pastoral bridges at least three spaces: the city, the manageable
natural world, and the wilderness. Wordsworth treats the city as the place
from which he retreats and the place to which he must return. He is on a
tour, and thus the ruin he visits is a managed and manageable Nature. A
third space the pastoral confronts, the wilderness, is all that is "other" and
beyond words, Nature fraught with the sublime awe of the awful and awesome. The parable of the lost sheep locates itself in this space as do the lovers outside the city gates in *The Song of Solomon*. For Wallace Stevens, the
wilderness is the unmeasured world, the "meaningless plungings of water
and the wind." The mind in conversation with itself constantly orders and
shapes the meaningless, but what persists always are questions and not the
balm of final thoughts:

Ramon Fernandez, tell me, if you know,
Why, when the singing ended and we turned
Toward the town, tell why the glassy lights,
The lights in the fishing boats at anchor there,
As the night descended, tilting in the air,
Mastered the night and portioned out the sea,
Fixing emblazoned zones and fiery poles,
Arranging, deepening, enchanting night.

Oh! Blessed rage for order, pale Ramon,
The maker's rage to order words of the sea,
Words of the fragrant portals, dimly-starred,
And of ourselves and of our origins,
In ghostlier demarcations, keener sounds.

The pastoral bridges even more times zones, allowing the speaker to move easily among temporal moments: the idealized past set against the hardship of the present moment, the idealized present harmonizing with the idealized past, the past's hardships rubbed up against the comfort and idleness of the present. In Virgil's fourth Eclogue, more a meditation than the conversation common to the Eclogues, even the future is bridged, revealing the hope of a splendid age to come, where "earth will shower you with romping ivy, foxgloves, / Bouquets of gipsy lilies and sweetly-smiling acanthus . . ." where "the ox will have no fear of the lion . . ."

"In the life we lead together," Robert Hass writes, "every paradise is lost." To fall from paradise is to fall into time. Into exilic time, post-lapsarian time. The hinge of such a meditation is usually the equation: Once . . . but now. . . . Innocence is cast then recast as experience. In Hass's "Meditation at Lagunitas" we find that language itself is an unstable medium, that "a word is elegy to what it signifies":

> After a while I understood that,
> talking this way, everything dissolves: *justice,*
> *pine, hair, woman, you* and *I.* There was a woman
> I made love to and I remembered how, holding
> her small shoulders in my hands sometimes,
> I felt a violent wonder at her presence

like a thirst for salt, for my childhood river
with its island willows, silly music from the pleasure boat,
muddy places where we caught the little orange-silver fish
called *pumpkinseed*. It hardly had to do with her.
Longing, we say, because desire is full
of endless distances. I must have been the same to her.
But I remember so much, the way her hands dismantled bread,
the thing her father said that hurt her, what
she dreamed. There are moments when the body is as numinous
as words, days that are the good flesh continuing.
Such tenderness, those afternoons and evenings,
saying *blackberry, blackberry, blackberry.*

The meditative mode attempts to slow time down, to hold it still, to condense it or stretch it or twist it, without diminishing its vitality or precariousness. The gradations of tense hot-wired into the medium of language allow the *now*, the *then*, and the *to be* to be put under the greatest pressure.

The meditative poet is not so much interested in rendering sequential experience, but in attending to the past, the present, and the conditional future as if a trinity embodied as one, as if a single moment, a single point on a plane. Hass writes at the beginning of "Meditation at Lagunitas" that "each particular erases/ the luminous clarity of a general idea," and yet his poem proves the opposite. The meditation merges the *now*, *then*, and *to be*, and the general and the particular into a single radiance of a mind at work.

The meditation as it has come down to us is an act, the act of the mind upon an object or idea. In the pastoral mode that object of meditation is often the landscape (and here I distinguish landscape from Nature: the landscape as the land "viewed" and arranged by the reflective and shaping mind). The habits of the meditative mode can be found in the variety of definitions one could give to the verb *to meditate*: to measure, to reflect on, to plan or project the mind, to design in thought, to practice religious or spiritual contemplation, to apply, to continue to apply the mind, to mete out (and if we look up "mete," we discover: to find the quantity, dimension or capacity by rule or standard, to appraise). To define boundaries. To judge.

Helen Vendler says that "Lyric is the genre of private life: it is what we say to ourselves when we are alone." That aloneness within the phenomenal world of a landscape and the noumenal world of the in-dwelling mind allows the pastoral-meditative poet to achieve what Samuel Taylor Coleridge calls the "grandest efforts of poetry . . . when imagination is called forth, not to produce a distinct form, but a strong working of the mind, still offering what is still repelled, and again creating what is again rejected. . . ." In "Mid-August at Sourdough Mountain Lookout," Gary Snyder, in his role as a fire watcher, oversees not only forest but also the intimate and wide expanse of the hours of his American solitude:

> Down valley a smoke haze
> Three days heat, after five days rain
> Pitch glows on the fir-cones
> Across rocks and meadows
> Swarms of new flies.

> I cannot remember things I once read
> A few friends, but they are in cities.
> Drinking cold snow-water from a tin cup
> Looking down for miles
> Through high still air.

Who knows how long the mind has lingered, ruminated, in the white space between stanzas. Charles Wright, alone in his backyard, alone in his never-resting mind, practices what he preaches. "Art," he says, "tends toward the condition of circularity and completion. The artist's job is to keep the circle from joining—to work in the synapse." That in-between-ness, that neither-here-nor-there-ness embodies the qualities of the pastoral-meditative state, as here in his poem "Returned to the Yaak Cabin, I Overhear an Old Greek Song":

> Back at the west window, Basin Creek
> Stumbling its mantra out in a slurred, midsummer monotone,
> Sunshine in planes and clean sheets
> Over the yarrow and lodgepole pine—
> We spend our whole lives in the same place and never leave,
> Pine squirrels and butterflies at work in a deep dither,
> Bumblebee likewise, wind with a slight hitch in its get-along.

Dead heads on the lilac bush, daisies
Long-legged forest of stalks in a white throw across the field
Above the ford and deer path,
Candor of marble, candor of bone—
We spend our whole lives in the same place and never leave,
The head of Orpheus bobbing in the slatch, his song
Still beckoning from his still-bloody lips, bright as a bee's heart.

This poem, like so many of Wright's poems, is at once static and head-long. "We spend our whole lives in the same place and never leave," he writes and then takes the time to catalog the particular moment, which is never the same moment and thus never the same place twice. The moment of meditation is, like mythic time, constant and ongoing. We are not surprised to find we have entered a mystical moment, to find in the American West of Wright's poem the head of Orpheus just lopped off and still singing.

William James describes the state of mystical experience, often a product of meditation, as characterized by ineffability, transiency, noetic qualities, and passivity. Echoing James, William Bevis describes meditative states of consciousness as rich with transience, ineffability, a sensation that time and space is changed or transcended, a sensation of self-loss (and the loss of self is not a negative here, but a way within the meditation). The retreat and return and the return and retreat of the meditation allows a poet to live in and sustain liminal space and time, to "work in the synapses." That work can happen in the gaps, as in Snyder's "Mid-August at Sourdough Mountain Lookout," or by way of the logical and associative leaps we find in Wordsworth and Hass, or like Stevens and Wright, by the naming and questioning of the world before them as they continue their lifelong inter-rogation of immanence. At once descriptive, reflexive, discursive, lyric, and narrative, the meditation gives density and gravity to moments of revelation.

Pastoral Matters

There's a literary story—probably apocryphal—that the eighteenth-century pastoralist James Thomson was once observed eating a peach off a tree on the estate of one of his patrons—George Lyttleton at Hagley, I believe—eating the peach, which must have been at the peak of perfection, with his hands in his pockets, like an ice-skater engrossed in figure-eights, likely with his eyes closed. If this smiling garden scene is true, it surely represents Thomson late in his career, after his great Claudian period of *The Seasons*, in which property and poetry mix to create both a sense of the pastoral work required in order to farm and the beauty of the result. Vistas *and* vitality. The Garden-of-Eden Thomson, however, is too often the character, and characteristic, of what passes for the ironic pastoral vision of postmodernism, just as Romanticism is now too often viewed as nature with an enlarged heart, plus various enlarged invisible parts, and too rarely as having the working weight of the rest of the body: hands, arms, feet, and much perspiration. Jonathan Swift, the anti-romantic, recognizes this lapse in mindfulness and labor in his preoccupation with Celia's bowel functions.

On the other hand, William Wordsworth, in the habit of rising before most of humanity, particularly when visiting London, looks out over the sleeping city from Westminster Bridge, September 3, 1802, and finds that "Earth has not anything to show more fair" than "the beauty of the morning; silent, bare, / Ships, towers, domes, theaters, and temples ... / Open unto the fields, and to the sky." He turns London into nature, or, if you will, an urban pastoral. "Ne'er," he says, "saw I, never felt, a calm so deep!" He links the towers and domes of the city directly to "valley, rock, or hill." Meanwhile, down on the ground, William Blake has his own experience with "London": "I wander thro' each charter'd street, / Near where the charter'd Thames does flow, / And mark in every face I meet / Marks of weakness, marks of woe." Of course, Blake is not looking at the cityscape from a perspective, but into the face of humanity close up, the face of despair, the face of the after-dawn, the afternoon, when the work of the day begins and grinds on. Nor is it the sweet Thames of Wordsworth and Edmund Spenser, but the dark, working river Charles Dickens would inherit in *Our Mutual Friend*. How does Wordsworth's pastoral vision come to terms with Blake's naturalism, where daily bread must not only be earned but too often begged for—bread blessed from the grain John Keats celebrates in "To Autumn"?

And how does Walt Whitman's elegiac American pastoral vision in "When Lilacs Last in the Dooryard Bloom'd" sort with the naturalism of his "The City Dead-House"—"Dead house of love—house of madness and sin, crumbled, crush'd" or "Come Up from the Fields Father"—"Lo, 'tis autumn, / Lo, where the trees, deeper green, yellower and redder, / Cool and sweeten Ohio's villages"? Whitman even has his Westminster Bridge moment in "Crossing Brooklyn Ferry" as he extols "stately and admirable ... mast-hemm'd Manhattan"—"what can ever be more ... to me"? Whitman's pastoral coming to terms is certainly best expressed in "This Compost," a poem that argues the matter in front of us.

1

Something startles me where I thought I was safest,
I withdraw from the still woods I loved,
I will not go now on the pastures to walk,
I will not strip the clothes from my body to meet
    my lover the sea,
I will not touch my flesh to the earth as to other
    flesh to renew me.

O how can it be that the ground itself does not sicken?
How can you be alive you growths of spring?
How can you furnish health you blood of herbs, roots,
    orchards, grain?
Are they not continually putting distemper'd corpses
    within you?
Is not every continent work'd over and over with sour dead?

Where have you disposed of their carcasses?
Those drunkards and gluttons of so many generations?

Where have you drawn off all the foul liquid and meat?
I do not see any of it upon you to-day, or perhaps
      I am deceiv'd,
I will run a furrow with my plough, I will press my
      spade through the sod and turn it up underneath,
I am sure I shall expose some of the foul meat.

    2

Behold this compost! behold it well!
Perhaps every mite has once form'd part of a sick person—
      yet behold!
The grass of spring covers the prairies,
The bean bursts noiselessly through the mould in the garden,
The delicate spear of the onion pierces upward,
The apple-buds cluster together on the apple-branches,
The resurrection of the wheat appears with pale visage
      out of its graves,
The tinge awakes over the willow-tree and the mulberry-tree,
The he-birds carol mornings and evenings while the she-birds
      sit on their nests,
The young of poultry break through the hatch'd eggs,
The new-born of animals appear, the calf is dropt from
      the cow, the colt from the mare
Out of its little hill faithfully rise the potato's dark
      green leaves,
Out of its hill rises the yellow maize-stalk, the lilacs
      bloom in the dooryards,
The summer growth is innocent and disdainful above all
      those strata of sour dead.

What chemistry!
That the winds are really not infectious,
That this is no cheat, this transparent green-wash
      of the sea which is so amorous after me,
That it is safe to allow it to lick my naked body all
      over with its tongues,

That it will not endanger me with the fevers that have
    deposited themselves in it,
That all is clean forever and forever,
That the cool drink from the well tastes so good,
That blackberries are so flavorous and juicy,
That the fruits of the apple-orchard and the orange-
    orchard, that melons, grapes, peaches, plums,
    will none of them poison me,
That when I recline on the grass I do not catch any disease,
Though probably every spear of grass rises out of what was
    once a catching disease.

Now I am terrified at the Earth, it is that calm and
    patient,
It grows such sweet things out of such corruptions,
It turns harmless and stainless on its axis, with such
    endless successions of diseas'd corpses,
It distills such exquisite winds out of such infused
    fetor,
It renews with such unwitting looks its prodigal, annual,
    sumptuous crops,
It gives such divine materials to men, and accepts such
    leavings from them at last.

Whitman's perspective, his "view" here, is well above and beyond Words-worth's view from the height of a bridge: Whitman's vision is essentially celestial as well as wholly terrestrial—distantly pastoral and darkly natu-ral at once. Typical of Whitman's idealism, this apparent contradiction is reconciled through empathy, patience, and forgiveness. In coming to terms with the "foul meat" just under the surface of the grave earth the "plough" has turned over, the poet realizes that the laden ground is also a compost, an opportunity for rebirth, renewal. His wholeness of vision completes the cycle and the circle.

One of the most wonderful moments in this thirty-seven long-lined great poem (fairly brief for Whitman) comes at the end in the recognition that the earth—the water planet, the flowering planet—may be the recon-ciler of all things good and evil, living and dead, but it is equally terrifying in its ability to distill and regenerate while turning "harmless and stainless on its axis": almost as if the literal ground of our being were well beyond us at another level entirely in both its indifference and/or caring. This vision sees the earth itself as the farmer, the gardener, the harvester, the keeper, with us merely an organic part of an all-encompassing organism. Thus the farmer *is* the field, the ever-returning lapsed meadow.

This tension between the actual and the imagined, the practical and the projected realities—between the run of unruly nature and the domesticating pace of a cultivated, nurtured nature—this tension is stretched to its limit in Wordsworth's sublime celebrations of mountain passages and wild common experience in *The Prelude* and reiterated in the Big Sur meditations of Robinson Jeffers, where wild is elevated to a standing superior to the feeble furrowings and corruptions of man. At such moments the pastoral consciousness seems to become something small, distant, even Lilliputian way down there in the commerce of the valleys. The question is: Can the pastoral ever achieve the depth and breadth of a richer, darker, perhaps ironic vision short of Whitman's "Compost" or Wordsworth's and Jeffers's interrogations? Or is the pastoral vision—countrified or urbanized—so endemic to the lyric that its potential wildness must be inevitably "cultivated" for consumption? Form itself is an expression of pastoral values—of sowing and reaping, measuring and making, symmetry and sympathy. Wordsworth and Jeffers each must return to Dove Cottage and High Tor Tower justified.

Pastoral is the civilizing voice of hearth and harvest, civility and city planning; culture is to cultivate; form is to run a furrow with a plow. Meditation is the shepherd at evening tending the flock; it is the idleness, if you will, in the *Idylls* of Theocritus; it is the mood and reflective beauty in Virgil's *Eclogues*. But sheep in the meadow, Ruth lost among the alien corn will not, in themselves, as tableaux, lift the heart of the pastoral to the heights. Only grief will do that. Only grief will bend nature to a will beyond indifference. Grief is the humanizing of nature, love's picked flower placed on the funeral bier. Whether it is Lord Byron's *Lament for Adonis*, John Milton's *Lycidas*, Percy Bysshe Shelley's *Adonais*, or Alfred Lord Tennyson's *In Memoriam*, nature, harmonized nature, becomes the deep emotional collaborator of the poet's need for correlative. The pastoral elegy, within the vast limits of its intimacy, seeks the sublime no less than the witness of great conquest, even when the conquest is writ small, "Silent, upon a peak in Darien."

What the pastoral elegy gives to lyric poetry is a piercing identification with longing, like the song of the nightingale, thorn at the heart. And transcending the particulars of birds, beasts, and flowers, and mountains and lakes, are the seasons—the sequence, the narrative of the seasons, that so perfectly mirrors the story of longing, of grief, and recovery, first as metaphor, then allegory, then archetype. We can read Whitman's magnificent elegy for Lincoln as a pastoral about rebirth, as a publication of national grief, as a reconciliation of life with death, as a celebration of the transforming power of simple, homely, domestic dooryard nature, as an homage to the pastoral elegy itself (especially Milton and Tennyson), as a spiritual journey into the heartland, and even as an elegy for a civil war whose dead are "not as was thought, / They themselves were fully at rest." However we read it, we cannot help but hear the almost clarion call of the hermit thrush nor miss selecting the sprig of lilac to lay on Lincoln's coffin nor not see the rising star in the gloomy dusk. The green pastures of the pastoral are reassuring; they are also defining as to our connection to and place in the nature of things.

Turn the earth a half-year back or forward to autumn—indeed, "To Autumn"—and we find no less an address to the constituencies and contingencies of this season of the elegy: the full cup of the harvest, the goddess herself resting, soon to lie down ("thy laden head across a brook"). Where, for sure, are the songs of spring? John Keats has already, months before, in the fragmentary "Ode to May," recommended a poetry "Rich in the simple worship of a day": "To Autumn" fulfills that recommendation, then surpasses it. This purest and greatest of lyric poems elevates the pastoral elegy by bringing it back to earth, to work, to balance, and to perspective—the intimate view, the total picture, the long vision. Structure and texture become transparent to each other as the rhythm of the day's harvest follows its fulsome "hours by hours" (note the plurals) formation from the dew-starred morning to the drowsy noon to the resonance of the "sinking" light of sunset; or from the cottage and "cottage-trees" to the low-lying fields and hills to the softly animated skies. The fact that Keats disappears into the poem only reinforces the internalization of the voice: the voice is the pastoral day itself unfolding from rise to fall, quietly, inherently. Whitman runs his furrow over the dead; Keats's goddess sleeps above her "half-reaped furrow" as if dreaming of the new life under her. The elegiac tone, by and large, must undergo the process of—in Yeats's phrase—death-in-life, life-in-death in order to achieve its emotional distance. "To Autumn" builds, from the beginning, both distance and intimacy, grand gesture and detail at once. Its rich, full heart runs over but never spills; Keats carries its cup through every line, "o'er-brimmed." The happiness in the poem comes as much from the quotidian "ripeness to the core" as from the broad "swath" through the landscape and workplace, the small, full moments intensifying the wholeness and roundness of the season.

It is, however, a season of mists, mellow and more. The refraction of sunlight, from morning fog to noon harvest haze to the "bloom [of] the soft-dying day," is the lens through which the gathering daylight proceeds and recedes, like the cycle of life, but life especially humanized by the work of hands. Whitman sees the human as only a part, though crucial, of a greater schematic. With Keats, this season, this human season, is about the human project on earth. "To Autumn" is like a psalm, a song sung by David the shepherd; a prayer for the day, the autumnal day. We have laid our store, we have brought in the harvest, we have tasted and savored the fruit of our labor, we have looked out over the "stubble plain" of the fields and are satisfied, we have earned our living, and now the sun, the "maturing sun," seems to bless the table in the house of our being, just as it slips and darkens the open window. This last of Keats's unique odes is the most unique of all in that its elegy is so self-reflective: it may be the pastoral of pastorals, but it is an elegy of itself. Its transparency before its subject, to paraphrase Walter Jackson Bate, is its subject. Its purity is its elegy. No one, not Tom nor Keats himself, is being grieved; but as well as gain there is loss, perhaps more loss than gain. That is the wonderful, tragic feeling that closes—but does not close down—"To Autumn": that ever so much, ever so little, loss adds up to more, fills more, empties more, than the heart of the harvest. And the poem represents this sense of itself at every moment, yet fills and fills to the very end.

Arcadia Redux

In the pastoral tradition, love appears in myriad forms. The pasture's ease and retirement are the attracting force when Virgil sings "let the country charm me, the rivers that channel its valleys, / Then may I love its forest and stream, and let fame go hang." Poets in the Latin Arcadian tradition choose contemplation and retirement—what Barry Weller calls a "pastoral retreat from responsibility"—so Virgil renounces corrupt city life in favor of an apparently private and peaceful existence in the country. Renaissance pastoral poets also invent timeless enclaves where lively shepherds, all body and no mind, attend to present pleasures. Here, though, an adolescent world predominates, playful, witty, and self-consciously fictive.

The idyllic, the pastoral, the *hortus conclusus* or enclosed garden, are rich but antique imaginative sites. So why do Eden, Arcadia, and the *locus amoenus*, the "beautiful place," maintain their hold on us still today? Each invites us into a world out of time, meant for leisure, contemplation, for free play and rapture without consequence. Enclosed in a safe haven, we sing of love, pastoral's abiding subject. What do our versions of paradise reveal about us? All narratives of paradise, Susan Snyder suggests, lead toward a familiar destination; in the end, the "story of Eden (from bliss to temptation, sin, knowledge, and expulsion into a harsh world demanding self-sufficiency) is . . . about growing up."

Both Latin and Renaissance pastorals play off the invisible backdrop of a tarnished world burdened with adult duty. Most pastoral poets of these periods write with an attending nostalgia for a golden age, for childhood's simplicity. They pair innocence with a frank erotic pleasure. Both circumstances, by implication, ought to be enjoyed while they are available. Robert Herrick's "The Argument of His Book" celebrates this bodily and spiritual aliveness despite time's encroachments. Our transience on earth intensifies the pastoral's necessity:

I sing of brooks, of blossoms, birds, and bowers,
Of April, May, of June, and July flowers;
I sing of Maypoles, hock carts, wassails, wakes,
Of bridegrooms, brides and of their bridal cakes;
I write of youth, of love, and have access
By these to sing of cleanly wantonness.
I sing of dews, of rains, and, piece by piece,
Of balm, of oil, of spice and ambergris.
I sing of times trans-shifting, and I write
How roses first came red and lilies white.
I write of groves, of twilights, and I sing
The court of Mab, and of the fairy king.
I write of hell; I sing (and ever shall)
Of heaven, and hope to have it after all.

Youthful pleasure lies at the center of this enchanted and enchanting bower. But "blossoms, birds, and bowers" surely ripen and decay, so Herrick hopes to keep both the ideal and real in balance, singing "of times trans-shifting" in the face of all our desires. So too sings Thomas Campion in "I Care Not for These Ladies." Here the poet praises direct and casual carnality, comparing the cold, cultured women of town to the more elemental and generous Amaryllis, ever-available, ever aroused:

I care not for these ladies,
That must be wooed and prayed.
Give me kind Amaryllis,
The wanton country maid.
Nature art disdaineth,
Here beauty is her own.
    Her when we court and kiss,
    She cries, "Forsooth, let go!"
    But when we come where comfort is,
    She never will say no.

Pastoral love is painless, guilt-free, grounded in a sex-world of delight. But of course this ideal haven "where comfort" abounds is fictive, an allegorical world where the players knowingly inhabit an illusion. As a holographic image shifts from one picture to another, so a reader of pastoral balances two different worlds. Perhaps because sexual pleasure itself is fragile and momentary, these idylls are temporary, threatened, and evanescent.

⁂

Medieval and Renaissance *hortus conclusus* gardens were built as living embodiments of the words of *The Song of Solomon*, spoken by the bridegroom to his bride ("My sister, my bride, is a garden close-locked, a fountain sealed."). A *hortus conclusus* encloses virginity, valorizes the Christian model of chastity, and is itself an emblem of the life of Mary. This version of pastoral locates chastity inside the garden, the fortified and secure space being also the most blessed and sanctified. With high walls and narrow passageways, orderly borders and self-contained fertility, the *hortus conclusus* can also serve as a stage set for the dramas of courtly love and the *fin amor* tradition. An unattainable woman, pure and chaste, waits at the center of this garden.

Poets who depict earthly paradise as a shaped landscape, separate from the messier, less productive system outside the garden walls, make a case for the civilizing forces of culture against the presumed wildness of nature. In terms of garden economy, enclosed gardens are simply more productive and therefore of greater real and moral value. Hard labor follows the fall from Eden, but labor leads in turn to spiritual reward. For instance, in *The Shepheardes Calender* (1579), Edmund Spenser uses seasonal metaphors of birth, growth, and harvest in order to describe the necessary transition from innocence to experience, infancy to full adulthood, along with a whole world of political and religious consequence to follow. And so the fall from innocence is allegorized in portraits of nature. In this way, pastoral grows up and becomes georgic.

⁂

Today all the old metaphors are new again. We still believe a garden is nature shaped to a human design. If the design is "good," then the garden will succeed. Current periodicals such as *Fine Gardening* or *Horticulture* promote orderly and well-bounded gardens as sites for restoration and renewal. Even a popular-culture maven like Martha Stewart steers her consumers toward this inherited pastoral tradition. Open the pages of any of these magazines and see how we define the "good life."

Indeed, much of what I would call contemporary georgic is actually written in prose; today's nature writers may describe their flight from city to country as a journey toward a moral or authentic life. A host of essayists (some of them are also poets) find their own spiritual health flowering inside the gardens they labor to create. Sue Hubbell, Michael Pollan, Maxine Kumin, Jamaica Kincaid: all of these writers have crafted miniaturized Edens, reforming untamed or fallow land through the work of their hands. Although the flower garden of Jamaica Kincaid and the heirloom kitchen garden of Martha Stewart are visually quite different, both embody the values of discipline, beauty and utility, as both writers wax nostalgic for a lost past where gardens were central to a community. Because they recognize how quickly beloved landscapes vanish, they place an intensified value on those that remain.

This is how heirloom vegetables and antique apple varieties become endowed with nostalgia; we long for the lost garden of "good" food. Turning food into fetish, epicurean consumers seek out rarities. For instance, when food writers elevated morels from wild fungus to culinary delicacy, their prices soared accordingly. Poet John Clare, shut out of once communally farmed fields by the enforcement of the Enclosure Acts of the nineteenth century, would surely recognize these economic circumstances. They demonstrate what William Empson called the "essential trick" of pastoral, "to imply a beautiful relation between rich and poor."

Despite all this, I must admit a real affection for these georgic essays of American life on the land. The words of most contemporary nature essayists are instructive and evocative, written from a position of genuine longing for the knowledge the land provides. But I'm troubled by how some gardens are situated not only as peaceful and contemplative places for their own sake, but also as sites where envy and aspiration gather. They model what life might look like in a pastoral retreat, but only for those with the taste and capital necessary to install ambitious gardens. Today, the good and beautiful place, or *locus amoenus*, exists for many of us as an airbrushed advertisement for a way of life to be found only in the pages of magazines.

So is it possible to write a pastoral poem today? We're still talking about how gardens produce pleasure. We continue to seek out spiritual retreat. How do these two directions—the garden as a bower of bliss and the garden as haven for chastity—play out in recent poetry about nature and gardens? Are there fresh ways to approach the pastoral metaphor of Eden? Why do we even bother to return to such a self-consciously artificial mode?

Steven Marx suggests that, despite the limitations of the pastoral landscape, we continue to yearn for a safe haven where contemplation and dream may flower:

> The motive of seductive rhetoric, no matter how artful or self-conscious, is real desire. The *locus amoenus* is a mythic rather than a merely rhetorical place. Like all myths, it means more than any interpretation can articulate, and whether consciously believed in or not, it shapes people's sense of the world and it motivates their behavior.

A powerful source and solace, nostalgia for lost time motivates anyone interested in memory's landscape. Again, Marx suggests why these ideas continue to stir us. Feelings of nostalgia stem from an impulse to idealize memory and history, not just the communal memory of place, but of our particular sense of childhood as a lost paradise:

> Whether manifested as the *locus amoenus*, the Garden of Eden, the Golden Age, or the land of Arcadia, the ideal of innocence is itself a metaphor for another world in the past that all people have inhabited: the world of adolescence, childhood and infancy, the world of their own youth recollected as different and dislocated from their present selves.

W. H. Auden's "In Praise of Limestone" speaks to the attraction we feel toward a fragile landscape, one, in this case, sculpted and shaped from limestone: "If it form the one landscape that we, the inconstant ones, / Are constantly homesick for, this is chiefly / Because it dissolves in water." Anthony Hecht argues that Auden's poem embraces the flaws in this fallen world even as it seeks consolation inside that same space. This double vision also occurs in Philip Larkin's lovely "When First We Faced, and Touching Showed":

> When first we faced, and touching showed
> How well we knew the early moves,

> Behind the moonlight and the frost,
> The excitement and the gratitude,
> There stood how much our meeting owed
> To other meetings, other loves.

The initial caresses contain not only the erotic charge of contact, but also "The decades of a different life," embedded with the history of other loves and with the gestures of romance learned from experience. Despite these present pleasures, so needed, so precious, the past will not disappear, though it might be held at bay:

> But when did love not try to change
> The world back to itself—no cost,
> No past, no people else at all—
> Only what meeting made us feel,
> So new, and gentle-sharp, and strange?

Engaged in a combination of erotic fantasy and an awareness of time, are we at our best, our truest? Or self-regarding and immature? Is pastoral a mode fated to be nostalgic? Or, as Larkin suggests, is it a necessary fiction where one willingly delights in—or rests a while under the spell of—illusion?

Nostalgic pastoral often seeks to reconfigure the body of the earth as a human body. In John Crowe Ransom's "The Equilibrists," the woman's body is "a white field ready for love," as if to make love meant *to plow*. In one sense, of course it does. When Ransom metaphorically merges topography and anatomy, he transforms a woman's body into a landscape over which to have dominion. This is essentially the same gesture, if in reverse, as one made by Christopher Columbus centuries ago; at the entry to the Orinoco River, he wrote to his patrons the King and Queen of Spain to announce his discovery of "a river flowing out of Paradise." The land surrounding it, he said, looked like "a woman's breast on a round ball, and [. . .] the part with the nipple was higher and closer to the air and heaven [. . .]; and it seemed to him that the Earthly Paradise might be found on this nipple" (from Bartolomé de las Casas's account of the conquest in his *Historia de las Indias*). Columbus's conflation of paradise, purity, and sexual prospect make a tantalizing panorama indeed, worthy of exploration and thus of further sponsorship.

If a *locus amoenus* comes to be seen as a trope for a woman's body, allegorized into landscape, if metaphors of conquest and imprisonment are linked to gender, then the pastoral's playful context disappears or becomes more difficult to deploy without irony or willed ignorance, as Susan Stewart suggests:

> They set before us their harsh taxonomy: true, steady,
> distant, tender, stormy, gone astray, love
>
> made less by being in time. Each had claimed to be the other's
> half-world—paltry haven or hermitage
>
> now bursting at the seams. We saw the garden "fill
> with leaves"; we heard "the wind rage
>
> at the bolted door while the spray drove
> back the brackish sea." It's always the same, one goes
>   and one stays, one turns his eyes
>
> from the awful scene and meanwhile the well-meaning,
> sincere one spies
>
> a flaw in the weaving the two of them have made. The task
> is repair, fray, tear, epitomize
>
> what metaphor could take the place of time's erosion.

(*from* "Nervous System")

The language inside quotations, the "paltry haven or hermitage" of their love, the knowledge that we are inclined in love to allegorize our actions, all send this scene into a downward spiral of failure. Stewart implies that we continue to follow the same old script of love, made no less affecting or "awful" despite its being "made less by being in time."

Real gardens throughout history have walled out wildness in order to hold and protect the sacred. Anyone who enters a garden enters via a gateway or threshold; journeys from outside to inside are full of ritual and magic.

But when contemporary poems include pastoral elements, or intentionally seek out an arcadia, it's often as part of a self-conscious or ironic performance, harking back to the scripted playfulness of Renaissance pastoral poetry. Many contemporary poets describe paradises now fallen, terrain ecologically damaged. Contrast Ransom's retrograde pastoral imagery with that of Australian poet John Kinsella, who writes what he calls "radical pastoral." He seeks to recognize, as he says, "The eclogic conversations between shepherds have become those between motorbikes and tractors, helicopters and light planes." In Kinsella's poems, environmental degradation coexists with beauty; the beauty of the land is politicized by the history of the people who live there. Nature is no longer a sympathetic haven, as in "Field Notes from Mount Bakewell," where "The guy from the chemical company / drinks a half-glass of Herbicide. / 'There you go, harmless to humans.' / The farmer, impressed, sprays / and gets his sheep straight back in there."

Poets who continue to engage with the pastoral tradition inevitably reexamine metaphors of Eden, asking not only personal but also environmental questions about gardens as well as questions of economy and access. Poets write themselves into gardened spaces at least in part because poems themselves are shapely and focused, relying on boundaries and the limitations of form to achieve breadth and beauty. Besides John Kinsella (*The New Arcadia*) and Susan Stewart (*The Forest, Columbarium*), contemporary poets examining the continuing possibilities of pastoral include Chase Twichell (*The Ghost of Eden*), Adrienne Rich (*Dark Fields of the Republic*), Jane Hirshfield (*The October Palace*), Carl Phillips (*Cortège, Pastoral, The Rest of Love*), Louise Glück (*The Wild Iris*), and Brigit Pegeen Kelly (*Song, The Orchard*).

Brigit Pegeen Kelly's darkly beautiful poems sometimes feel as if they should be illustrated by Edward Gorey. Shaded by Gothic elements, her paradise is more graveyard than garden. In *The Orchard*, monuments to the past lie scattered across the poems' grounds. And though the spooky atmosphere retains a sexual quality, eros in "The Satyr's Heart" is debased and damaged:

> Now I rest my head on the satyr's carved chest,
> The hollow where the heart would have been, if sandstone
> Had a heart, if a headless goat man could have a heart.
> His neck rises to a dull point, points upward
> To something long gone, elusive, and at his feet
> The small flowers swarm, earnest and sweet, a clamor

Of white, a clamor of blue, and black the sweating soil
They breed in. . . .

With no head, no heart, a body made of stone, the satyr makes an entirely
unsatisfactory lover. His neck "rises to a dull point, points upward" to a lost
heaven, or perhaps merely a vacant spot left where his head once was. As
the poem proceeds, its images confirm and extend the feeling of corrupt
emptiness, the "birds turning tricks in the trees," "the wind fingering / The
twigs," while at her feet, flowers seem merely childish, "earnest and sweet."
She has no time for them, and instead uproots a stone to uncover "what is
brave." Only beneath ground does she locate "armies of pale creatures who /
Without cease or doubt sew the sweet sad earth."

Kelly's poems merge Christian and Classical tropes, and in her garden
of earthly delights death, chaos, and destruction are as fully present as
love. If you can't look with confidence to heaven, it might be worth looking
earthward, beneath the surface of the ruined garden. The success of traditional pastoral depends on a conflict between the simple and natural, and
the urbane and cultivated. But now this opposition exists not between innocence and corruption, or the garden and the city, but wholly within the
complicated garden itself. It's as if the garden now contains multitudes,
ghosts from the past who insist upon making themselves heard.

Some of the most complex pastoral encounters recognize the need for
magic in our lives, even as they acknowledge the limitations of old metaphors. Carl Phillips's poems often dramatize scenes of eros played out as
performance and, in the next moment, just as simply put away. Phillips contends with difficult contradictions; in his poems the pastoral idyll is longed
for and occasionally achieved, but also abides alongside a contingent daily
life with its pain, its social reality. "Against His Quitting the Torn Field"
calls up idyllic images, locating them in a contemporary context. Desire is
drawn from Classical tropes but takes form in an urban city park:

the mouth that says *You can do anything,* here;

the arm tattooed with—
as obviously as if this were
dream—the one word:
    Paradise. . . .

Phillips's erotic encounter is ritualized even as it is made strange, quickened into fragment. Likewise, in "Afterward," the boundaries of waking and dream are not fixed, not settled:

> In the long dreaming, the old gods are again
> with us: some in the guise of ordinary
> light through the green leaves they love
>
> . . . .
>
> your body not your body any longer, nor mine
> mine to give thought to, but the gods':
> theirs, the hands that cast out; theirs,
>
> the hands to fetch, surely, us back . . .

As with Kelly, Phillips's lost Arcadia is a dream land, a magic space. Fragile, momentary, these scenes are haunted by the ghosts of other arcadias.

Regarding dreams, dreamers have a choice: analyze the dream or leave the magic intact. If pastoral lives today, it does so in images of private meditation, in poems marking out the boundaries and limits of a sacred interior space, and in rituals of privacy between lovers. That pastoral occurs in the context of ritual and transformation reminds us of its origins in ecstatic encounters. That it often takes the form of allegory, as in Phillips's "Teaching Ovid to Sixth-Graders," tells us "how any myth / is finally about the lengths the mind will / carry a tale to, to explain what the body // knows already." And that pastoral continues to allow poets to live in two realms at once demonstrates how much we need such imagined interior landscapes.

2. On the Sublime: The Problem of Beauty

Once again
Do I behold these steep and lofty cliffs.

WILLIAM WORDSWORTH

The Sublime: Origins and Definitions

My task of exploring the poetic sublime will take us up to, and into, the heights of the American nineteenth century. To do so I need to make three stops: to look at early Classical origins of the sublime, to consider a relationship of the British nineteenth-century Romantic sublime to certain eighteenth-century poetic constructions, and finally to propose points of distinction between the English and American sublime in the nineteenth century. Thus, what *is* the sublime? A natural landscape? A poetic mode? From where does it originate, how does it evolve, and how does it become nationalized on these shores?

Before I tackle these questions though, I need to perform a quick act of lexical alarm. The best restaurant in the whole county where I live, according to my teenaged daughter, Katie, is a greasy spot called, merely and with generic pride, Restaurant. Globs of mashed potatoes, warm pies on the counter. They oven-roast their own cashews and make their own chocolates. And on the menu they proudly feature a dish called Pork Chop Sublime. This involves, I believe, a lot of canned mushroom soup. The word *sublime* has been drained of its richness and its ferocity, and remains today a synonym for *great*, or *dandy*, or worse, a kitsch hyperbole: think of Lisa Douglas on *Green Acres*, standing in her Tiffany jewels speaking to a pig as "the sublime Arnold." At least Terry Eagleton, coining in 1990 his term "the Marxist sublime," and Jonathan Bate with his "industrial sublime," in 2000, retain some of the psychological complexity and linguistic tension that Keats generated in his own term "the egotistical sublime" nearly 200 years earlier.

A long time before Keats, someone we refer to as Longinus wrote something we translate as *On Great Writing*, or *On the Sublime*. This Longinus may have been a third-century philosopher, Cassius Longinus, though some manuscripts show the author to be Dionysius Longinus, from the first century. One translation reveals the author to be "Dionysius *or* Longinus"; but even this is iffy, since the oldest-known extant manuscript dates from the tenth century, and it is incomplete. What is uncontested is the audacity of this writer's thinking, as it flies in the face of the Classical Greek rhetoricians. Rather than declaring poetic inspiration a "dangerous divine madness," as Plato did in banishing certain poets from his Utopia, Longinus asks how such inspiration is best employed. Great writing, he asserts, is more than skillful rhetoric and well-ordered sophistry. Sublimity itself must "[flash] forth at the right moment [scattering] everything before it like a thunderbolt."

There is much to glean from Longinus, but I want only to recall from his eighth chapter his five "causes" or "sources" of great writing. Great writing must have 1) vigor and nobility of mind—the power to grasp and form great ideas. Sublimity is, thus, "the echo of a great soul." 2) It must be made from, and must be able to elicit, strong emotion; he calls this "vehement and inspired passion." His final three features are characteristics of the poem itself. 3) It must make the right use of metaphors; 4) it must employ "noble diction"; and finally, 5) it must attend to "dignified and elevated composition." The first two causes here—vigor and nobility of mind, vehement and inspired passion—are the fundamental elements driving Longinus's profound and original theory. More about this soon.

Or not so soon, to be historically accurate. In fact, Longinus's *On the Sublime* vanishes for an entire millennium. One or two doubtful references are found in a thirteenth-century Byzantine rhetorician, as G. M. A. Grube points out, but the first modern edition doesn't appear until 1554 in Basel. Milton mentions it in his essay "On Education," the first English translation appears in 1652, and finally the famous French translation, by Nicolas Boileau, appears in 1674, and watch out. When the late-eighteenth-century pre-Romantic philosophers retrieve the text, they raise a huge new aesthetic sensibility up from Longinus's ruins.

Ruins indeed. The Romantic sublime scene stands in our imaginations so clearly it is cliché. The dimensions are vertical and vast—steep cliffs, great wild trees and hanging mosses, the haze and fog of distance, high clouds and filtered sunlight. Whatever architecture there is—whatever is man-made—is fallen, in ruins and decay. We are struck, and dumbstruck, by the intense dimensions of the place, the amplitude of nature, the shrunken size of our power and imaginations in the presence of a colossal, spiritually charged, meaningful landscape shaped by capital B, Beauty. We are tiny, we are alone, we are mortal, and we are without a sound:

Dizzy Ravine! and when I gaze on thee
I seem as in a trance sublime and strange
To muse on my own separate fantasy,
My own, my human mind, which passively
Now renders and receives fast influencings,
Holding an unremitting interchange
With the clear universe of things around;
One legion of wild thoughts, whose wandering wings
Now float above thy darkness . . .

These lines from Percy Bysshe Shelley's "Mont Blanc" identify a fundamental scene of the Romantic imagination. The landscape links the supernatural with the aesthetic, and the primordial with a potential extinction of self. It is a perilous place, and vertigo, fear of losing control, is met by the paradox of "passive" pleasure. Denis Donoghue says

> The sublime makes the sense of beauty fear for its security, just as genius sends taste and pleasure into abeyance. In the sublime, the mind is beside itself, thinking defies its limits, forms stare into formlessness, and the aesthetic faculty shudders. It is best to think of these states of feeling as secular versions of religious experience, peremptory intuitions of the holy, of mystical rapture, and of transcendence. The sublime transgresses grammar and syntax in its collusion with the unsayable.

Rainer Maria Rilke, suddenly faced with an angel in *Duino Elegies*, expresses a sublime vision: "I would perish from his powerful being, for the Beautiful is nothing but the onset of Terror we can scarcely endure."

This is what I first want to restore to our term: the inevitable, necessary accompaniment of Beauty with Terror. The terrible potential of the sublime, according to Kant, depends essentially on the scale of things. That is, beauty for Kant implies shape or boundary—the pleasing form and use of a finite entity—while the sublime stretches beyond the beautiful into the unbound, the formless, the "absolutely great." Thus when Shelley gazes into the sublime abyss before him, the "Dizzy Ravine," he is made to fear for his security and identity. But contemplation of the sublime, with its ratio of beauty to terror, also leads him to "still and solemn power." Such is the tangible result of "vehement and inspired passion," as Longinus describes it.

But again, what *is* the sublime? I've associated it here with a landscape. But it is not a landscape—nor a mode of poetry, nor a trope, nor gesture. I need to transgress the lexical to make a connection.

The *limbic lobe,* to use neurologist Paul Broca's term from the nineteenth century, is the area surrounding the primal brain stem. The limbic *system* defines the larger structure—the cerebral layers—of the brain, from the reptilian to the early mammalian to the later mammalian, as our evolution demanded an increasingly complex apparatus to assure our survival. We experience—in the order of our evolution—reactions, emotions, then finally cognition. A *limb* derives from the Latin noun *limbus,* indicating an edge, a border: if something is sub-limbic, it is beneath the complex apparatus of the brain. The word *sublime* suggests a parallel meaning, though it derives from a different root. *Sub limen* translates from Latin as "up to the lintel." Something sublime is noble, majestic, inspiring awe; it is lofty, heightened; it is purified. But the subliminal also takes us below the threshold of consciousness. Conflation of these two word origins gives us a good definition. The neurologist Rhawn Joseph concurs: "Maybe the ability to experience God and the spiritually sublime is an inherited limbic trait. Maybe we evolved these neurons to better cope with the unknown . . . because they would increase the likelihood of our survival." This may provide, he says, a neurological, even genetic, basis for religious or spiritual belief. Or aesthetic belief.

The sublime, I contend, is a cognitive, or pre-cognitive, *circumstance,* like ecstasy: an emotional state. In Kant, Donogue reminds us, the sublime has nothing to do with art. It's a *feeling* in someone, Donogue says, "provoked by an object in nature before which her imagination trembles, till her reason reasserts itself." Kant calls this transcendental procedure the "dynamical sublime," moving from fear of erasure in the presence of a great natural force, to comprehension, regaining of balance, and thus a greater magnitude of understanding.

The Romantic poets radically alter the literary imagination passed to them from the eighteenth-century classicists and rationalists. Let's note— for John Keats and William Wordsworth, Samuel Taylor Coleridge and Percy Bysshe Shelley—some fundamental adjustments: a valorization of nature over the social text, as over the machine; a preference for the experi-

Romantic innovations?

ence of the individual over the group, or subjectivity over cultural wisdom; a tone of high seriousness—melancholy being the "sublimest" tone—instead of wit, satire, learnedness; a tendency toward the clarifying, the vernacular, or the plain, instead of the baroque; a faith in inspiration and spiritedness instead of reason's logic.

And yet I propose that the sublime Romantic imagination derives directly from some central eighteenth-century aspects. I think of the virtues of the age of reason as being order, balance, a notion of the perfectible or ideal shape. But in important ways the dominant literary mode of the eighteenth century is satire. Why does the rude genre of satire accompany the stately Neoclassical ideal? What better way to measure the ideal than to juxtapose the misshapen, outsized, the proportionally skewed? What better way to critique the culture of high-learnedness (and high-handedness) than with the low-comic? In the work of Jonathan Swift, the Earl of Rochester, Alexander Pope, satire is a hyperbolic fun-house mirror of the idealized. Things are funny, and we are hyperaware of their funniness when things are the wrong size: physically, tonally. Too loud, too big, too grotesque. Such is the formal nature of the mock-epic itself: the tiny swollen to immense stature. Satire is thus a type of instruction by means of comedy, its driving trope being hyperbole.

I contend that the sublime is as misshapen as satire. It may very well be a Romantic translation of satire. Do away with the tone—change wit to awe—do away with the fixation on social narratives, but keep the dimensional exponent. If satire is instruction by means of social comedy, then the sublime is instruction by means of solitary terror. Both of them depend absolutely on a magnified sense of out-of-proportionality.

Late-eighteenth-century England, like all of Europe, was shrinking before the world's eyes. Its empire was radically diminished, by war, by the coming of democracy and equality: more people crowded into a smaller space, a claustrophobic sense of agedness, moldy ruins among Alpine heights, and the persisting hierarchal political order. The sublime is mimetic of the interplay between "a kind of vertical mobility," as Angus Fletcher says, and fixedness or paralysis. Imagine a topography of such history: the strata, the stacked and heightened perspective of damage and rot. Waste up and down.

The sublime emerges from that sense of personal peril amid cultural ruin or folly. Among its greatest articulations must be Shelley's "Mont Blanc" and Wordsworth's "Tintern Abbey":

> And I have felt
> A presence that disturbs me with the joy
> Of elevated thoughts; a sense sublime
> Of something far more deeply interfused,
> Whose dwelling is the light of setting suns
> And the round ocean and the living air,
> And the blue sky, and in the mind of man . . .

In "Tintern Abbey," the terror that accompanies Wordsworth's "joyful" sublime transcendence is, of course, history: the bloody presence of the French Revolution. Details of the war are suppressed in his serene poem, but barely so, and may be the real source of his compulsion to "[fly] from something that he dread[ed]." Keats's own related source of terror is mortality; Shelley's terror is foolishness, fear of triviality; as Coleridge's is sanity. We each have our own.

The sublime makes its journey across the ocean, to America, thanks greatly to Ralph Waldo Emerson, Crèvecoeur, and Edgar Allan Poe. The same features obtain here: the dramatic or serious tone; the interiorized narrative of perception; the valorization of nature and of the self, or self-seeing, self-discovery—here translated as self-reliance. But there are, I contend, two significant adjustments to the sublime made during the American mid-nineteenth century.

The high tone and terror of the European sublime is maintained in America, especially in Poe, Herman Melville, and Nathaniel Hawthorne. The transcendental sublime, however, which we see in Emerson, Walt Whitman, Henry David Thoreau, some of Emily Dickinson, marks a significant national adjustment. Here is the Romantic sublime, but without the guilt, the dread, the sin, or shame. Even in a poem as perilous and aggrieved as Whitman's great elegy, "When Lilacs Last in the Dooryard Bloom'd," the new flavor of American hope, of self-reliant and progressive capability, is eventually discovered, like a new land. In this poem Whitman plumbs his life's greatest challenge, figured both by the assassination of Lincoln and the potential failure of the American experiment. Here he faces not merely doubt, "the thought of death," but obliteration, "the knowledge of death." In the primordial swamp, where he flees, we find all the elements of the sublime—the treatment, the shocked awe, the overgrowth—though the topography itself is markedly different, its sunken "swamps" and flattened "recesses." He must go

"Down to the shores of the water, the path by the swamp in the dimness, / To the solemn shadowy cedars and ghostly pines so still" where he discovers the healing song of the hermit thrush. But even more surprising, when Whitman finds his revitalization and eventually vacates the site of the sublimely erasing swamp, he reactivates two important qualities: his lost physical momentum, and a new, articulate capability and optimism.

> Passing the visions, passing the night,
> Passing, unloosing the hold of my comrades' hands,
> Passing the song of the hermit bird and the tallying song of my soul,
> Victorious song, death's outlet song, yet varying ever-altering song
> . . . .
> Passing, I leave thee lilac with heart-shaped leaves,
> I leave thee there in the door-yard, blooming, returning with spring.

Like the European elegy, the sublime poem rarely finds impulsion, remaining stricken, in awe or in stasis. But in the lilac elegy and in many other instances, the American sublime text pushes off, continues its journey. Huck on the raft, Thoreau going back to work.

A second significant difference in the American sublime emerges from America's landscape and geography. In the Hudson River School of painting (Albert Bierstadt, Thomas Cole, Asher Durand), as in so many popular images depicting the newly explored Grand Canyon and Rocky Mountains, we find works of art that clearly locate their precedent in the European sublime. James Fenimore Cooper, Washington Irving, and other writers often mimic the vertical magnitude, the massive natural blur, of such paintings. But I think a second distinct configuration is original to the American imagination. If Europe was stacked, ancient, diminishing, this new America was both promising and terrifying for its horizon, its horizontal features. The new land seemed never to end, stretching across prairies, plateaux, mountains, all the way to the vanishing point of the ocean, which continued the linear destination beyond measure. Consider the relative size of a cliff to this whole landscape spreading out, hopeful, so sweeping it seems eternal. The godly, the heightened, is brought down to earth. Recall, as an example, Emily Dickinson's great erotic elegy, "Because I could not stop for Death." Where is the future? Where is Dickinson's promise? Not upward, but to the West, where the sun is leading and where her destined journey points her: "'tis Centuries," she says, "and yet / Feels shorter than the Day / I first surmised the Horses' Heads / Were toward Eternity—" Her "toward" is very significant: an unarriving, unending procedure. As Joseph Addison writes in the *Spectator*, "a spacious horison is an Image of Liberty." Gazing across Dickinson's and Whitman's "democratic vistas," we discover a new form of social potential where power is invested at the level bottom, not top-down.

The archetypal American sublime may not be elevated. Like the language, like the political aspiration, like the landscape itself, the terror and promise of the American aesthetic just might be a flat, even playing surface. What is more representative, more accurately sublime, at last, than Moby-Dick? Perhaps a great whale is our national limbic hero: "the wonderful comparative smallness of his brain proper is more than compensated by the wonderful comparative magnitude of his spinal cord." When Ahab finally is swallowed by the equalizing waters, to Ishmael's witnessing terror, I can't help but see a landed parallel: "Now small fowls flew screaming over the yet yawning gulf; a sullen white surf beat against its steep sides; then all collapsed, and the great shroud of the sea rolled on." Europe found its sublime in its terrifying heights and decay. America has its own aesthetic problem: it never stops.

The Gay Sublime

What became of the sublime in those long centuries between late antiquity and the eighteenth century? The great Italian humanists turned to Aristotle, Horace, and Plato well before they turned to Longinus. The first Latin translation of *On the Sublime* appeared only in 1612, the first English translation in 1652. The major philosophical elaborations of Longinus did not emerge until the Enlightenment, in the work of Edmund Burke (1729–1797) and Immanuel Kant (1724–1804). It took the so-called "Pre-Romantics" (William Collins, 1721–1759; William Cowper, 1731–1800; Thomas Gray, 1716–1771) to revive Longinus as a significant theoretical model for poetic practice. We generally understand the Renaissance, like the Middle Ages, to be a period when the sublime went missing.

But had the concept, the durable human apprehension of sublimity, simply adopted other vocabularies? Sometime in the fourth decade of the seventeenth century, when England was struggling to contain the theological splintering set in motion by the Reformation and was on the verge of civil war, a family physician in Norwich wrote a remarkably resilient and optimistic contribution to the disputes of his day and called his tract *Religio Medici*, a doctor's religion. And in Part One, section 9 of his tract, Thomas Browne wrote as follows:

> As for those wingy mysteries in Divinity and ayery subtilties in
> Religion, which have unhindg'd the braines of better heads, they
> never stretched the Pia Mater of mine; me thinkes there be not
> impossibilities enough in Religion for an active faith; . . . I love to
> lose my selfe in a mystery, to pursue my reason to an *o altitudo*.
> 'Tis my solitary recreation to pose my apprehension with those
> involved aenigma's and riddles of the Trinity, with incarnation and
> Resurrection. I can answer all the objections of Satan, and my

rebellious reason, with that odde resolution I learned of Tertullian, *Certum est quia impossibile est* (it is certain because it is impossible).

Altitudo in Latin means both height and depth, and Browne's reference appears to be to the Latin Vulgate, in particular to a passage in St. Paul's letter to the Romans: *O altitudo!* "O the depth of the riches both of the wisdom and knowledge of God! How unsearchable are his judgments, and his ways past finding out!" (Romans 11:33). The context is a paradox, the foundational figure of thought in the Christian gospels as also, I would argue, in the prose and lyric poetry of early modern England. How is it, Paul asks, that the Christian revelation, born of the Hebrews' failure to recognize the path of truth, can rebound as salvation for Hebrews and Gentiles alike? Paul writes to the Romans, the Gentiles, among whom he pursues his ministry or apostolic office, but he finds he must enlarge his office, to spread the gospel among the Hebrews ("them which are my flesh," Romans 11: 14) as well. "For as ye in times past have not believed God, yet have now obtained mercy through their unbelief: Even so have these also now not believed, that through your mercy they also may obtain mercy. For God hath concluded them all in unbelief, that he might have mercy upon all. O altitudo . . . ," etc. Paul's point is the unfathomability of God's ways, the paradox of grace, God's ability to draw good from bad, faith and salvation out of faithlessness.

When I asked my friend Marjorie Levinson to give me an emergency tutorial on the sublime, the part I felt I understood best was her explication of the opposition between the beautiful and the sublime. This opposition holds whether one imagines, with Burke, that beauty and sublimity are properties that attach to certain classes of objects, or insists, with Immanuel Kant, that the opposition is cognitive rather than empirical, that we are talking about different modes of perception. When we experience the beautiful, my friend explained to me, we are made to feel at home in the world, as though the world were made for us and we for it; we seem to "fit." When we experience the sublime, we face instead the limits of our ability to imagine: the sense data exceed the organizing capacities of our mental apparatus or conceptual "categories."

In sixteenth- and seventeenth-century England, the foundational apprehension about humanity's place in the world, about humanity's cognitive apparatus and its suitability to the world, was of a "poor fit." That apprehension was construed primarily in theological terms, to which the aesthetic was mere corollary. The mediating structures of Medieval Catholicism (the consoling surrogacies of penance, eucharist, remission of sins, the priests and nuns and saintly intercessors, all the go-betweens who brought the holy down to human scale) had been done away with by the Reformation, leaving the individual believer with a terrifying double injunction: you yourself are responsible for comprehending the divine, and you must recognize your immutable incapacity for such comprehension; hence the need for grace. As religion moved more and more to the forefront of lyric address (think of John Donne, think of Henry Vaughn and Thomas Traherne), the characteristic lyric aesthetic came more and more to exhibit the aggravated disproportions Dr. Johnson labeled "metaphysical." Epistemological struggle manifested itself in the ungainly, the disproportionate, the violent yoking of unlike and unlikely elements, until it reached its culmination in the mannerism (think Crashaw) of Counter-Reformation art. In the aesthetics of the early seventeenth century, Catholic as well as Protestant, Reformation trumps the Renaissance.

Can the aesthetics of paradox and mannerism help us to look for a contemporary American sublime in the right, unlikely places? The sublime as I understand it should involve an epistemological vista that disrupts and disavows smooth mastery of any sort ; it should be a crisis for the artful, the knowing, the literate, the urbane. And so I turn by instinct to poetry of consummate urbanity and to the rupture or crisis urbanity masks. My first example is by James Merrill, a poem of the mid-1960s:

Charles on Fire

Another evening we sprawled about discussing
Appearances. And it was the consensus
That while uncommon physical good looks
Continued to launch one, as before, in life
(Among its vaporous eddies and false calms),
Still, as one of us said into his beard,
"Without your intellectual and spiritual
Values, man, you are sunk." No one but squared
The shoulders of his own unloveliness.
Long-suffering Charles, having cooked and served the meal,
Now brought out little tumblers finely etched

He filled with amber liquor and then passed.
"Say," said the same young man, "in Paris, France,
They do it this way"—bounding to his feet
And touching a lit match to our host's full glass.
A blue flame, gentle, beautiful, came, went
Above the surface. In a hush that fell
We heard the vessel crack. The contents drained
As who should step down from a crystal coach.
Steward of spirits, Charles's glistening hand
All at once gloved itself in eeriness.
The moment passed. He made two quick sweeps and
Was flesh again. "It couldn't matter less,"
He said, but with a shocked, unconscious glance
Into the mirror. Finding nothing changed,
He filled a fresh glass and sank down among us.

The vessel is finely etched: masterful syntax, a flexible iambic pentameter, minutely calibrated oppositions and overlays of diction. And all, apparently, in the service of social satire: postprandial philosophizing, a series of glaring faux pas that throw into relief the better manners of the general company and also, perhaps, their vanity. Why has one who must stipulate that Paris is in France been allowed to crash this elegant symposium in the first place? He is young, we are told. Young men at symposia are generally expected to be blessed with uncommon good looks; personal beauty and an unformed mind are meant to be their entry tickets. I'm not certain the experience of the sublime must inevitably be a solitary encounter—that may be more conventional than definitional—but social satire would seem to lodge at the other end of the spectrum: its chattiness, its foursquare descriptive engagement, its sheer this-worldly knowingness would seem to be antithetical to the transformative, sublime encounter of soul with universe. But the company that so comfortably, so self-revealingly patronizes the young man in Merrill's poem sees its fabric torn, first by blunder, then by otherworldly visitation: the world of spirits erupts into the complacent ceremonies of food and drink and class consolidation. From this perspective, that eruption seems to anticipate *The Changing Light at Sandover*, Merrill's grand *commedia* of a decade later, in which the spirit world will speak to the poet, at considerably greater length, via domestic sessions at the Ouija board. Is this the sublime? Or is it some sort of anti-sublime? The answer probably depends on how truly we take the veil of appearances to be torn, how seriously the ordinary cognitive faculties thrown into crisis. What is too readily assimilated is unlikely to be the thing we're after.

My second example is a poem of the early 1990s, written by another poet of conspicuous urbanity and technical virtuosity. Like "Charles on Fire," Richard Howard's "Writing Off" introduces itself by way of an archly cast philosophical debate, in this instance about the nature of art and artistic "signature." The poet announces he shall be rebutting Mark Strand's *ars poetica* in "Keeping Things Whole": "In a field / I am the absence of field ... / I move / to keep things whole" (from *Reasons for Moving*, 1968). The field Howard chooses to adduce by way of counter-argument is the scene of superabundance, of densely inscribed urban decay:

> [H]ere is a wall
> and at its base a ruined car
> filled with spray-cans that strew the ground as well,
>
> and every inch of wall and car and ground
> is covered, cancelled, *encrusted*
> with the spirit-writing known as graffito,
> cursive abuse, cacography
> which by its very glut becomes glamor,
>
> a collaborative chaos of uncials,
> illegible and thus elect.
> . . . .
> (How many times we must peruse
>
> these depths before the deepest impulse floats
> to the surface and is legible:
> the inenarrable FUCK which appears
> only after the eye has long
> frequented more decorous instances!)

But slowly the poet begins to infer the absence in surfeit. He compares the "self-immolating" labors of his urban graffiti artists to the labors that built the pyramids of Egypt and the great cathedrals of Europe. In the "wasted splendor of an empty / lot in East Los Angeles," he begins to see cognates to Luxor and Lascaux,

> Sacred places where we learn we can change
> > our faith without changing gods (and
> vice versa) . . .

Until at last he acknowledges the paradoxical triumph of the "absence" he began by opposing. His primary piece of evidence, "the wall / the filthy field, the gutted car engorged // with the spray-cans" turns out to be itself at least twice-removed, accessible only by means of a snapshot and then by means of words on the page, "an unvisitable shrine . . .

> where obscure artisans have succeeded

> in transcending the five destinies
> > by which we claim to be guided:
> *mind body nation language home.* This is
> > how we learn, by just such unseen
> art, to approach the divine.

The final half-line of Howard's poem ("Next slide please") serves simultaneously as deprecating discard and as poetic signature. It echoes the throwaway world-weariness the poet has inscribed in the title of his book. *Like Most Revelations*: as who should say, the momentous is business-as-usual too; we've seen it all before.

We are certainly not in the Alps. And yet, amidst all the insider polemic, the pedantry, the flagrant self-display, despite the insistence on the made world to the utter exclusion or destruction or despair of "nature," this poem does stage the one encounter requisite for the sublime: an encounter with the incommensurate. The very gestures of urban discard, of trashing and decay, of dissonant mediation, a palette made of abandoned edifice and immobilized modes of transport, a brush made of aerosol that poisons the earth and thins the ozone, the cheap technology of photograph, the computer-programed typeface on the page, all testify to our simultaneous ephemerality and stubborn insistence on leaving a trace. The world and the self are incurably at odds. But passionately at odds.

My final example is a poem called "Crêpe de Chine" from Mark Doty's fourth collection:

> That's what I want from the city:
> to wear it.
>
> . . . .
> Look how I rhyme with the skyscraper's
> padded sawtooth shoulders,
>
> look at the secret evidence of my slip
> frothing like the derelict river
> where the piers used to be,
>
> look at my demolished silhouette,
> my gone and reconstructed profile,
> look at me built and rebuilt,
>
> torn down to make way,
> excavated, trumped up, tricked out,
> done, darling,
>
> in every sense of the word. Now,
> you call me
> Evening in Paris, call me Shalimar,
>
> call me Crêpe de Chine.

The aesthetics of drag, the metaphysics of drag, demand the embrace of paradox, the preemptive ironizing of mortal decay: we tear our pleasures with rough strife. The emphasis on artifice, the made rather than the given, is taken one or two steps further than in Richard Howard's poem. Doty give us not merely "art," the art of cathedrals and pyramids and vacant lots, but the art of wearable surface, of fashion, and of fashion queered.

I have begun to wonder about an American canon of the gay sublime.

Its landscape is urban; its characteristic vistas are the intricate fields of social nuance, material surface, manners, wit, and cultivated artifice. At home in the world is a status denied, not merely by the provisionality that characterizes all that is mortal, but by additional overlays. For all our fitful progress, homosexuals must still come of age in a climate of hostility and incomprehension: think of Doty's "Homo Will Not Inherit," think of Howard's "What Word Did the Greeks Have for It?" Even those gay people who might choose them are often denied the ordinary social vehicles by which we are accustomed to process mortality: socially sanctioned pairing and reproduction. The gay community has been stricken by the AIDS epidemic and subsequently by a painful generational chasm between those for whom AIDS was an inevitable death sentence and those for whom it is a way of life, albeit one dependent upon medications and a precarious social safety net. Homosexuality in our culture has had to construct its discursive and presentational styles under seige; its styles as a consequence are among the most brilliant and complex we have. *Mind body nation language home:* and none of them a natural "fit." "I have my kingdom," writes Doty in "Homo Will Not Inherit." And he speaks in concert with Thomas Browne: it is certain because it is impossible.

The Intimate Sublime

As an example of onomatopoeia, even the very word *sublime* sounds sublime: a term of breathtaking, soaring, awe-inspiring fear and fascination, a
traveling word evoking out-of-the-body. *You're the top! You're the Coliseum,*
says Cole Porter; you're the awful shadow of some unseen power that floats
among us, the everlasting universe of things that flows through us, says
Percy Bysshe Shelley. Can a civilizing garden be as sublime as an undecon-
structed space, a wild space? Does it depend on the nature and dimensions
of experience? Does the sublime make of nature art, say in a landscape,
or does art require the right proportion of nature to achieve even a sense
of the sublime? William Wordsworth, standing at dawn on Westminster
Bridge looking to the north over the spread of the city, states that nature
has nothing more fair to show. Would his sight be sullied if he were looking
from the perspective of noon? Do human beings mess up the picture—too
many human beings? Is a mountain, a mountain of ice, a Mont Blanc, more
sublime than a live oak in Louisiana? Is size the question, natural or aesthetic scale?

One thing the English Romantics taught us is that scale is a measurement that finds its dimensions within us; proportion is an interior, subjective experience in which, says Wordsworth, "the mind of man is fashioned
and built up/Even as a strain of music." In Wordsworth's greatest poem,
The 1799 Two-Part Prelude, first published in 1970, he fashions a sequence
of young experiences that serve him ever after as archetype: from the night
theft of the shepherd's boat, to the secret witness of watching a drowned
man being lifted "with iron hooks and with long poles," to the winter day of
his father's death that he associates in memory with an earlier seminal set
of scenes:

Dismounting, down the rough and stony moor
I led my horse, and, stumbling on, at length

Came to a bottom where in former times
A man, the murderer of his wife, was hung
In irons; mouldered was the gibbet-mast
The bones were gone, the iron and the wood,
Only a long green ridge of turf remained
Whose shape was like a grave. I left the spot
And, reascending the bare slope, I saw
A naked pool that lay beneath the hills,
The beacon on the summit, and, more near,
A girl who bore a pitcher on her head
And seemed with difficult steps to force her way
Against the blowing wind. It was in truth
An ordinary sight, but I should need
Colours and words that are unknown to man
To paint the visionary dreariness
Which . . .
Did at that time invest the naked pool,
The beacon on the lonely eminence,
The woman and her garments vexed and tossed
By the strong wind.

"Visionary dreariness" is the phrase that sticks out as the sublime characterization, and as the stand-in for the "colours and words [. . .] unknown to man." Sometime before in this great poem (a thousand total lines), Wordsworth has referred to "a grandeur in the beatings of the heart," and later, when he summarizes his feelings toward his experience of these "spots of time," he concludes that "All these were spectacles and sounds to which / I would often repair, and thence would drink / As at a fountain": perhaps because these "recollected hours . . . have the charm / Of visionary things . . . on which the sun is shining." In the eyes of the sublime, darkness, dreariness, if visionary, is light. And "ordinary" sights, if transformed in imagination, are emotionally sized—lifted, though not exaggerated.

Wordsworth's more ordinary sightings complement rather than contradict his "larger" experiences in the full-length *Prelude*—in the Alps and on Mount Snowden, where nature is like a monument to our feelings. Nevertheless, the sublime tends to be a one-time, first-time level of experience, though if we leave it at that, says T. S. Eliot, we'll have missed the meaning.

The memory, the transformation of the sublime experience is what makes it meaningful. The sublime, re-experienced, becomes a fountain, a muse-experience, finally internalized, evaluated, assigned its proper emotional, spiritual size. And as Wordsworth, in his spots-of-time moments suggests (and as Eliot later echoes), whether remembered as ordinary or grand, such experiences are infused with "fancies that are curled / Around these images, and cling: / The notion of some infinitely gentle / Infinitely suffering thing." Eliot reiterates in *Four Quartets*:

> For most of us, there is only the unattended
> Moment, the moment in and out of time,
> The distraction fit, lost in a shaft of sunlight,
> The wild thyme unseen, or the winter lightning
> Or the waterfall, or music heard so deeply
> That it is not heard at all, but you are the music
> While the music lasts.

The music heard so deeply that it is not heard at all Eliot stole from John Keats's "Heard melodies" that are sweet, while those "unheard / Are sweeter," which is memory compounding memory, art inspiring, inspiriting, art. And while speaking of Keats, and of ordinary, intimate sights, we should observe that the purity of "To Autumn" comes mostly from the fact that even though it's nothing more than a rendering of an English harvest scene—such as a detail from a Thomas Gainsborough painting—it is, in every fiber, a complete sublime experience, word for saturated word. Words, indeed, ordinary words, as the sublime, in a sublimation achieved from the outset as a rhetorical question: "Where the songs of Spring?" "Ode to a Nightingale," on the other hand, is about experience *becoming* sublime, a still journey from the transitive evening into the transcendent dark, a vision *and* a waking dream. It needs its eighty lines. The autumn scene of the harvest and the spring night of the nightingale are both small moments in small places. They claim no greatness in nature; instead they create greatness by projecting into what they perceive.

The American poets make of the English intimate sublime still smaller, more subjective moments. Emily Dickinson's entire best work is the epiphanal sublime reenacted, over and over, dressed in the funereal, looking through the lens of a window. She sees a slant of light and feels a funeral in her brain.

I don't know that I agree — D's 'epiphanies' are so coy + confounding. But maybe he's suggesting these are anti-epiphanies, implosions rather than exaltations.

She tastes a liquor never brewed and likes a look of agony. She dies for beauty, then hears a fly buzz. And she cannot live with us because it would be life. And life?—life is a white sustenance, despair. Like all Romantics, she monumentalizes the moment in order to find the moment, to see it, feel it, celebrate it, even to endure it. Her compression is her compassion; her empathy is with intimacy, the interior of the construct, where the meanings are.

And Whitman, for all his bravura and bigness, can be even smaller than Dickinson, since it's not the grass or the narrow fellow in it, but the leaves of grass themselves that metaphorize his attention. The visionary in Whitman never forgets the view, the ground from where the sublime starts, where the divine is inside, as the grain of sand is in a diamond. "It is not upon you alone the dark patches fall," he says in "Crossing Brooklyn Ferry," "The dark threw its patches down upon me also." In Whitman the rhetoric itself can take on or compete with the sublime as it lifts language onto another level of recognition, or lowers it to an ur-level of a first language: "Expand, being than which none else is perhaps more spiritual,/Keep your places, objects than which none else is more lasting." The antecedent for this appositive is "dumb, beautiful ministers"—cities, I suppose, and the stuff of cities, such as Manhattan, on the lower East Side, at the South Street seaport. Whitman's ferry crossing is another case of his multitudes finding enough oratory to suffice. Yet Whitman's most sublime moments can tend to get lost in the great mix of things he masters. In section 3 of "Crossing," the list of what he is looking at proceeds at an anaphoric rate of operatic sound, but not so fast as to miss "the Twelfth-month sea-gulls . . . high in the air floating with motionless wings, oscillating their bodies,/[. . .] the glistening yellow" lighting "up parts of their bodies," leaving "the rest in strong shadow." This momentary detail of a vision is answered in his own image of himself at the rail of the ferry with "the fine centrifugal spokes of light round the shape of my head in the sunlit water." The whole is staged as a series of small, subtle connections and fluid connectivity, the traveler of time in time. And here at the sublime time of the day, the sunset hour, the speaker is but a part of the fine centrifugal shining, no more or less than the gulls, or the great city objects.

Perhaps more than anything, the real intimacy of the sublime is not so much the way in which it connects us to what we perceive and judge in the value of things and their nature but to the ways in which it connects us to community and humanity, the humanity in ourselves, and especially, in Wallace Stevens's great lyric phrase, to the voice that is great within us. After all, the casual flocks in the isolation of the sky, with their ambiguous undulations and their sinking down to darkness, at the end of "Sunday Morning," are only pigeons on those extended wings. And—now that the Irish poets have become American poets—that greatest of modern American lyrics, "Among School Children," is founded on the least of things: a face, an image and a memory of a face—on an isolating walk among the future and the past, and on a daydream. This great poem is built upon the inseparability of this daydream and its dreamer, the very perishability of that moment. The sublime cannot be left locked inside the cold heart of a mountain or the giant entanglements of a bridge, but must be recognized within our own hearts, and within our small circumference—the circumference, for one example, of form, poetic form, our terza rimas, our ottava rimas, our odes and elegies, where the sublime is primarily manifest. Form is the ultimate internalization of the sublime: Whitman's full-bodied free verse embrace, Dickinson's exquisite concentration of energies, Stevens's majestic blank-verse stride. Form is where the texture of our feelings of and feeling for transcendence is acted out. Form is the mountain, and also the tree and the wing.

ANN TOWNSEND

The Technological Sublime

I. "what to make of a diminished thing"

David Baker's genealogy of the sublime suggests that as prior versions of the sublime become outmoded, writers must abandon or reconfigure their definitions. I'd like to craft a genealogy of my own, tracing an evolution away from nature as the primary source of sublime feeling, toward the emergence and eventual domination of a twentieth century technological sublime. Most simply put, today we either can't experience the sublime at all, or at least we can't experience it using the same sources or the same psychological basis points as the Romantic poets did.

Wallace Stevens addresses our contemporary unsteadiness in his poem, "The American Sublime," published in 1935. He asks "How does one stand/ To behold the sublime?" Perhaps this is simply a question about the writer's position. If you were going to write directions for capturing the sublime, you might say "Please stand at an edifying middle distance. Choose an elevated place. Step a little closer to the edge." These are measures traditionally taken by painters and poets so they might see more clearly, be awakened to the awe and fear that immensity, vacancy, or overwhelming natural force ought to provoke. In his *American Technological Sublime*, David Nye says "the early American landscape, with its immense scale and natural resources, invited such views. And so Americans have traveled, for instance, to Niagara Falls in the east, and to the Grand Canyon, in the west, to get a taste of the sublime." But when the wildest nature has become tamed, when there's little left to discover and conquer, landscape may no longer call up the sublime in us. Now go back to Wallace Stevens's question: "How does one stand/ To behold the sublime?" The sublime as such never resides in any object; it is an effect, says Immanuel Kant, occurring solely within the subjective mind. So, Stevens implies, how capable is the contemporary mind? How will our mind work to keep up or to contain this effect? As the pace of technological wonders increased in the twentieth century, the American mind needed to shift to accommodate technology as a central source for the sublime.

We shouldn't think that only in contemporary America is sublime feeling called up by technological wonders. In the eighteenth century, Nye says,

> Burke took it for granted that two basic categories of the sublime, namely difficulty and magnificence, particularly applied to architecture.... In the following century Victorian cities were filled with structures that were not meant to be beautiful or picturesque, but rather awesome, astonishing, vast, powerful, and obscure, striking terror into the observer. The new railway stations, aqueducts, factories, and warehouses were rhetorical structures, demonstrating the power of the builders.

But the vast crowds drawn to massive public works projects like the Hoover Dam, the Brooklyn Bridge, and the Empire State Building suggested that, in America, the experience of the sublime was democratic and communal rather than solely an individual psychological experience:

> Where Kant had reasoned that the awe inspired by a sublime object made men aware of their moral worth, the American sublime transformed the individual's experience of immensity and awe into a belief in national greatness. (*David Nye*)

This version of the sublime is also tied to consumer culture; just as I get tired of my last new pair of jeans, so the sublime image can cease to have an impact when it ceases to be "new."

So, go back to nature for a moment. If the sublime feeling depends, in part, on the shock of the new, of virgin apprehension, what happens once an allegedly sublime landscape has been seen, described, and experienced by many? What happens when we become tourists of the sublime? In Carl Phillips's recent collection, *The Tether*, the speaker in "The Pinnacle" refuses a potentially sublime moment, because he knows that the landscape that might produce such feeling has already been overencountered, overdescribed, and is no longer capable of producing that so-called "peak" experience. At the end of the poem, after hiking with some difficulty the trail through woods and valley and up a winding path, the speaker understands the limits of the experience he is about to have, even though he hasn't had it yet:

> [he] began,
> like that, to feel cooler, more
> sure: the pinnacle we'd been
>
> told the trail led to would
> come, the trail would end
> in what they usually do,
>
> a view. There are limited
> choices. Already *Go*
> *down or Don't*, in my head.

This narrator doesn't particularly want to experience the sublime. What he wants is to feel sure of the view. Because he anticipates it, sublime feeling is not available to him.

So, what to make of a diminished thing? That is the question Robert Frost poses in "The Oven Bird," and he asks it not only about the bird's non-sublime song, but also about himself, non-sublime poet. What is the function of poetry in an age where the sublime is a dead aesthetic? Frost, who sets his poem in jaded midsummer rather than in the first rush of spring flowering, says that nature's song has grown old. "The Oven Bird" argues that the moment for the sublime has past. Even though we are still engaged in naming what we see ("And comes that other fall we name the fall"), Frost's diction implies that autumn should be read not only as a season, but also as emblematic of Eden's fall, the imminent end of life. This gesture comes at the midpoint of the poem, after the octave. At this volta, the sonnet structure puts particular emphasis on the words "the highway dust is over all." By 1916, when the poem appeared, railroads linked the East Coast to the West, and an emerging highway system had begun to bisect and define the spaces that previously seemed immense, even limitless. It's no accident that Frost has chosen a bird whose actual call, whose birdsong, sounds a lot like "teacher-teacher." The bird is schooling us on what he sees as he flies across the land. This is a singer "everyone has heard." Even in 1916, it's an old story, a lesson learned. Frost's bird will not sing a sublime song, so the poet must make, instead, the poetry of a diminished thing.

Another poet who reaches for the sublime even as she undercuts it is Elizabeth Bishop. In "The Moose," the narrator travels by bus through Nova Scotia, surrounded by the voices and stories of her fellow travelers as the land-scape unfolds outside her window. When a moose emerges from the woods and the bus stops (stanza twenty-three), the speaker has all but fallen asleep, lulled by the voices around her. The men and women on the bus are plain-spoken, not given easily to transports of amazement, but when the moose, "grand, otherworldly," "looms" massively in the middle of the road, the people on the bus give in to their astonishment. If the moose, approaching to sniff the bus, seems to encounter something for the first time, so too do these passengers. Bishop asks the simple, resonant question:

> Why, why do we feel
> (we all feel) this sweet
> sensation of joy?

Together they are "awakened" by the presence of the moose. Rob Wilson has suggested that the sublime may take the form of a conversion narrative, that shared sublime experiences are "communally adhesive," even redemptive. But even though Bishop makes a point to say that "we all feel" this joy, the feeling is fleeting, and when the moose disappears into darkness, the mundane and comforting conversations simply continue, and the bus drives away. Shared awakenings like this are disorienting and don't last long. What remains is the lingering smell, and because that smell is in part composed of gasoline fumes, Bishop might be asking us to see that technology works to distract us from the sublime moment. The poem closes down on these words:

> For a moment longer,
>
> by craning backward,
> the moose can be seen
> on the moonlit macadam;
> then there's a dim
> smell of moose, an acrid
> smell of gasoline.

It's the gasoline that remains, lingering in the air and overriding the smell of the moose, as the mechanized world overshadows the natural world—as if one no longer exists without the other.

II.

Why do we like to be part of a spectacle? Why do we cheer at the sight of particularly good fireworks? Why do I feel pleasurably dwarfed by my neighbor's two-storey high combine that threshes his corn every summer? Part of the pleasure I take in feeling fear must come from the combination of being at once insignificant and powerful. Perhaps our grandparents derived the same fear and pleasure from beholding the Hoover Dam. Perhaps early travelers experienced it at the Grand Canyon. But technologies and sublime landscapes are ephemeral. Railroads and monumental structures that seemed amazing on first encounter soon became commonplace. Thus do we strive to replace the once-sublime with the newly apprehended, the bigger and better sublime.

But in 1945, the boundaries of the sublime changed perhaps for good when the atomic bomb was first tested at Alamogordo, New Mexico. On that July day what we imagined and created was not simply powerful. The bomb exceeded and devastated all expectations. The men who felt the revelation of its power first hand were awestruck at what they witnessed. They found themselves at a loss for adequate terms and tropes by which to explain themselves. Robert Oppenheimer, director of the Los Alamos lab, quoted Hindu scripture: he said "I am become Death, the destroyer of worlds." Brigadier General Thomas Farrell suggested that not even poetry could capture his experience:

> No man-made phenomenon of such tremendous power had ever
> occurred before.... The whole country was lighted by a searing light
> with the intensity many times that of the midday sun.... It lighted
> every peak, crevasse, and ridge of the mountain range with a clarity
> and beauty.... It was that beauty the great poets dream about but
> describe most poorly and inadequately.

And atomic-test director Kenneth Bainbridge said, perhaps most resonantly, "Now we are all sons of bitches."

If we traditionally describe the sublime as emotion arising from "terror beheld and resisted," as Rob Wilson configures it, how do we resist a terror larger than our capacity to contain it? If the sublime takes us to the edge of chaos, and then allows us the clarity of understanding, how can we step away from the chaos that threatens us now? In Jorie Graham's 1987 collection *The End of Beauty*, the poem "What the End Is For" describes the B-52 bombers stationed on constant alert, "running every minute /of every day," at the Grand Forks, North Dakota, air force base. While she can't directly experience the awesome force of the bomb, the noise that announces the bomb's presence surrounds her. B-52 bombers have eight very loud engines, and in the poem the airfield is hyperbolically crowded with five hundred planes. This "eternity of engines never not running," like the smell of gasoline in the Bishop poem, drowns out everything. It obliterates even the sound of the wind, even her companion's voice as he tries to speak, even the sunlight that seeks a way out, away from this overwhelming sound, even the grass in the field, "every last blade of grass [. . .] wholly possessed." The tensions and dangers of the Cold War are embedded in this sound, awful, impossible to ignore.

The poem enacts a struggle to maintain identity in the face of all of this noise. Not everyone is strong enough to survive it, including the two men in the poem whom she simply calls "boys." One boy takes her to see the planes, offers an inadequate bouquet of grasses and "torn pods," and the other stands passively in a darkening room as their relationship dissolves. Both "go out" with the sun, both boys disappear in darkness. For these two, the fragmentation of the world induces a vertigo of the soul, when we are lost without what Susan Stewart calls the "anchoring capabilities of touch." But Graham's speaker alone keeps pressing against the noise, and the ending of this poem resists closure, keeps moving forward on its path of consciousness.

When, at the conclusion of "What the End Is For," Graham tells the ending of the story of Orpheus, she tells it in present tense, the only part of the poem to be thus. Against the noise of the ocean, Orpheus, the allegorized figure of the poet, continues to sing even when he's been decapitated. Nye claims: "The classic form of the technological sublime has broken down not because the objects of our contemplation have ceased to be fearful but because terror has become their principal characteristic, and we have no sense that we can observe them in safety." Graham's poems address the moment when the sublime dissolves into the chaotic, and so Orpheus contends with the sound of the overwhelming waters that threaten to swallow him:

> When the Maenads tear Orpheus limb from limb,
> > they throw his head
>
> out into the river.
> > Unbodied it sings
> all the way downstream, all the way to the single ocean,
> > head floating in current downriver singing,
> until the sound of the cataracts grows,
> > until the sound of the open ocean grows and the voice.

As a stand-in for the poet, for the precious individual voice, Orpheus has the final say in this poem. When technology itself has eclipsed our mastery of it, when all we hear is an unbearable noise that separates us not only from nature but from each other as well, how do we make ourselves heard?

The sublime as such never resides in any object; it is an effect, says Kant, occurring solely within the mind. It is subjective and it is ephemeral. If sublimity is possible at all, it is not a socially created experience but a solitary and fundamental encounter with reality, one perhaps doomed to failure against the burden of contemporary noise, but necessary nonetheless. Now remember David Baker's archetypal American sublime landscape that stretches on and on. And so the loudly singing head of Orpheus keeps floating toward the open ocean, toward the endlessly extending horizon.

3. On Meditation and Mediation: The Problem of People

Life is an affair of people not of places.
But for me life is an affair of places and
that is the trouble.

"I'm Nobody": Lyric Poetry and the Problem of People

That we mourn. That we ache. That we want. That we lie. That we forget. That we fail. That we kowtow. That we deceive. That we covet. That we love. That we die. That we remember.

This chapter considers lyric poetry and the problem of people. My list, of course, denotes the problem, some of the problems, *with* people. I want to press on this proposition for a moment before I turn my attention more fully to another part of the title.

The problems with people have provided poets with their subjects for millennia. In our investigations of three primary lyric modes, we have previously considered the love poem (and the problem of passion, heartbreak, betrayal), the elegy (and the problem of death and loss or forgetting), and the ode (and the problems of social rhetoric and lyric progression). In parsing these three categories into more specific rhetorical modes or landscapes, we have looked at other problematics within the lyric: pastoral poetry (thus, the problem of nature), the sublime (the problem of beauty), and narrative and syntax (the problem of time). Our present issue finds its focus in lyric meditation and the problem of people. Wallace Stevens prepares us in "Adagia": "Life is not people and scene but thought and feeling."

To be sure, people are a real problem for the lyric poem. Conventional definitions of the lyric poem generally abide by critic Roman Jakobsen's assessment: "lyric poetry speaks for the first person, in the present tense—a present toward which lyric always impels any past or future events." Isn't this the case? I turn to works of literature for many things, in many needs. But I seek lyric poetry specifically for its meditation, for the example of its music, the solace of its radical interiority. Harold Bloom goes so far as to assert that the main value of literary study is "to enlarge a solitary existence." Such is the dream of the lyric in particular, that the self shall be revealed and enlarged.

Immediately, a problem. In a narrative of self, what is the place of the other, of others, of people? From here the problem extends in many directions. Does the lyric possess a political aptitude? Can it protest, criticize, convince? What is the place of the popular in a seemingly hermetic site? How do communities, indeed how do urban and technological constructions, fit into the private or pastoral space of the lyric? These are real and delicious problems to tackle, for don't we want a lyric poetry capable of cities, populations, politics, testimony, exchange, social engagement?

I am going to limit my own discussion to a more basic problem of people and the lyric. I wish to consider the center of both the social and lyric cosmos: the self, that conscious or self-conscious entity speaking from the singular and personal present. If a lyric poem is a song of oneself, what *is* that self? What is its relation to the collective? Has the lyric poem always extended outward from the center of the solitary self to the "others"? The answers range vividly.

Sometimes we hold that the self is an autonomous and independent entity, a body and a psyche of measurable dimensions, the fixed hub around which our perceptions and relationships orbit. This is consistent with Bloom's notion of the lyric's function: to enlarge a solitary existence. Ralph Waldo Emerson identifies this version of the self in its most pure and central state: "I see all; the currents of the Universal Being circulate through me."

Sometimes we think of the self as a more fluid or deconstructed thing: an artifice formed by convenience and language, a social construct, a fiction. This attitude dissolves the self into the social collective. Likewise, critic Anthony Easthope disperses the genre of lyric poetry into the overall category of discourse; hence, all exchanges engage equally in "a process of enunciation." The poet's presence—and the anthropomorphic trope of the poet's "voice"—is hereby recuperated into a symptomatic of ideologies, power struggles, and destabilized structures. In her essay "Coherent Decentering," Annie Finch agrees with this critique of the notion of the stable self:

> Like many contemporary writers, I find the Romantic poetic construct of the fixed, central self and its point of view to be extraordinarily limited. . . . I am aware that my own selfhood, let alone the self voicing my poems, is not a clear and simple unit separate from everything else in the world.

I agree, too. I know I am, as Whitman says, "part and parcel of the whole." I am no more independent from the water and wind of the world than a hair is independent from my head. But I sense a problem here as well. Note how Finch begins her next paragraph: "When I was a child, my family would spend several months a year in an isolated cabin." And on she goes, in a complex study of Cartesian logic, Buddhist selflessness, and subjectivity, to destabilize that "romantic construct of the fixed, central self." And she undertakes her study, persistently, in the first person singular. Erasure and assertion are part of the self's paradox, as in Jane Hirshfield shows in these lines from "A Day Comes":

A day comes
when the mouth grows tired
of saying "I."

Yet it is occupied
still by a self which must speak.
Which still desires,
is curious.
Which believes it has also a right.

What to do?

Here is my first point: the self exists. It is a vexed, changing, elusive, and fictive—a linguistic—construct. But linguistic constructs are real. We make the world when we say it, and it's the only world we have. The poet and philosopher John Koethe is succinct: "I know that *I* exist, but what about that place we lived? Is it still real? // —Of course it is." That is to say, we have a self because we insist to refer to an "I" as separate from a "you" or a "she." And when we say "I," we all seem to agree more or less on what that word signifies.

How did the issue become so complicated? I wish I could propose a tidy linear, historical explanation: that the first lyric poetry was private and coherent, and that poetry has become more complicated or contaminated as it addresses its social and postmodern mien; or that the history of privacy in the lyric has moved from fact to irony to utter impossibility; or vice versa. But these are false propositions. The issue has never been stable, just as the self has never been stable.

When I turn far back to the classical Greek poets, I find it significant that already the literary arts have gravitated into discreet genres. Epic poetry embraces the expansive history, the continuity, of a whole culture. Dramatic poetry serves as a more narrowed—in the narrative sense—performance of voices and types. And lyric poetry sings the song of the self. But is this the case? Michael Schmidt reminds us that there are actually three basic modes of Greek lyric poetry. The "coarsest," he says, is *iambic*. Old Greek iambic poems were typically recited, not sung, and were an important feature at festivals. Bawdy, playful, slangy, but also highly formalized, they are the root of satire. The oldest practitioners are poets like Archilochus and Semonides. In such poems there's no self, interior stance, or personal point of view, anywhere in sight.

The second category of *elegiac* poems does not indicate a poem sung in mourning, but rather a metrical structure. Greek elegiac couplets are made of a line of dactylic hexameter followed by a line of dactylic pentameter. These, too, are intended for public recital and performance, as Schmidt notes, are hortatory in nature, and often are not lamenting or memorial but erotic. Only much later does the rhetoric of the dirge overtake the metrical origin of the elegy, thus shifting the term from a formal to a thematic designation. As practiced by poets like Mimnermus and Theognis, these are even more highly conventionalized, ritualized poems.

And finally, the third category is *melic*, a lyric composed in meters. Schmidt says that melic poems "take the form of a monody, a single voice perhaps with musical accompaniment." Here Sappho and Anacreon are forebears of what we conventionally refer to as lyric poetry. Most speak from an "I" and address a single listener. Critics have suggested that in melic poetry we find a point of departure for the first-person subjective lyric; Sappho's apparently intimate perspective, for instance, often marks the origin of the personal lyric. But, Schmidt points out, this overlooks three significant things: the entirely public context for which melic poems were composed, the necessity of instrumental accompaniment, and the fact that the emotions and the "personal" elements were "shared" by the symposium participants. It is thus dangerous to assume a too-similar relationship between those ancient lyrics and ours. Schmidt reminds us that Yeats says lyric poems are overheard, not heard. Yet Greek melic poetry *is* heard.

It is in fact dangerous to assume a too-similar relationship between those ancient *people* and us. A fascinating difference between the Greek lyricists and ourselves derives from the entity we label "the self." How did the self come to be? Have we always been self-conscious, of two or three or four minds, a stew of self-aware voices? Julian Jaynes thinks otherwise. In *The Origin of Consciousness in the Breakdown of the Bicameral Mind*—that famous book my poetry friends adore and my psychologist friends shrink from—Jaynes surmises that the early Classical mind, still bicameral, shows us the coming-into-consciousness of the modern human, shows our double-minded awareness as, originally, a haunted hearing of voices. To Jaynes, thinking is not the same as consciousness: *"one does one's thinking before one knows what one is to think about."* That is, thinking is not synonymous with consciousness or introspection; it is rather an automatic process, notably more *reflexive* than reflective. Jaynes proposes that epic poetry, early lyric poetry, ritualized singing, the conscience, even the voices of the gods, all are one part of the brain learning to hear, to listen to, the other.

I am interested in the progression, then, from those "bicameral" Greek poets to the present. The development seems to be from social and public to private and personal. Indeed the significant differences between the Greek odes of Pindar and the later Latin odes of Horace support Jaynes's theory. It's no small act of guesswork to deduce the conscience—and quality of consciousness—of a culture's people from its lyric poetry, and yet it does seem true that the grand, impersonal, highly formalized Pindaric ode represents the Greek citizen's subsumed relation to the group. The fifth Isthmian ode is typical. Here, ostensibly to praise Phylakidas (victor of a strength competition), Pindar sings more so of the public good:

I have come with the Graces
For the sons of Lampon

To this law-loving city.
If she has turned to a clean path
Of god-given actions,
Grudge not to mingle fitting praise
With song for her labours.

The high esteem for law, the gods, and decorum corresponds to the heightened public discourse of the Greek ode. But as early Greek culture with its emphasis on civic duty evolves into the Roman world, notice how Horace—

five hundred years after Pindar—enjoys the pleasures of a singular body and personal experience. His ode to Phyllis is a clear step toward the modern individual; Horace is more a self than an arm (or voice) of the *polis*:

> I have saved for the day a full bottle of old
> Wine from the Alban hills. Phyllis, out in the garden
>   There's parsley, and ivy, for fillets and coronets
> To bind up your hair and make you look still more
>   Beautiful than you looked even before.

[handwritten margin note: If you compared this with a Sappho poem it wouldn't be so easy to formulate this supposed shift from public to private.]

If the early Greek culture—so different even from the Roman world—shows a kind of coming into the complexities of consciousness as we think of it now, then the early seventeenth century shows us coming into early modernity. Harold Bloom calls Shakespeare's achievement nothing less than the invention of the human. By this he refers to the psychological interiority, the self-referencing, the meta-narrative of the early modern mind: "What Shakespeare invents are ways of representing human changes, alterations not only caused by flaws and by decay but effected by the will as well, and by the will's temporal vulnerabilities." In other words, before Shakespeare there was characterization—types, allegorical categories—as seen in Homer, Chaucer, and later still in Spenser. After Shakespeare, there were characters, men and women with highly individuated personalities. William Logan agrees that the "invention of personality" is a literary achievement as well as a step in psychological evolution, and that this phenomenon occurs in the early seventeenth century. But Logan nominates Milton as the inventor: the anxious Milton of *Paradise Lost*, of course, but more so the Milton of those sonnets "drawn to real events," the Milton who "did not fit." His agony is a personal agony—neither typical nor archetypal. Rather his is the discomfort of a man acutely aware of himself in the wrong time, surrounded by wrongheaded others of wrong faith.

[handwritten margin note: Wray credits Col w/ this!]

In the early Romantic era, the self's evolving interiority becomes even more fully textualized. Here it is transcribed into a landscape that itself takes the shape of the human psyche. William Wordsworth represents an example of the power of self-realization, but also embodies the peril of solipsism—both traits of the mind in modern literature. In Book VIII of *The Prelude*, he admits his potentially self-enclosed dilemma: that the extent of his solitary "Love of Nature Leading to Love of Man" is so consuming that he cannot present a vision of social complexities. "Though he had the best of intentions, he could never handle close-packed, present, human crowds in the mode of imagination," notes Frederick Pottle. Across the Atlantic from Wordsworth, a similar Romantic conundrum stews. When Edgar Allan Poe's House of Usher crumbles, the old mansion's architecture suggests the rotting psyche of Roderick Usher, poisoned by his family's fate and his own self-destructive behavior. Where Milton's earlier garden serves as a social paradigm, a cultural problem allegorized, Poe's house is the inte-rior world of a single, modern mind.

We might find a similar social withdrawal or debility in our home-grown hermit, Emily Dickinson. Who better embodies the lyric's self-containment and self-reliance, with her pathological fear of those "close packed human crowds"? "I'm Nobody! / Who are you? / Are you— Nobody—too? / Then there's a pair of us!" she virtually brags. "The Soul selects her own Society— / Then—shuts the Door," she decides. "Except to Heaven, she is nought. / Except for Angels—lone." But throughout her work, the radical paradox of Dickinson's self-imposed privacy is its articu-lation not apart from but *through* the tropes of community. Privacy is a precious entity, a mark of the mind's increasing valorization of the self; but Dickinson's privacy is also itself a "Society," a populous "Heaven." Her very solitude—powerful, empowering, embracing—contains others. The self is a self only as it resists, but relates to, all the others. Helen Vendler makes a related assessment: "Although in the usual lyric the speaker is alone, this solitude does not mean that he is without a social ambiance."

And what of that most social and democratic of poets, Walt Whitman? No one represents the paradox of the highly realized self and the unavoidable social world better than Whitman. On one hand he demands and defines the "song of the self," praising autonomy and self-realization above all else. But in "Song of Myself" we find him also "mad to be in contact" with the body of the world, mad to be "quiver[ed] to a new identity" by the simple touch of one to another. In virtually all of his great poems, the connection of body to body serves a number of functions. It is a form of personal acknowledgment or va-lidity, a form of knowledge, a form of political action, and a connection—like a fuse, an electrical circuit—that engenders a power at once political, artistic, sexual, and personal. This personal lyric poet isn't troubled by other people, is he? Rather, he seems most himself when he is measured and identified in the group; his song of himself is, gloriously, "a call in the midst of the crowd."

Whitman's songs of himself are underscored by the paradox of the public. Those things that seem to separate us—making each self distinct from each other self—are precisely those that most connect us, that we most recognize in ourselves, that we most share. "I too knitted the old knot of contrariety, / Blabb'd, blush'd, resented, lied, stole, grudg'd, / Had guile, anger, lust" and on and on—no sin "wanting," he confesses in "Crossing Brooklyn Ferry." Yet we are not shocked, not repulsed by his transgressions, but rather stricken with self-recognition. We literally are Whitman, and he knows it: "I was one with the rest," he says, this self among selves, this socialized modern man.

I know of few better articulations of this fundamental problem of the self or personality than T. S. Eliot's comment in "Tradition and the Individual Talent." "Poetry is not a turning loose of emotion, but an escape from emotion; it is not the expression of personality, but an escape from personality," Eliot writes. Lest he be misunderstood, he continues, wryly: "But, of course, only those who have personality and emotions know what it means to want to escape from these things."

The story of the self in lyric poetry is the story of such contradictions. The progress of lyric poetry—like the progression of personhood—seems to have moved from outward to inward, from social function to self-realization. But have changes in the psyche led to changes in poetry, or has poetry's increasing interiority help to create the modern mind? Certainly the development of writing has contributed to our capability to meditate. It's important to remember that Pindar sang but Horace wrote. And as poetry moved from voice to page, likewise we moved inward, solitary in our enjoyment of poetry. With a book we can read slowly, partially, even backwards; we can study, not merely overhear. As books have flourished, so have an increasing number and variety of written genres, many of which have absorbed or overtaken some of the purposes of the oldest poetry. I sympathize with Czeslaw Milosz when he mourns the apparent loss of a public function, a social discourse, in lyric poetry: "The poets of the past were not 'pure.' That is, they did not assign poetry a narrow territory, did not leave religion, philosophy, science, and politics to ordinary people who supposedly were unable to share in the initiations of the elite." But newscasts and sports pages, political novels and thrillers, creative nonfiction and biographies—to say nothing of gossip columns, self-help memoirs, and blogs—have become part of our literacy and our imagination; as a result, poetry has found its own specialized but urgent function. Lyric poetry is largely a poetry of the self.

Why apologize? Lyric poetry with its frequent intense interiority is still, and is powerfully, a public art. This is the final paradox. The very history that I briefly recounted here becomes the shared communal text underwriting each individual private text. We *share* in poetry's privacy, as we share in poetry's history. This privacy is a social act or, as Matthew Arnold points out, "a dialogue of the mind with itself." Helen Vendler usefully extrapolates "dialogue": "Insofar as every human relation-of-two entails an ethical dimension (of justice, estimation, reciprocity, sympathy) so, too, does every lyric representation of the linkage of two persons." "Two persons" can be as well two parts of one mind.

Lyric poetry is never merely about a self but is always also a social performance, just as the linguistic and formal material of poetry is a social achievement. As Whitman and Dickinson represent in their work, self-interest—both the figure and fact of the self—is a vital feature of cultural identity, even perhaps of collective survival. The more the self is identified, in detail and in context, the more connective and sympathetic is its relationship to others. Interiority is—the ultimate paradox—one of our most conjoining gestures.

Life among Others

The lyric poem is a form of social speaking. This simple, self-evident feature has often been obscured or overshadowed by the lyric's prized affinity for inwardness. But the very trait we prize—the public face of privacy—is paradoxical, reminding us that the social and the solitary, the plural and the personal, are interdependent and mutually sustaining realms. What follows is a highly unsystematic effort to examine the lyric as a site for investigating the reciprocal pleasures and obligations, treacheries and fidelities of life among others. One of my examples is drawn from the sixteenth century, one from the twentieth century, one from the very recent past; two were written by women and one by a man; one makes much of the poet's real or ostensible autobiography; two are silent, or all but silent, on just that point. All are poems I admire. Together they seem to me to delineate a landscape of possibility: the varied means by which the lyric poem may seek to address its own entanglement in social life, an entanglement both moral and epistemological. Together they debunk a romantic stereotype: far from thwarting or impinging upon the apprehending self, life in the clamorous social world affords the self its meaningful occasions for coming into consciousness and contour. Or so these poems attest.

❧

Isabella Whitney was the first woman in England to publish a volume of poetry. She published not one but two: *The Copy of a Letter, Lately Written in meeter, by a younge Gentilwoman to her unconstant Lover* (1567) and *A Sweet Nosegay or Pleasant Posy* (1573). Whitney seems to have been a member of the minor gentry; we believe we know the family to whom she was born; she spent some years "in service" in a London household. Her precise class position and thus the nature of the service she is likely to have performed are difficult to ascertain: she would not have been a charwoman, but neither would she have qualified as an all-but-equal companion to aristocrats, like Maria in *Twelfth Night* or Nerissa in *The Merchant of Venice*. She seems to have known the nature of real domestic chores: her writings display familiarity with the boisterous commercial and material life of sixteenth-century London, the noise and stench of the streets, the haggling with butchers, apothecaries, and pawnbrokers, the harried contracting of petty loans, the everyday business of getting and spending. Whitney lost her employment in the early 1570s, or so we conclude from her published work, and was forced to leave London for lack of means.

Upon her departure, she wrote a 364-line poem in which she bids farewell to the city and makes a series of mock bequests. Thus begins "The Manner of Her Will & What She Left to London, and to All Those in It, at Her Departing":

> I Whole in body, and in minde,
> but very weake in Purse:
> Doo make, and writ my Testament
> for fear it wyll be worse.

Much in the manner of François Villon, Whitney construes her departure from the city as a kind of social death and builds her poem upon the rhetoric and method of a Last Will and Testament. In Whitney's era, as in Villon's a century earlier, the Last Will was a document of both legal and religious force. Villon, despite the mock liberality with which he disposes of worldly goods in his famous "Testament," grants considerable space to that which we recognize as belonging to the soul: he tempers lyric satire with extended meditations on mortality, lost love, lost chances, and regret. Whitney's tonal and sentimental range is considerably different, more like that of Villon in his shorter "Legacy." Whitney dispenses with the soul rather briskly, for instance. And once she has dispensed with it, she doesn't look back: the conceptual and rhetorical leverage that interests her is that which she can achieve by working entirely within her principal conceit:

> I first of all to London leave
> because I there was bred:
> Brave buildyngs rare, of Churches store,
> and Pauls to the head.

As conspicuous as the conceit itself is the punning and tautological spirit in which it is deployed. The speaker is leaving London because she is no longer able to support herself there; she leaves *to* the city that which she must leave behind, that which is not, in the usual sense, hers to give, that which the city owns already or keeps in circulation, that which makes the city what it is.

When she turns her beneficence from the city itself to its denizens, the poet lets loose an expansive and proliferant body of detail:

> For Nets of every kynd of sort,
> I leave within the pawne:
> French Ruffes, high Purles, Gorgets and Sleeves
> of any kind of Lawne.
> For Purse of Knives, for Combe of Glasse,
> or any needeful knacke
> I by the Stoks have left a Boy,
> wil aske you what you lack.

Would you have luxury fabrics and ornamental sleeves or ruffs? I leave you, says the testator, a world of such things in the pawnshops. Would you have mirrors and trinkets? I leave you hawkers on every street corner who will gladly provide them, cheap. "What do you lack?" is the street hawker's cry, distinctive as the church bell or the alehouse sign. "Lack" is hawker's slang for "wish to buy." Lack is the fuel of commerce and also its undoing; lack for the buyer means appetite and for the one who cannot buy means destitution. The stocks, near which the hawker plies his wares, betoken the threat beneath enticement: for those who fall outside the law or the margins of economic competence, the city has prepared a disciplinary corrective.

But note how the poet turns an empty purse to plenty. She who lacks everything but mother wit, whose extreme lack has occasioned both her departure from the city and her metaphorical death, writes a poem whose method is that of *copia*. She contrives, by the sheer force of speech act, to make the whole burgeoning inventory of urban plenty pass through her hands:

> To all the Bookebinders by Paulles
> because I lyke their Arte:

They evry weeke shal mony have,
when they from Bookes depart.
Amongst them all, my Printer must,
have somewhat to his share:
I wyll my Friends these Bookes to bye
of him, with other ware.

Isabella Whitney is not the first to expose the legal document ("will") as a vehicle for the capricious exercise and intractable constraint of individual purpose ("will"), but the particular pressure she puts on the paradox, her complex staging of personal insufficiency and resilience, is like no other I know. The city, she writes in a preamble to her Will, "never yet, woldst credit geve" nor "help wold finde, / to ease me in distress," and yet, in the spirit of forgiveness and witty one-upmanship, she makes London her "sole executor." What is more, she makes London the unrivaled darling of her poem: she addresses the city as one might address a cruel beloved (thou "never yet . . . hadst pitie," she writes); she blazons the city's noises, textures, and rhythms as one might blazon the beloved's eyes and lips.

Isabella Whitney wrote for money at a time when women in England did not do such things, though some few aristocratic women translated Psalms or circulated Petrarchan lyrics in manuscript. Whitney published her intimate acquaintance with the topography and commerce of the city when such details were thought to be sordid and knowledge of them discrediting to her sex. At a time when women had very limited powers under the law to own or convey "real property" at all, she contrived in "The Manner of Her Will" a proprietary interest in the material life around her. She made social and economic vulnerability the ground of rhetorical strength:

And though I nothing named have,
to bury mee withall:
Consider that above the ground,
annoyance bee I shall.
And let me have a shrowding Sheete
to cover mee from shame:
And in oblvyon bury mee
and never more mee name.

Imagining, and forcing the reader to imagine, the naked display of her own dead body, the poet turns shame to moral advantage. She is no confessionalist, God knows; she works at the opposite end of the spectrum. But she pioneers a salient technique: undressing in public, strategically.

Whitney's prosodic choices are telling as well. She composes "The Manner of Her Will" in ballad meter, a popular and populist verse form: iambic tetrameter alternating with trimeter, the trimeter lines end-rhymed. The lowly origins and ubiquity of the form are well-suited to the urban traffic Whitney takes as both her subject and her setting: ballads were sold on the street in Whitney's London like other cheap consumer goods. Ballads were also the repositories of folk memory and popular performance, very much at odds with the sheltered decorums thought to be appropriate for literate women in the sixteenth century, at odds also with the sobriety and high seriousness expected of last wills and testaments.

In a world that measured privilege by the power to withdraw from common public life, Whitney flaunted her immersion in the color and noise of urban commerce. In a world that measured womanhood by its powers of modulated restraint, Whitney practiced exorbitant indecorums. She wrote in her poetic "Will" an oppositional portrait of the system that ruthlessly preserved disparities of privilege and well-being. She invented a public self and a mode of public speaking-on-the-page that England would not see again for nearly a hundred years. To the city that rejected her, she wrote a knowing and exuberant love letter, a letter, and a love, that left that city considerably richer than she had found it.

❦

In 1935, Yale University Press published a book called *Theory of Flight*, the newest winner of the Yale Younger Poets Award. Like many a first book, it was built around the story of the poet's coming-into-consciousness. But this particular poet, whose aptitude for inwardness and finely calibrated lyric cadence are manifest throughout her book, scorned to trade on the easy beauties of private sensibility. Or, more precisely, she scorned to think that consciousness worth the name had been born in familial or ruminative isolation. "Prinzip's year bore us," she writes in "Poem out of Childhood"; "see us turning at breast / quietly while the air throbs over Sarajevo." Gavrilo Prinzip, Serbian nationalist, assassinated the Austrian Archduke Ferdinand in

Sarajevo in 1914, plunging Europe, by a series of missteps and inadvertencies, into a disastrous world war. Muriel Rukeyser—it is she who writes—was six months old at the time.

"Not Sappho. Sacco," she writes. Nicola Sacco, of Sacco and Vanzetti, Italian anarchists executed in Massachusetts, 1927, for murders they may never have committed. Presiding over the poet's coming-into-voice-and-awareness was not an esteemed lyric forebear, "with her drowned hair trailing along Greek waters, / weed binding it, a fillet of kelp enclosing / the temples' ardent fruit," not the muse of erotic fecundity and victim of erotic passion, but the symbol and victim (as was widely believed) of ethnic and political hatred, of American justice shamefully perverted. "[W]e were a generation of grim children," writes the poet; a violent world was "smearing [its] centuries upon our hands."

Rukeyser was a journalist as well as a poet. She covered the Scottsboro trial in Alabama, the eve of Civil War in Spain, the opening of the Golden Gate Bridge in San Francisco. In 1936, she traveled to Gauley Bridge, West Virginia, to cover an outbreak of silicosis among the miners there. What she saw in Gauley Bridge she could not contain in either the journal article or the lyric poem as she had heretofore construed it. What she saw required her to shatter old decorums and forge a new poetic form; what she wrote was "The Book of the Dead." The sequence records not only the spectacle of harrowing illness and impoverishment but the more invidious spectacle of indifference and collusion: while the miners were breathing the silicon dust that would kill them, their employers were suppressing information about the danger in their mines. Rukeyser wished to find a place in poetry for the experience of people who did not produce a literature of their own, who had neither political, social, nor economic power. She wrote in a quasi-documentary mode, using materials from her own interviews with the dying and their families, from letters and news reports, from transcripts of congressional hearings, from stock reports in the *New York Times*.

One section of the poem is cast as a blues ballad, art form of the dispossessed. The poet juxtaposes clinical description with highly personal testimony. She allows herself very few moments of direct commentary, affecting instead the transparency of an archivist or court reporter. This transparency is a fiction, of course, but one that is immensely important to Rukeyser, both ethically and aesthetically. It gives her control over tone; it allows her to step aside and say, in effect, this is not my story, I am not the one who is important here, but I (and you, too, Reader) are emphatically responsible.

Sometimes in "The Book of the Dead," an embedded stage direction will suggest a private interview, or a private moment in public deposition:

> This is the X-ray picture taken last April.
> I would point out to you: these are the ribs;
> this is the region of the breastbone;
> this is the heart (a wide white shadow filled with blood).
> . . . .
> Come to the window again. Here is the heart.
> More numerous nodules, thicker, see, in the upper lobes.
> You will notice the increase : here, streaked fibrous tissue—
>
> Indicating?
>
> That indicates the progress in ten months' time.
> And now, this year—short breathing, solid scars
> even over the ribs, thick on both sides.

Other passages speak directly through the voices of the victims:

> "It is growing worse every day. At night
> "I get up to catch my breath. If I remained
> "flat on my back I believe I would die."

Yet others mimic the subdued adversarial pull of a formal deposition or courtroom interrogation:

> It gradually chokes off the air cells in the lungs?
> I am trying to say it the best I can.
> That is what happens, isn't it?
> A choking-off in the air cells?
>
> Yes
> There is difficulty in breathing.
> Yes.

> And a painful cough?
>
> Yes.
>
> Does silicosis cause death?
>
> Yes, sir.

The victims of the Gauley Bridge silicosis disaster were black and white, men (the miners) and women (their wives and mothers), old (dependent parents) and young (dependent children). Those who died were in the prime of life; their death was the by-product of economic and social class. "Yes, sir" is a line of painful penetration: the deference of the witness, the protocols of deposition, the stateliness of the law stand in ghastly contrast to the broken social contract. And so it is throughout "The Book of the Dead," whose abutments and oppositions capture the interlocking logic of deathwatch and market watch, capital and labor, free breathing and the breath that will not come. The poem's faceted panels of genre and point of view aspire to something like wholeness, insisting that wholeness is never abstract but grounded and material. "I remember being asked what grit was," wrote Rukeyser of her school days, "and I said 'number 4 gravel' when I was supposed to say 'courage.'" She wrote "The Book of the Dead" without sentimentality, without condescension, without the consolations of private disavowal or easy irony. It must have been hard to keep irony under wraps sometimes: the 1930s rural poor still spoke with respect to authority.

Rukeyser's active writing life spanned more than forty years. She wrote about love, about war, about slave revolts and labor strikes, philology, physics, and Harry Houdini. She distrusted, even mocked, the model of poetic calling that depends upon privileged sensibility and sanctified retreat from the ordinary run of human affairs:

> All the voices of the wood called "Muriel!"
> but it was soon solved;   it was nothing, it was not for me.
> The words were a little like Mortal and More and Endure
> and a word like Real, a sound like Health or Hell.

Rukeyser's lifelong commitment to social activism was born, in part, of her particular historical moment, of place and time and intellectual context, but it was also in her DNA, as central to cognitive process as were her gifts for image and idiom. The murderous inequities of power and well-being that afflict the social landscape were as constant in her consciousness as in the world around her. When she wrote, she wrote in the syntax of human affairs as natively as in poetic line. This deep marriage of political and lyric consciousness will always, I expect, be rare. Rukeyser's example is not, in any straightforward sense, a model for emulation. It is nevertheless a tonic example. Take "Islands," a late poem, quarreling with its title: "O for God's sake / they are connected / underneath."

⁂

A book entitled *Citizen* might seem to fall too easily into the present survey, but there is nothing easy about the book in question or the spirit in which it bears its name. The author, Andrew Feld, is well and wittily aware of the contradiction thought to exist between poetic contemplation and civic solidarity. "You think of Thoreau," he writes, "steering his solitudes / through the fields . . . of the Lower Cape," eschewing the roadways that betoken "habit / and a slavish disposition." Thoreau of the independent view, Thoreau the Georgic anchorite. "So it comes as a surprise," writes the poet, mildly, "to learn that he had / a companion." Not to mention a mother who did the wash. "He had / a companion, as I did." As to the alternate posture, the writer-immersed-in-the-lives-of-the-masses, Feld is equally wry: "At this point," he writes, apropos of nothing much more than hanging out with the locals after the tourists have gone, "I would like to state my solidarity with the working classes."

Citizen: the word derives from city, one who dwells there and enjoys its rights. Historically, the term has been used to distinguish civilians from soldiery, masters from apprentices, denizens from transients, those who live by commerce from those who own the land. "A man of trade," wrote Samuel Johnson in his dictionary, "not a gentleman." The word therefore is shot through with division: inside is preferred to out, wealth preferred to poverty, greater wealth to wealth. Feld's readers, of course, will understand the term more broadly, in the modern sense: the citizen is one who belongs to the nation, not merely to its densest settlements; the citizen has rights and obligations not governed, in theory, by guild or regulated trade. But the commonwealth is still a common good that depends upon exclusions, exclusions as ruthless as were London's when Isabella Whitney lost her place.

The country to which Feld belongs, the—or is it these?—United States, is built like any other on contradiction: inclusiveness and xenophobia, "equality" and envy, unity and severalness; note the ambiguous grammatical number that characterizes our very name. Contradiction can be generative, a kind of tensile strength or provocation. It can also be a sorry liability, productive of nothing but shame, inaptitude, and incoherence. Of one particular period when incoherence seemed to reign—morass in Cambodia and Vietnam, break-ins and cover-ups and payoffs at home—Feld has written a national portrait-in-verse, part satire, part lament, and three parts paradox: a study of the treacheries that bind us. The poem is "Best and Only"; its first part is "The Ship of State." Which sails on a river, as if to escape the clamor of public affairs:

> The way a carp's speckled brown and white head
> flashes just below the surface of the Potomac
> night waters, Richard Nixon's penis almost enters
>
> the national consciousness, as a thin gold thread
> of urine stitches him to an August night in 1973,
> on the stern of the *Sequoia*. Standing beside him
>
> is the Cuban financier Bebe Rebozo, who is also
> pissing into the river. The image is a small shame
> in the middle of many greater ones: the damp dots
>
> on his pants as he shakes off with an awkward
> drunk step back and zips up: the president pissing
> on the Republic, over which he stands.

Pastoral was always the genre of city folk, the simple life a fantasy of power elites.

"The Ship of State" is all third-person, a telling choice for a portrait of intimate friendship, but the voice passes through a series of shifting perspectives, allied now with one accidental witness and now with another. From narrative omniscience, endowed as it is with hindsight and opinion, the stanzas migrate to the sight line of the on-call secret service agent, "trained to see elsewhere" while guarding the men on the boat, and then to the hippie playing Frisbee on the riverbank, who

> mistakes the drunken laughter
> of two old men in a boat for the drunken laughter
> of two old men in a boat, unaware that History
>
> is passing so close he's breathing its exhaust . . .

As are we all, the poem would say; it has blackened our lungs. Along the poem's Potomac, each corroborating extra adds his bit of the night to the whole.

The title "Best and Only" refers in the first instance to the friendship between the poem's two center-stage personae: Bebe Rebozzo and Richard Milhaus Nixon. One of these men also happened to be the president of the United States: we only get them one at a time, so each is for his time perforce the best we have. One man, fallible like the rest of us or even, it seems, more fallible than any other score of us, comes for better or worse to stand for the whole. Feld does not dwell on the unhappy commonplace: the incommensurate scales of moral stature and political consequence. He does dwell upon, or rather ruefully performs, the import of that commonplace, its effect upon the dynamic construction and reformulation of community. Historically, Richard Nixon was a master of paranoia: his secret enemies list became a not-so-exclusive club of doubters and dissidents, investigative journalists, critics of the war in Southeast Asia, social progressives, "Eastern elites," and public intellectuals. The secret leaked: to appear on the list became a badge of honor; to be left off came to feel like a slight. The enemies list was a scandal and a joke, but Nixon was not wrong about the league he fantasized: of people whose motives varied widely and were even at odds, of people joined in action and people acting separately, of activists and contemplatives, of people with nothing in common but loathing of his policies and methods, the president made a nation. From section 2 of "Best and Only":

> Protesters under the cherry trees: notice
> how each fallen petal rots from the inside
> with a small brown dot on its delicate center-seam,
> like a piece of used toilet paper:
> so corruption is essential in us. It's in our guts.
>
> ("From the Apocrypha of Bebe Rebozo")

Nothing is more common than the community forged by contempt. Default, oppositional, the social body is also retroactive, grounded in common memory of a shameful era.

And even a shameful era is profoundly mixed: bad and better, harmful and innocuous, funny and lame, all of it food for nostalgia. The third and final section of "Best and Only" is an abecedarian elegy for the whole of the gorgeous, botched, youth-fearing, youth-idolizing, contradictory American century:

> Apollo. Bebe Rebozo. Beatniks.
> The Car. . . .
>   . . . The century
> when Oral Sex came into its own.
> The Overdose. *People*. Peaceniks.
> Plutonim. Post-. Pop-. Plastic-wrapped
> bundles of cocaine washing up
> on Florida beaches. . . .
>   . . . Watergate. World Wars. The X ray.
> Yeah Yeah Yeah. Zen Koan. Ground Zero.

The choral refrain does not resolve to a solace of hail and farewell. Fellow feeling is here, to be sure, and pity for our shared and chronic adolescence, but so is the sting.

Feld is especially deft at rendering the complexities of common cultural reference and private divides, the process by which the self discovers its own nature in the social field. In poem called "Two Chapters," in the resonant nave of San Giorgio Maggiore, buoyed by their fragmentary memory of Euclidean optics and Palladian perspective and every art historical book they have ever consulted on transept and vault, the speaker and his companion eavesdrop on another pair of tourists. They hear enough to be appalled, to think they've glimpsed the desiccated heart of the others' relationship, and to thank their lucky stars for that which makes them different. The moment unfolds, the couples exchange no word or overt glance. And after all, the pair that guides us through their poem, the pair with whom we feel allied, discover they have misjudged. What had seemed like one thing was something else altogether; our pair catches the trace of sorrows and kindnesses they had not been generous enough to read for. A small moment, and no open transgression or harm. But a moment worthy of Henry James in what it reveals of the soul. "Awful," writes the poet, "and unasked for, these sudden, sidelong glimpses of the self."

⚜

In their different methods and different cultural moments, Whitney, Rukeyser, and Feld cannot be made to add up to a single poetic; their example is neither unified nor prescriptive. But their work, in all its agility and conceptual range, does free us from a debilitating premise about the self. We may, though we needn't, consult high theory to find what we find in the lyric poem: that the self or first person is not, in the first instance, singular. Like language, it is social at inception. It *emerges* as singular in the process of social encounter and social thinking-through, in the byways of longing and recoil, in the shocks of recognition. The first person is born of the second and born again of the third. It is learned, it is made, it is less a home than a mode of navigation. In this it resembles the poem.

A Place for People in Lyric Poetry

You may remember from some twenty years ago the PBS series entitled *Voices & Visions*, which set about presenting documentaries of thirteen classic American poets—from Walt Whitman to Sylvia Plath. Not all the presentations are of equal value, though the one on Wallace Stevens is, I think, especially good. And its beginning, its opening interview, is especially revealing. The first interviewee is a salty old New Englander who worked with Stevens for many years at the Hartford Accident and Indemnity Company. You will recall that Stevens was an executive in and a lawyer for the company, his legal opinions themselves achieving a kind of rationalist poetry and ranking as models of judgments. (And there is a picture, by the way, taken in 1938, of all the officers of the company posing as if graduating. In the picture, it is clear that Stevens's reputation for intimidation of his colleagues is not based simply on an intellectual superiority; he literally towers, in height, over his fellows.) Anyway, the retired old fellow being interviewed starts off, in answer to the question: What do you remember most about Wallace Stevens? by saying, in one of those inimitable Connecticut Yankee accents, "Well, if you don't count his personal life, I guess you could say Stevens was a happy man."

The term *personal* comes, of course, from the same root as person, persona, and personality, all of which, at their base, harken to the common sense of saving face, putting a face on, wearing a mask, and so forth. W. B. Yeats speaks of the poet—the first person of the poet—as revealing him or herself only through the manifestation of the mask—perhaps, even, the manipulation of the mask: the way he, W. B. Yeats, personally, writes acutely from intense autobiographic, ennobling experience, yet writes theatrically too, as if he and Maud Gonne and Robert Gregory and whomever were dramatic personae or characters on the stage of the event we create as a poem.

We sat together at one summer's end,
That beautiful mild woman, your close friend,

And you and I, and talked of poetry.
I said, "A line will take us hours maybe;
Yet if it does not seem a moment's thought,
Our stitching and unstitching has been naught.

What does it matter that the two women in this poem, "Adam's Curse," are real people—Maud Gonne and her, in fact, sister, Kathleen Pilcher? In the poem they are figures, masks of their real-life selves, so to speak. What does it matter that they are not named as such—though the naming of literal figures in our poems would become an American habit with William Carlos Williams—that they have only an implicit identity? What does matter, I think, is that these two women are not inventions, are not expressly anonymous ("That beautiful mild woman"), are not made up for some imagined convenience for the author, who himself is the speaker-actor in the "drama," and who is musing over what, at this moment, he is doing, which is the writing of and perfection of a poem—employing, I might add, an analogy of perceived women's domesticity: their happy art of stitching and unstitching; like the work of the real teaching nuns in "Among School Children," teachers he observed when Yeats was an Irish senator checking out the quality of Irish education.

What does matter is that, like language itself, the people, the human figures in and of our poems, testify by their authenticating presences to a real etymology, a true history, an actual source in our experience, whatever necessary transformative powers intervene. The distortion, refraction, mask, or protective coloring of our sources should not lead us away from the truth of the face under the face, the fact of what is behind the mask. How much difference does it make that Maud Gonne's "friend," in the example above, is in real life her sister? The truth of the poem is that Kathleen Pilcher is also Maud's "close friend" and that "friend" rhymes with the monosyllable "end."

Our concern here is what to do with how the people in our lives live in our poems. Stevens lamented once—and I paraphrase—that life is a problem of people and that that was what was missing in his poems: this problem, those people. Warm bodies. I happen to think that there are lots of warm bodies in Stevens; even the snow man, it seems to me, is a warm body. What Stevens may be, indirectly, lamenting is his "personal" life, the other person in it, and who knows how many missing persons. As a young man, Stevens fell in love with a face, the mask of a face on the Liberty Dime: Elsie Moll was her name, and she became, for this poet, his chief antagonist, a living manifestation of the illusion of beauty, even the necessary angel of the imagination. They were, apparently, completely incompatible. Yet she serves Stevens's poetry as a kind of inspiriter, a conspirator, if you will, an antithetical muse, who underwrites what I find to be Stevens's deep emotional stoicism. "It is an illusion that we were ever alive," he writes in one of his last poems. "Regard the freedom of seventy years ago. / It is no longer air. The houses still stand, / Though they are rigid in rigid emptiness." These poignant lines are from a poem that immediately follows, in the *Complete Poems*, "Final Soliloquy of the Interior Paramour," Stevens's most beautiful lyric of self-reference and isolation, and his singular embrace of the reader who is or is not there:

Light the first light of evening, as in a room
In which we rest and, for small reason, think
The world imagined is the ultimate good.

This is, therefore, the intensest rendezvous.
It is in that thought that we collect ourselves,
Out of all the indifferences, into one thing:

Within a single thing, a single shawl
Wrapped tightly round us, since we are poor, a warmth,
A light, a power, the miraculous influence.

Here, now, we forget each other and ourselves.
We feel the obscurity of an order, a whole,
A knowledge, that which arranged the rendezvous.

Within its vital boundary, in the mind,
We say God and the imagination are one . . .
How high that highest candle lights the dark.

Out of this same light, out of the central mind,
We make a dwelling in the evening air,
In which being there together is enough.

When John Keats, in the nightingale ode, makes reference to the world "Here, where men sit and hear each other groan;/Where palsy shakes a few, sad, last grey hairs,/Where youth grows pale, and spectre-thin, and dies:/ Where but to think is to be full of sorrow"—when Keats sets the stage this way, we know he is alluding to his brother Tom, dead just months before of the "wasting disease"; and we know that he knows that he is becoming ill of likely the same symptoms, symptoms that have and will have consequences within his family; and we know how much of his medical training is backed up behind the image of the sad, last grey hairs of the old and dying, an age he will never be. I believe it is not so much the degree to which the people in our lives show up in our poems, but the degree to which they stand behind them. The degree to which those who inspire us or conspire with us can become powerful and useful archetypes—not with a capital A but a quieter, intimate lower case tension, antagonism, or presence, someone wholly other.

Robert Lowell asks: "Yet why not say what happened?" Which, I think, is different from asking, to whom did it happen. Lowell's good and great poems, for me, become less good the more they literalize, or claim to, the people breaking his heart or whose hearts he is breaking. And it may sound absurd that John Berryman should disavow any autobiographic connection to his Henry figure in the *Dream Songs*. But he does, and I see his point: of course the poems are about Berryman, but Berryman as Henry, no less than Berryman as Mistress Bradstreet. The actual people, places, and things name-dropped in *Dream Songs* are coincidental to the double identity of poet and persona. Just as there is no such point of view as omniscience in poetry, there is only the limited knowledge of the first-person pronoun, however that pronoun is manifested through its various masks: I, you, he, she, Henry, et al. And that knowledge is limited by and to those people in those landscapes, in those houses, in those rooms we share and suffer. The protagonist-antagonist relationship is the fundamental meaningful tension in a poem, whether the human arrangement is between us and other people directly or us and other people indirectly, with a bird or an urn or a god intervening. "I cannot live with you—/ It would be life," writes Dickinson, but the poem, #640, cannot live without the "you." I know lots of things, says Stevens, including "noble accents" and "lucid, inescapable rhythms;/ But I know, too,/That the blackbird is involved/In what I know"; and what I know is that "A man and a woman/Are one," even if you add a blackbird.

When Stevens asks us to take off our square-hats and put on our sombreros, he is asking us to forgo our four-cornered superior rationalism in favor of the roundness, the connectiveness, the familiars of the imagination. For the literalists who see Sylvia Plath as a confessional poet and her poems as therapy for a lost father, an obsessive mother, or an unfaithful husband—they should look again at the brilliant art of the brilliant poems. Should look again at the living hand of the poet at work, shaping her material out of the clay that represents the flesh and blood of her life. Should look again at the conversion of the material into the archetypal, the father, for instance, into figure. The imagination makes from its sources, not the other way around. No poet, however manifest, is ever alone in his or her poem. Sonnets, elegies, odes, the textual landscapes of the love, grief, and thought as feeling: none of these forms are possible without other people, whether announced, alluded to, or acknowledged by their absence. People are where the narrative comes from, even when language apparently supersedes every motive behind the poem's making: narrative is the movement of and between sentences, fragments, the words themselves.

Stevens, of all poets, asks:

> What is the function of the poet? Certainly it is not to lead people
> out of the confusion in which they find themselves. Nor is it, I think,
> to comfort them while they follow their readers to and fro. I think
> that the poet's function is to make his imagination theirs and that he
> fulfills himself only as he sees his imagination become the light in the
> minds of others. His role, in short, is to help people live their lives.

And how does the poet reconcile this apparent high-minded intention with the high calling of art?—well, one way is by making sure that the people in and of our poems are worthy of the attention of the people reading them. But not because, as subjects, they are virtuous, but because they are vital: because our imaginations have made them—and ourselves—worth the bother of our art.

And worthy in the way that "It is not upon you alone the dark patches fall, / The dark threw its patches down upon me also," as Walt Whitman puts it. And worthy in the way that you broke your appointment and "did not come ... as the hope-hour struck its sum, / You did not come," as Thomas Hardy says. And worthy in the way that

> For most of us, there is only the unattended
> Moment, the moment in and out of time,
> The distraction fit, lost in a shaft of sunlight,
> The wild thyme unseen, or the winter lightning
> Or the waterfall, or music heard so deeply,
> That it is not heard at all, but you are the music
> While the music lasts

as Eliot writes in the third of the great *Four Quartets*.

A Mind for Metaphors

Drawing diagrams I measured
Movements of the stars;
Though her tender flesh is near
Her mind I cannot measure.

Sometime in the seventeenth century, the sixth Dalai Lama wrote this brief but revealing poem about the problem of people. The poem's orderly division in two neat halves enacts the struggle to impose a form, or "measure," upon the unknowable woman sitting right beside the narrator. We long to take the measure of someone else's mind, but lack the tools for gaining the access we seek. Need to solve or settle your lover's essential strangeness? Sorry, no measuring device exists. The devices and strategies we count on to chart the stars are quite useless under love's circumstances. Does it matter that the brief life of the sixth Dalai Lama was as divided as this little poem? Dalai Lama by day, he was a lover of women, intoxicants, adventure by night. It would be easy to draw a connection between the life of his poems and the facts of his life. But one of the problems with people is that we all too often misinterpret. When poetry addresses the difficulty of knowing others, or even of knowing ourselves, what is at the heart of the problem? The tools we use, of course.

Fundamentally alone, reliant on our senses and on how we interpret what the senses provide, still we seek connection and contact, we crave the touch of those we love. Mistakes abound as we reach toward others. The eye has a natural blind spot, so we never stop reconfiguring what we see, and our revisions inevitably impose forms or narratives upon experience. Governed by a restless interior life, we interpret, reflect, and re-enact a wealth of sensory information, comparing new impressions, revising older ones. To record these impressions is our human compulsion, our homage to the world as it passes through us and disappears. And besides, this comforts us. We structure and compose our lives, in part, to interpret and calm the chaos that assaults our nervous systems. We know, like Milton, that "The mind is its own place, and in itself / Can make a heaven of hell, a hell of heaven." But a single sensation, a neurological perception of a stimulus, like an odor, lasts only an instant. It is episodic rather than narrative. Because no one apprehends sensory impressions in quite the same way as I do, you are mistaken if you believe you see what I see. But when we make language out of sensation, we reach across the boundaries between us. Representing the world alters it, even transforms it, and that transformation allows others to make sense of our sensations. So when I seek to represent the world, I turn intentionally toward metaphor.

Derived from a Greek word that means "carrying across," metaphor brings something new into being by linking two known things, and by insisting upon the similarity embedded in difference. The connections we forge suggest how two things are alike, but the success of metaphor depends on essential difference. In other words, to make metaphor is to insist on a necessary error. In "In Memory of W. B. Yeats," Auden makes such a gesture, endowing Yeats's poems with their own life and agency in the lines "By mourning tongues / The death of the poet was kept from his poems." Absent their maker these poems scatter across the world, take on new interpretation, are internalized and digested by new readers. And more than that: what Franz Kafka says in a letter to Felice Bauer ("I am made of literature") is how Auden transforms Yeats after death:

> Now he is scattered among a hundred cities
> And wholly given over to unfamiliar affections,
> To find his happiness in another kind of wood
> And be punished under a foreign code of conscience.
> The words of a dead man
> Are modified in the guts of the living.

Now the poet's body is changed, utterly; witness Auden mapping it, laying out an electrified country that zone by zone fades and loses power. Here he underscores how the body shuts down even while Yeats's poems live:

> But for him it was his last afternoon as himself,
> An afternoon of nurses and rumours;
> The provinces of his body revolted,

The squares of his mind were empty,
Silence invaded the suburbs,
The current of his feeling failed; he became his admirers.

Poetry asks its readers for a species of double vision, as two things become a third and yet continue to remain themselves. Etymologically, the word error, or errancy, is related to the Latin *errare*, to wander (which, according to Linda Gregerson, provides the source for the phrase "knight errant"). Mental wandering, the mind at play, and the seemingly accidental associations that emerge from wandering: these are the tools we use to create the collage that corresponds to our selves. In this way, both metaphor and contemplation arise from the same fertile ground. Poetic leaping has long been recognized as conceptually illogical, even irrational. For evidence of this, look to Aristotle, who says those who make metaphor embrace a necessary madness. Anne Carson explores these ideas in her poem, "Essay on What I Think about Most":

Lots of people including Aristotle think error
an interesting and valuable mental event.
In his discussion of metaphor in the *Rhetoric*
Aristotle said there are 3 kinds of words.
Strange, ordinary, and metaphorical.

"Strange words simply puzzle us;
ordinary words convey what we know already;
it is from metaphor that we can get hold of something new & fresh"
(*Rhetoric*, 1410b10–13).
In what does the freshness of metaphor consist?
Aristotle says that metaphor causes the mind to experience itself

in the act of making a mistake.

Later in the same poem she extends the field of discussion even further:

So a poet like Alkman
sidesteps fear, anxiety, shame, remorse
and all the other silly emotions associated with making mistakes

in order to engage
the fact of the matter.
The fact of the matter for humans is imperfection.

Our lapses, our missteps, our omissions, our errors of the mind, all of these
deeply engage us. But "fear, anxiety, shame, remorse, / and all the other silly
emotions" do not cease to be present in poetry simply because we aspire to
understand ourselves. Indeed, self-understanding often conflicts with the
contrary evidence the senses provide.

Through multiple encounters with flux and contingency in John Berryman's *Dream Songs*, but particularly in "Dream Song 29," Berryman's poems
capture states of psychological confusion. In "Dream Song 29," Henry is
alert and worried, the poem emerging out of confusion, the weight and pressure of sorrow:

> There sat down, once, a thing on Henry's heart
> só heavy, if he had a hundred years
> & more, & weeping, sleepless, in all them time
> Henry could not make good.

It's as if he's emerged in terror from a psychotic state, a hallucination, or a
dream, and now wonders what he's said or done, whom he's killed, or failed
to save. He seeks the error that has yet to happen. He knows he's the cause
of some trauma, but cannot locate the event. In the middle of the poem, he
struggles to interpret the images insistently present in his head:

> And there is another thing he has in mind
> like a grave Sienese face a thousand years
> would fail to blur the still profiled reproach of. Ghastly,
> with open eyes, he attends, blind.
> All the bells say: too late. This is not for tears;
> thinking.

Dreams emerge into daylight not whole but filled with gaps in the narrative. How much is he responsible for remembering? What responsibility does
he bear for the lives of other people in the poem? What kind of emotional
work must he do in order to preserve those people he might unintentionally

kill? What are his dreams telling him? There is a story trying to emerge in this poem, and Berryman's achievement lies in how he thwarts its emergence. The sensory details in the poem support this confusion: a "little cough" here, "an odor" there, "a chime," so that all memory-making filters through a complex and uneasy synesthesia. The past is at the edge of recall, is not easily manifested, and certainly not to be relied upon. No wonder Berryman's poems so frequently adopt a role to play or a mask to wear. Under pressure, the face we present to the world depends on the course of the weather.

Critics and psychoanalysts who talk about the connection between dreams, free association, word play, and "hidden" truth, often link creativity and chaos, as Adam Phillips does in *Promises, Promises:*

> Our dreams and the poetry we write (and speak) verge on incoherence and nonsense; the moments when sense begins to turn, or fade, also define us. Going out of bounds might be as close as we can get to that recurrent fear of being other-minded which seems also to be a wish. The unconscious describes an apprehension that there are other minds—other, that is, than the one we easily recognize—going on inside us; that there is something inside us, and between ourselves and other people, that is forever verging on incoherence and nonsense.

Berryman's Henry both knows and fails to know his own mind. The *Dream Songs* play out this unreliability, suggesting that not only do we not know our closest companions, we do not know ourselves in a fixed or daylight manner. In these poems knowledge is momentary, and our only assurance is that the next poem's truth will have mutated. Dream images: how real are they, how much weight do they have in our waking lives? How are the landscapes of dreams like the landscapes created by poetic metaphor? In their compression, weight, and symbolic logic, dreams are our nighttime errancy.

> He knows: he went over everyone, & nobody's missing.
> Often he reckons, in the dawn, them up.
> Nobody is ever missing.

As long ago as 1621, Robert Burton recognized that how we describe ourselves depends on the circumstances, the audience, and on the shifts and tides in our emotional lives. While hallucinations and paranoid visions certainly take place on sanity's far edge, Burton knows that emotional experience occurs over a large continuum. We are all subject, at one time or another, to wrong impressions: sometimes we misunderstand each other, sometimes all the "senses are troubled, [we] think [we] see, hear, smell, and touch that which [we] do not...." (*Anatomy of Melancholy*) Going further along the spectrum of symptoms, Burton describes a series of patients who can no longer distinguish between the metaphoric and the material world: some are afraid that "they are all glass, and therefore will suffer no man to come near them: that they are all cork, as light as feathers; others as heavy as lead; some are afraid their heads will fall off their shoulders, that they have frogs in their bellies, etc." One definition of madness: to believe one's own body has the capacity to be utterly transformed, indeed, made metaphoric.

If metaphor is the necessary semantic mistake, the madness that connects us, then it might be useful to consider two contending theories of mind, one lately espoused by Daniel Dennett, one by the contrarian philosopher Galen Strawson. In brief, the argument looks like this: Dennett and others like psychologist Jerry Bruner and neurologist Oliver Sacks suggest that we construct identity around the stories we tell about ourselves, and to ourselves. Writing in 1988 in the *Times Literary Supplement*, Dennett claims that "we are all virtuoso novelists, who find ourselves engaged in all sorts of behaviour, and we always try to put the best 'faces' on it we can. We try to make all of our material cohere into a single good story.... The chief fictional character at the centre of that autobiography is one's self."

Galen Strawson doesn't mind the notion that some of us seek to create coherent narratives about our lives. Of course we do. What he disputes is the assumption that such a narrative-driven life is the best or most moral way to live—because, as Dennett believes, it provides a structure by which we achieve mature personhood. Instead, Strawson seeks to operate under another framework, as an "episodic" personality rather than a "narrative personality." He says:

> If one is Episodic ... one does not figure oneself, considered as a self, as something that was there in the (further) past and will be there in the (further) future, although one is perfectly well aware that one has long-term *continuity* considered as a whole human being.

Episodics are likely to have no particular tendency to see their life in Narrative terms.

Genuinely disinterested in narrative self-fashioning, Strawson believes instead that episodic personalities prefer to live more exclusively in the present tense. I'll leap here and suggest that an episodic frame of mind is also a lyric frame of mind. Reading a lyric poem, we experience an illusion of stopped time, of radical subjectivity. The subjective lyric "I" is not traveling on a straight road of progress toward a good life, but is more likely to be in the midst of momentary drama or crisis, to be, in fact, in the midst of a mistake. Or, as Adam Phillips says, "We are not continually making mistakes, we are continually making alternate lives" (*On Flirtation*). Or, as Randall Jarrell says, "And yet, the ways we miss our lives are life" ("A Girl in a Library").

One further claim about the nature of both metaphor and perception comes from Victor Shklovsky, in his 1917 essay "Art as Technique," in which he advocates an art of "defamiliarization":

> The purpose of art is to impart the sensation of things as they are perceived and not as they are known. The technique of art is to make objects "unfamiliar," to make forms difficult, to increase the difficulty and length of perception because the process of perception is an aesthetic end in itself and must be prolonged.

Perception: how do you represent it? Here is Anne Carson again:

> Sokrates' central argument, as he goes on to reevaluate madness, is that you keep your mind to yourself at the cost of closing out the gods. Truly good and indeed divine things are alive and active outside you and should be let in to work their changes. Such incursions formally instruct and enrich our lives in society; no prophet or healer or poet could practice his art if he did not lose his mind, Sokrates says. (*Eros the Bittersweet*)

Someone with a narrative sensibility might be inclined to see fragmentation or defamiliarization as symptoms of madness. But the nature of metaphor itself leads us toward an episodic understanding of a poem. Berryman's poems give us the experience of living in the midst of perception. This is a feature of his lyric personality. It's the wellspring of both pain and the beauty that emerges from pain. Unreliable, momentary, subject to interpretation, not bound to be final and fixed from one version to another, from writer to reader, each poem is a translation of selfhood.

When we are feeling at a loss in a poem, metaphor comes to the rescue. Metaphor is instructive, tactical, and interactive; it succeeds when its audience sees it as both strange and true. We need metaphor to make the error that allows us to reach beyond ourselves. As a final example, consider Sally Mann's recent photographs of the landscape of the American South. "Using damaged lenses and a camera that requires [her] to use her hand as a shutter, these photographs are marked by the scratches, light leaks, and shifts in focus that were part of the photographic process as it developed during the nineteenth century" (from the PBS documentary). These "light leaks" around the edge of the images create an effect of haze known as "vignetting." What are the implications of haze? Can haze suggest a method of perception? In *Deep South: Landscapes of Mississippi and Louisiana*, Mann's images are scratched, blurred, tear-glazed. They compel us to look intently at subjects that can be difficult, at first, to identify or interpret. In one photograph, a tree is scarred by a horizontal wound across its trunk, as if it had been slashed by a bayonet and left standing. In the background, prosaic wire cattle fencing marks a field's boundary and provides a horizon line for the photograph. We want to be able to "read" this image coherently, but a landscape can tell many stories. It's like seeing with eyes that are flawed, and emotional; these photographs invite us, much as Berryman's poems do, into a world damaged by the past and confused in the present. These photographs bear the marks of both their method and their maker. If indeed "the fact of the matter for humans is imperfection," Mann forges a direct link between emotion and imperfection. In the same way, the lyric poem stands in the present with all the attendant errors of perception that immediacy and emotion permit.

4. On Subject, Story, and Style: The Problem of Time

Send me out into another life
lord because this one is growing faint
I do not think it goes all the way

W. S. MERWIN

To Think of Time

Time defines us. Time binds us. Yet time is not an element of nature. It does not exist in and of itself, as a material substance, like a sycamore does or a muon. It is an immaterial measurement of the relationships of material substances; and—this is important—it is an entity wholly of our own making. It is a figment, a metron, a device by which we measure the elements of nature. Or, more exactly, it is a device by which we measure the changes among natural substances. The tides sweep in and out, our hearts beat, atoms fuse and decay, and all the great galaxies spin around at unimaginable speeds across unimaginable space. Space, the cosmologists remind us, is merely another word for time.

We see and distinguish the materials of nature because we see them change. We ourselves change. Over and over we are born and grow and perish. Deep within the hypothalamic nuclei of our brains, our biological clocks oscillate in circadian rhythms. Because we are time-bound creatures with an awareness of our "changing face," as W. B. Yeats writes, we are naturally also driven or tantalized to imagine ourselves outside of time. A central facet of our survival instinct seems to depend on our reluctance to accept our mortality. We fantasize about time stopped, time eliminated; we sing about the inexorable turned as if by magic into the contingent. If we can halt time, as John Donne sings, then "death shall be no more."

Such is the dream of the lyric poem. Poetry wishes. Poetry wants to grant our wishes—for a lover, for a better world, for eternal life. Or if we are realists, poetry wants to grant our wishes *to be heard*, as we imitate, critique, praise, and argue with the world.

> *There are two abiding theories about the nature of time and the universe. One holds that time is circular or cyclical; the other that time, like an arrow, is straight and linear.*

> *The hands of a clock turn around. Grains of sand fall in an*
> *hourglass.*

Our deepest wish is to prevent time. This wish has enchanted poets from the beginning. "Beyond all hope," Sappho sings in a fragment to Atthis, "I prayed those timeless / days we spent might be made twice as long." Two millennia later, Chidiock Tichborne's wrenching self-elegy exposes with unmatched pathos the paradox at the heart of time and the lyric instant. His execution in the Tower imminent in a few hours, Tichbourne knows he is a man outside of time, and his poem demonstrates the collapse of temporal meanings:

> My tale was heard and yet it was not told,
> My fruit is fallen and yet my leaves are green,
> My youth is spent and yet I am not old,
> I saw the world and yet I was not seen;
> My thread is cut and yet it is not spun,
> And now I live, and now my life is done.

The instant of understanding is the instant of death. Here the usual temporal marker of syntax—verb tense—shows the anxiety and then the breakdown of narrative sequence. As Tichbourne indicates, when time is rendered nonexistent, only death or obliteration can abide.

> *Plato held that the heavens were "a moving image of*
> *eternity." Likewise, Aristotle believed the human race and*
> *the world had always existed and would exist forever.*
> *Both thought that time, while not necessarily abiding by*
> *Pythagoras's doctrine of "eternal recurrence," was cyclical.*
> *So did the Indian philosophers of the Vedic period, the*
> *early Chinese, and the Mayan and Aztec cultures, among*
> *many others. To them all, the universe undergoes an eternal*
> *pattern of creation, destruction, and recreation. This is not*
> *unlike some contemporary physicists' metaphor of an "oscil-*
> *lating" or "bouncing" universe, as it expands and contracts.*

I'd like to look at another classic poem to show how fully the subject of time infiltrates the lyric genre, even in lyric poems that appear or claim to have other subjects. Elsewhere in this book I have offered Christopher Marlowe's "The Passionate Shepherd to His Love" as an example both of a pastoral poem and an erotic love poem. The shepherd woos his potential lover by gradually amplifying his fund of goods and gifts:

> And I will make thee beds of roses
> And a thousand fragrant posies,
> A cap of flowers, and a kirtle
> Embroidered all with leaves of myrtle;
>
> A gown made of the finest wool
> Which from our pretty lambs we pull;
> Fair lined slippers for the cold
> With buckles of the purest gold . . .

He saves his ultimate presentation, however, for the poem's conclusion, where he tempts his audience with the ultimate promise. If only she will yield her treasures, he might then bestow eternity—a lasting fertility—on her: "The shepherds' swains shall dance and sing / For thy delight each May morning." Thus, he says, love defeats the ravages of time by suspending its passage, keeping the lovers forever in their springtime Eden.

Among two of the most famous replies to this poem, John Donne's "The Bait" continues the heavy conceit-play of Marlowe's lyric, attempting to defuse the shepherd's advances by outdoing his poetic skill: "For thee, thou need'st no such deceit, / For thou thyself art thine own bait; / That fish, that is not catched thereby, / Alas, is wiser far than I." But in "The Nymph's Reply to the Shepherd," Sir Walter Ralegh cuts more precisely to the heart of the matter by recalibrating the subject itself:

> If all the world and love were young,
> And truth in every shepherd's tongue,
> These pretty pleasures might me move
> To live with thee and be thy love.
>
> Time drives the flocks from field to fold,
> When rivers rage and rocks grow cold;
> And Philomel becometh dumb;
> The rest complain of cares to come.

The flowers do fade, and wanton fields
To wayward winter reckoning yields;
A honey tongue, a heart of gall,
Is fancy's spring, but sorrow's fall.

Thy gowns, thy shoes, thy beds of roses,
Thy cap, thy kirtle, and thy posies
Soon break, soon wither, soon forgotten—
In folly ripe, in reason rotten.

Thy belt of straw and ivy buds,
Thy coral clasps and amber studs,
All these in me no means can move
To come to thee and be thy love.

But could youth last and love still breed,
Had joys no date nor age no need,
Then these delights my mind might move
To live with thee and be thy love.

The multiple subjects of Marlowe's poem include love, temptation, nature's beauty, all the enchantments of comfort and ease. But Ralegh makes a brilliant and fundamental adjustment, not just to Marlowe's poem but to all erotic discourse. He shows that, even if Marlowe's ostensible subject is something else—love, death, splendor—the deeper informing critical issue is always time, which "drives the flocks from field to fold." Point by point Ralegh defuses the "folly" of the shepherd's "shallow" promises with "reason," with constant reminders of time—its passages, its damages, its corrosive inevitability. The shepherd's promise of eternal spring comes with too great a price. As Maurice Blanchot formulates: "Dead—immortal."

> Linear time is an Old Testament trope, according to
> physicist Richard Morris, and extends into later Christian
> doctrine: "To imply that similar events had taken place
> on numerous occasions in different cosmic cycles would
> be to destroy the meaning of the redemption." In The
> City of God, St. Augustine argues that man and thus

the universe have a recent history. He observes that since
civilization is clearly progressing, and since we remember
who performed this or that deed or action, we need only
trace the history of events backwards to the origin, about
5000 BC. Even more precise, James Usher—appointed in
1642 as the Archbishop of Armagh—determined that
the universe was created at exactly 6 p.m. on Saturday,
October 22, 4004 BC. To make his calculations he corre-
lated the genealogy of recorded history, Nebuchadnezzar's
death, the second book of Kings, and the book of Genesis.

Poetry wishes. It may wish to stop or eliminate time by its eternal promises or by replacing chronology with epiphany. But my argument here is to
show that time is an inevitable, central element in lyric poetry, even poetry
that intends or proposes to be outside time's frame. That is, time provides
the subject, the story, and the style of lyric poetry.

Here is a rather extreme test case. If, as I suggested previously, the temporal engine of a poem is its verb, then what happens to time in a poem
without a verb? Pound's famous Imagist poem, "In a Station of the Metro,"
poses just that question:

The apparition of these faces in the crowd;
Petals on a wet, black bough.

In the place where a verb would likely reside, Pound substitutes a semicolon
(originally a colon, in an earlier draft). He wants the poem to be an instant
of recognition or epiphany, an instant of likeness, so he snips out the temporal marker and puts in something like an equal sign. Thus, the image in
line 1 *is like* the image in line 2. The poem doesn't seem to advance, or evolve,
without a verb to enact. The poem thereby embodies Pound's interest in a
"pure" image. In "A Few Don'ts by an Imagiste," Pound and the essay's coauthor, F. S. Flint, argue against temporality in the new "imagist" lyric: "An
'Image' is that which presents an intellectual and emotional complex in an
instant of time.... It is the presentation of such a 'complex' instantaneously
which gives that sense of sudden liberation; that sense of freedom from
time limits and space limits...."

But time limits and space limits are precisely the elements that give the poem its dramatic vigor. Surely we must include the important information and context provided by the title as we consider the poem's time and space, its narrative. The juxtaposition of spring (when petals bloom) and a dark unseasoned subway, the ghostly human faces and a rain-dampened branch, the hurry of rush hour and the slow growth of a natural object—these things find force through the procedures of their gradually revealed relationships. Even the aura of wartime Paris and the serenity of Chinese haiku abide in this juxtaposition of "time limits and space limits."

Time mitigates. Syntax and syllable, line and line break, sequence and duration mitigate: So we experience the gradual focus of cognition and recognition in Pound's poem. In other literary forays into the "instant," we might find similar results. James Joyce's epiphanies must be contexualized by the larger surrounding ennui of Stephen Hero's life. William Wordsworth's "spots of time"—those focused instants of memory and understanding—are intensified and envalued by the larger sweep of history so present in Wordsworth's conscience and his work. A poem's local narrative, even its objectivist or imagist "instant," must be read within the larger cultural narratives brought to bear in the exchanges of reader, poet, their language(s), and the epochs at hand.

Time is the fundamental subject of the lyric poem. In the elegy, time is the harbinger of death and erasure. In the erotic poem, time is the inevitable enemy of lovers, the source of decay, of betrayal. Time provides the occasion of celebration or ritualization in the ode; time is measured and memorialized by festivals, rites, and rhetoric.

> *According to radiometric dating, the oldest rocks on earth are 4.031 ± 0.003 billion years old. It has been that long since the earliest detectable molten rocks solidified. The age of the Earth—about 4,500,000,000 years—is based on the radio-metrically measured age of meteorites, which is about 500,000,000 years older than the oldest rocks.*

If time is the lyric poem's subject, it is also the stuff of the poem's story. I want again to explore the nature of the lyric, this time in its supposed opposition to story and narrative. These are two of the diametrics by which contemporary poetry is frequently defined: the lyric and the narrative. But an important problem arises from simple grammar. These two words each operate, variously, as two different parts of speech, a qualitative adjective and a quantitative noun. We may say: "I admire the spare lyric clarity of that hymn by Arvo Pärt"; or "I have written a lyric for my friends in the mosh pit." We may say: "Your narrative is suspicious for its overdetermined ending"; or "The narrative tension in that advertisement for Ford trucks is contrived." The terms are not interchangeable any more than are the sentence-functions ignorable. We misapply the term "lyric" in many cases when we wish to indicate qualities of a thing. A lyric is a poem defined by particular generic conventions, as this very book explores. A thing that is *not* a lyric may possess lyric-like characteristics and thus may be "lyrical" though not a lyric.

My definition of a narrative poem is also specific; nor is it idiosyncratic. Here is the Princeton Encyclopedia's take on things: "A narrative poem is one that tells a story. The two basic types are epic and ballad." I tend to hold to those two distinct modal components of a narrative poem. A narrative poem is usually very long, with a sustained and foregrounded narrative procedure; with a dramatic, active plot (often hyperbolic or symbolic); with a vivid linear trajectory to that plot; and with characters who may operate as individual "people," but also often function as symbolic or typal figures. Time passes, things change, and we learn something in the process. A narrative implies a moral—a culminating gesture that articulates a moral announcement or ethical lesson. Narratives are naturally didactic.

Nearly everything we call narrative poetry these days is more accurately lyric poetry with story-like or narrative elements. What we often identify as contemporary narrative poetry is really lyric poetry with poor lyrical aptitudes. Of course we love stories. Stories are basic to our imaginations, our ways of treating each other, even to our survival. But just as basic is our compulsion to sing. Song is story driven out of its head.

> *Charles Darwin and Alfred Russel Wallace, independently, showed that biological species are not static but change, and change so slowly that the time-span of their evolution must be huge. Geologists and paleontologists demonstrate that most of the species the earth has known are long gone.*

I contend that every good poem always contains both lyric and narrative procedures, the elements of song and story. The story in Marlowe's poem is complex but clear, a proposal of erotic exchange: goods for services. It contains the conventional elements of narrative—character, setting, plot, action—and proceeds by a linear rhetorical design. Each aspect of this design leads, or wishes to lead, to an inarguable consummation. Likewise Pound's imagist poem offers enough narrative details for the poem to exist as a mini-narrative. We know the who, what, when, and where of the scene, as well as we know the brooding tone and imaginative power of Pound's transformative structure. The poem is not, as Pound claimed, "[free] from time limits and space limits," but, in fact, finds its meaning and music in the interplay of those very structures as well as in the larger cultural narratives and genres from which the language extends.

Poetry is about the varieties of measuring, telling, and thinking about time. Thus the nature of its stories varies from poem to poem. The interesting question is not *whether* a poem has a story in it, but rather *what kind* of time-telling the poem undertakes. Time may be suppressed, elongated, distorted, or abbreviated. It may be spotty, circular, or linear. It may, as in a palimpsest or a bad photograph, be multiply exposed. Time may be a field of concurrent times. Susan Howe's poems, while appearing radically experimental, are often rather simple three-dimensional renderings on a two-dimensional plane. Her sequence "Scattering as Behavior toward Risk" is a gloss based on William Tyndale's sixteenth-century *Pentateuch*, and subsumes the free play of individual "soliloquy" within a larger canvas of "political literature." Here is one section:

Howe posits a concurrency of times. To make history apparent, to make history's continuing presence felt, and activated, Howe inscribes one moment or story over or within another moment or story. It's as though we can look down, into the strata of language, to where it is partially rubbed away, where it continues to glisten, where its uses merge and evolve. She wants to show that her texts are "as old as the people." George Steiner says, in concurrence, "There is a common sense in which any human production, articulate concept, or aesthetic act takes place in time. This time has evident historical, social, and psychological components." Even the most inward, instantaneous, or concrete lyric poem, Steiner continues, arises out of a "matrix of temporal circumstances and social contours. [T]he condition of language . . . is always a result of diachronic and collective forces." Thus the "untimely" lyric operates, if in tension, "against the historicity of the moment in which a thought is emitted or a work created."

> *In his letter to the editor of the* Columbus Dispatch, *on December 28, 2005, Hugh Miller descried "an ignorance of historical geography and archaeology." This ignorance, to an incredulous Miller, has led many people to believe that "man and dinosaur did not live at the same time." A 2005 Harris poll confirms the extent of Miller's stance, showing the following results. A majority of American adults (54%) do not think human beings developed from earlier species, up from 46 percent in 1994. Forty-nine percent of adults believe plants and animals have evolved from some other species while 45 percent do not believe that. Adults are evenly divided about whether or not apes and man have a common ancestry: 46 percent believe we do and 47 percent believe we do not. Again divided, 46 percent of adults agree that "Darwin's theory of evolution is proven by fossil discoveries," while 48 percent disagree.*

If time is the subject and the story of lyric poetry, time also provides the material of its style. Poetry wishes to defray the damages of the inexorable, or at least to clarify and perhaps to exploit them; to accomplish this, poetry proposes alternate methods of making and keeping time. Much of a poem's style is designed to delay, to defer, to remind—to create a companion world where the reader may linger before the inevitable ending.

A poem's most obvious method of temporal measurement is meter, that ticking clock. Meter—a *metron*, a thing by which we measure—formalizes the naturally uneven rhythms of language into a heightened regularity. We "mete out" time in poetry. Even the metrical choices a poet makes determine the velocity of time's passing. For instance, a poet may impede time with heavy, halting, monosyllabic stress. A poet may hasten time with anapestic speed, elision, or sonorous phrasing. Alexander Pope famously demonstrated such effects in a mere four lines of "Essay on Criticism":

When Ajax strives some rock's vast weight to throw,
The line too labors, and the words move slow:
Not so when swift Camilla scours the plain,
Flies o'er th' unbending corn, and skims along the main.

If meter and free-verse phrasing measure time, then syntax establishes and configures time. Language itself—grammar itself—is narrative. I do not mean simply that grammar and syntax are durational, though that is part of what I mean. It does indeed take time to shift from word to word, meaning to meaning. But also the relation of subject to predicate, and modifier to object, compels the genesis of chronology through the issue of difference and change. Every word and every phrase imply, and require, time. Syntax is a time-born and time-bound construction.

> *Using the Doppler effect, measuring the red-shift of distant stars, cosmologists estimate the age of the universe to be fourteen and a half billion years. That is the measurable space/time that light has traveled from the farthest reaches of the cosmic background radiation, the faint remnant of the Big Bang. This is the "edge" of the known universe. If the universe is indeed open—if it does not contain enough matter to halt or reverse its expansion— the supplies of interstellar gas that produce new stars will extinguish in about 100 trillion years.*

Meter measures time. Syntax establishes time. And a poem's difficulties, its tactics and impediments, slow it all down. Many of a poem's effects are designed to delay or retard time. The line and the line break formalize this effect. Even inside a single line, devices such as caesuras and hyphenates enhance the effects of impediment:

O the mind, mind has mountains; cliffs of fall
Frightful, sheer, no-man-fathomed. Hold them cheap
May who ne'er hung there.

Here the interior of Gerard Manley Hopkins's lines shudder with weight and waiting. The sentences shut down, halted, in midline. Yet the enjambed line breaks assure the "fall" of the mind into the poem's subject, grief. The second line above is especially freighted with heavy syllables and simply cannot be read quickly, while the short next sentence with its lighter rhythm, its shorter and elided words, seems fatally quickened.

These verbal tactics conspire to control the poem's timing. But further, rhetorically, a poem's troping, its allusive density, its difficulty, require and delay time. All of these tactics are evident in the opening octave of Hopkins's famous sonnet:

No worst, there is none. Pitched past pitch of grief,
More pangs will, schooled at forepangs, wilder wring.
Comforter, where, where is your comforting?
Mary, mother of us, where is your relief?

My cries heave, herds-long; huddle in a main, a chief-
woe, world-sorrow; on an age-old anvil wince and sing—
Then lull, then leave off. Fury had shrieked 'No lingering! Let me be fell: force I must be brief.'

At hand is a virtual catalogue of poetic impediments designed to delay, to linger. Even his sentence-inversions slow us, as in the first sentence, which more simply might read "There is nothing worse." That opening spondee, however, serves to emphasize the gravity of the sentence's meaning as well as to frustrate or defray any more facile insight. Following, the heavily stressed monosyllables in the first line ("none. Pitched past pitch") further heighten the deliberate pacing, as do his repetitions ("where, where"), his intense alliterative music, and the frequent medial caesuras. Sometimes, in fact, we have to stop entirely just to parse the grammatical function of a single word.

"[H]uddle" is a verb here, "Main" looks like a noun but functions as an adjective, "wince" is a verb, "lull" a verb. And what is "fell"?—a predicate adjective? Or a critical pun on the verb "befall"? And "force"—a foreshortened version of "perforce"? The weight and the waiting of things become so severe that line 7 snaps off from the pressure. Even this hyphenate, which elsewhere might hasten a reading, instead extends and amplifies the intense, slow rhetoric of the scene.

Hopkins makes my thesis. Even in a lyric poem whose ostensible subject is something else—love, death, or here the angst of faithful intensity—the subject of time underwrites the experience. Time is subject, story, and style of the lyric poem.

A poem may propose a temporary alternative—be it a dream, a wish, or a warning—to the world. But a poem intends not so much to stop time as, instead, to formulate a parallel universe with its own temporality. In *Audubon*, Robert Penn Warren delineates the interplay I have been trying to identify between story and time, between a poem's local history and a culture's larger narrative, as between a reader's moment and a poet's desire:

> Tell me a story.

> In this century, and moment, of mania,
> Tell me a story.

> Make it a story of great distances, and starlight.

> The name of the story will be Time,
> But you must not pronounce its name.

Mortal Time

Temporality in the poem is a question of limits. We may refer ourselves to that which is conceptually unbounded—to godhead, the expanding universe, the goodness or the perfidy of paradigms—but the poem can only unfold on a human scale. Which is to say, the only time available to the poem as method or substance is bounded time, time hedged and underwritten by its terminus, by death. It is this boundedness that gives time its value and its measure, that gives the poem, like other forms of consciousness, its poignancy and proportion.

The poem measures time in syllables, accents, metrical feet. In the contractual expectations and fulfillments, which is to say, in the forward momentums and earned stops, of syntax. In the variable concord and tension between grammatical unit and line. Time in the poem manifests itself to eye and ear at once. It requires the eye and the ear to consult each other, to register their native sympathies and their native propensity to be at odds. Time and its intractable limits may assume thematic presence in the poem: the poet bemoans the brevity of time and treasures the transient moment, the poet rails at death, the poet is half in love with death, the poet mounts in words his counterargument to extinction. No matter. Time and limit are the stuff of which the poem is made.

1. Time, Death, and Poetic Form

The two poets we habitually construe as bracketing the thinkable limits of the English Renaissance—Edmund Spenser the Tudor colonialist, John Milton the revolutionary—work with inherently opposed figurative fields when they take death for their explicit subject: Spenser habitually renders death by means of fixed anatomy and sharpness of outline, most famously in his description of the Munster famine:

Out of every corner of the woods and glynnes they came creeping
forth upon their hands, for their legges could not beare them; they
looked like anatomies of death, they spake like ghosts crying out of
their graves; they did eate the dead carrions, happy where they could
find them, yea, and one another soone after, insomuch as the very
carcasses they spared not to scrape out of their graves.

In Spenser's poetry, descriptions of death abound, death in progress (a
beheaded corpse venting its "streame of cole black blood"), death recently
inflicted ("a rusty knife fast fixed" in an open breast), and death about to
happen (a "pined corse" consumed with ghastly wasting):

> His sad dull eies deepe sunck in hollow pits,
> Could not endure th'unwonted sunne to view;
> His bare thin cheekes for want of better bits,
> And empty sides deceived of their dew,
> Could make a stony hart his hap to rew;
> His rawbone armes, whose mightly brawned bowrs
> Were wont to rive steele plates, and helmets hew,
> Were clene consum'd, and all his vitall powres
> Decay'd, and al his flesh shronk up like withered flowres.

Here in *The Fairie Queene*, these protean variations, however, bespeak a single
premise: it is the recurrent argument of Spenser's writings that death *has* a
body, that it is legible.

Milton, by contrast, configures death as a species of formlessness. In
what is a theological as well as a representational position, Milton insists
again and again upon the derivative status of death, its belated and contingent appearance on earth, its founding and perdurable absence of form. In
Paradise Lost, the allegorical figure of Death has no proper body:

> The other shape,
> If shape it might be call'd that shape had none
> Distinguishable in member, joint, or limb,
> Or substance might be call'd that shadow seem'd,
> For each seem'd either; black it stood as Night,
> Fierce as ten Furies, terrible as Hell,

And shook a dreadful Dart; what seem'd his head
The likeness of a Kingly Crown had on.

Loosed upon creation, Death stuffs his "Maw, [his] vast unhide-bound
Corpse." In Milton's unfallen Paradise, eating is a measured ceremony, both
a corporal and a social form of sustenance. In the fallen world, Death's feast-
ing exceeds all measure, quite literally knows no bounds. Death's appetite is
never satisfied: it is tautological (the body Death feeds is already a corpse);
it is dispersive or entropic rather than consolidating (the body Death feeds
has no binding integument). Death's force may gather to a point (the dart
can "sting"), but that force is a radical loosening. The power of the dart, like
the power of the maw, is dissolution.

Moving from figuration in these two great Renaissance poets to the
realms of syntactical and musical form, we contemplate a kind of double
chiasmus or crossover. The poet gravitates toward antidote, each his own,
and, according to the logic of inversion, each adopts prosodic formulas conspicuously at odds with those of the other. The poet writes against death
not in general but in particular, against death as he instinctively apprehends
it. And because Milton's formal propositions are the easier to describe, I
shall ignore chronology and begin with them.

Milton's prosodic command is the firmest in the language. It is mindful,
it is unwaveringly deliberate, it treasures the rigor and the suppleness, the
orchestrated expectation of the line as one might treasure life itself. Phrase
by phrase and syllable by syllable, Milton generates the conscious "sense" of
his verse by means of a variable opposition between syntax and poetic line,
"the sense variously drawn out from one Verse into another." The clarity of
this prosodic method, the key to its simultaneous freedom and its control,
depends in the longer poems upon the suppression of competing composi-
tional units, the suppression, that is, of stanza and rhyme.

Even within the distilled expectations of a shorter form—the sonnet—
we can see this formal imperative at work. Take, for example, the famous
sonnet "On His Blindness":

When I consider how my light is spent,
    Ere half my days, in this dark world and wide,
    And that one Talent which is death to hide,
    Lodg'd with me useless, though my Soul more bent

To serve therewith my Maker, and present
  My true account, lest he returning chide;
  "Doth God exact day-labor, light denied,"
  I fondly ask; But patience to prevent
That murmur, soon replies, "God doth not need
  Either man's work or his own gifts; who best
  Bear his mild yoke, they serve him best; his State
Is Kingly. Thousands at his bidding speed
  And post o'er Land and Ocean without rest:
  They also serve who only stand and wait."

In the Italianate sestet, the separation of end rhymes is compounded by an aggravated enjambment until the stabilizing symmetry of rhyme words (need, best, State, speed, rest, wait) is almost entirely withdrawn from immediate auditory apprehension. This by a poet for whom visual rhymes—eye rhymes—had withdrawn to the realm of shades. The injunction Patience delivers to the man of faith is that of unrelenting vigilance: no soothing, sonorous reiterations will pass for action in the harsh light cast by eternity; you must stand (at attention) and wait.

For a structure fully as rigorous as that of the sonnet, but as far from the traditional sonnet in pacing and proportion as verse may be, we may consult the slightly more than sonnet-length passage that constitutes the first sentence of *Paradise Lost*:

Of Man's First Disobedience, and the Fruit
Of that Forbidden Tree, whose mortal taste
Brought Death into the World, and all our woe,
With loss of Eden, till one greater Man
Restore us, and regain the blissful Seat,
Sing Heav'nly Muse, that on the secret top
Of *Oreb*, or of *Sinai*, didst inspire
That Shepherd, who first taught the chosen Seed,
In the Beginning how the Heav'ns and Earth
Rose out of *Chaos*: Or if *Sion* Hill
Delight thee more, and *Siloa's* Brook that flow'd
Fast by the Oracle of God; I thence
Invoke thy aid to my advent'rous Song,

That with no middle flight intends to soar
Above th'*Aonian* Mount, while it pursues
Things unattempted yet in Prose or Rhyme.

We call this syntax Latinate, by which we mean to refer to the firm architecture of sub- and super-ordination of which Latin and other highly inflected languages are capable. And, indeed, the architectural solidity of this sentence is all but palpable, as an old-fashioned schoolroom device makes wonderfully clear (see pages 252–253). "Blueprint" is too weak an analogy for the structural revelation a diagram of this sentence affords: its power is more like that of a CAT scan.

The poet builds an elaborate edifice of interlocking modifiers cantilevered (brooding) over the abyss, secured at one point only by the narrowest possible main clause, by *sing,* a single monosyllabic word in the imperative mood. *Muse* is not the grammatical subject; *muse* is an appositive. The grammatical subject, as is all but universally the case in the imperative mood, is "understood," which understanding is both the premise and the project of the poem. "Something understood," writes George Herbert in the ravishing breakthrough that constitutes the soul in prayer. Milton's speaker summons the divine second person (or His attendant emanation, which is all to the same effect; the god is required to exist) by an act of will, the sheer coercive act of grammatical address, and simultaneously by an act of complete submission, by conceding power to a second person who must always be construed as first, the single underwriter of the universe. And under the (unspoken) name of this single underwriter the poet claims to stand.

The imperative mood has no tense and therefore is not bound by the ordinary divisions of time. The heavenly intercessor the poet summons is eternal, as is the vision this intercessor is summoned to provide. Yet Milton's sentence unfolds in time and, in its temporal contours, enacts a compressed version of the epic poem it launches, a cognitive progress in which prolepsis and retrospection are inseparably entwined. The story the poet proposes to tell is that which made the present what it is and what, except for this story, it need not have been: a time inflected by mortality. Death enters the world, and the sentence, as a contingency, the grammatical object of *brought,* which action is governed by the grammatical subject *taste,* which is itself the property of *fruit* and, conceptually if not grammatically, of *disobedience.* So Death, which to those of imperfect apprehension seems

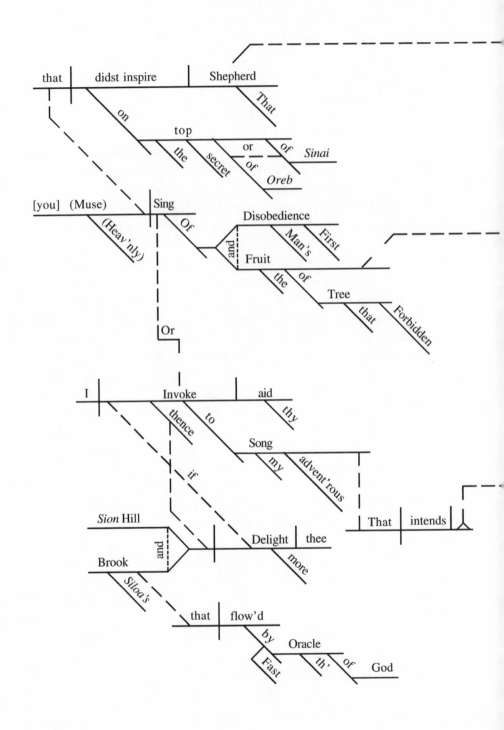

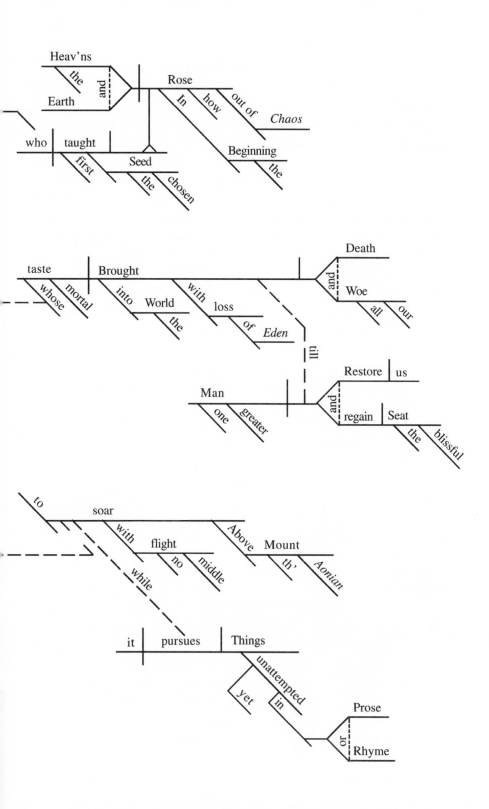

to impugn the perfect goodness of a perfectly powerful and perfectly know-ing God, is unveiled in the context of its proper subordination: as the mere by-product of sin.

The invocatory sentence unfolds in a meantime, the time between first disobedience and final redemption: "till one greater Man / Restore us." Much is elided here, not least the whole of history. Redemption is problematically lodged in a deferred time all its own. The Incarnation, which Christians have been taught to construe as their redemption, has retreated into an ever more distant past, while the promised defeat of death this Incarnation was sup-posed to entail has retreated to an ever more difficult-to-imagine futurity. Is it futurity at all? The clauses that posit a limit to death and "all our woe" may be imagined to contain a suppressed auxiliary verb: "till one greater Man / [shall] Restore us, and regain the blissful Seat." But they may as plausibly belong to the realm of the subjunctive, the grammatical mood that governs wish, hypothesis, and conditions contrary to fact.

This much of the traditional sonnet the sixteen lines of the anti-sonnet retain: the vocational foundation, the production of poetic voice as an at-tempt to conjure the beloved into being. The beloved, in this case the Creator, is addressed not by name nor attribute nor local habitation but by "meaning." You: you know who you are; you spoke to Moses as now I ask you to speak to me. Do you prefer Siloa's brook to Sinai? Do you prefer to be imagined as a muse? an angel? the third part of Trinity? May I call you Light, or Urania, and not be misunderstood? "The meaning, not the Name I call," lest you re-fuse me on a technicality.

The first sentence of the first book of the story that comprehends all oth-ers pivots at its center on a double beginning: "who first taught [. . .] / In the Beginning." In the beginning the heavens and earth rose out of Chaos. In the beginning of their life as a nation of faith, the chosen were taught the story of creation, which story has been gathered in a book. In the beginning, when death was still unknown and, more, was not inevitable, there was a Word where now are only words, which obsessively reiterate the breach in meaning even as they attempt to heal it. First causes are beyond our immediate appre-hension, on the other side of the division made by sin; beginnings can only be inferred retroactively. What can be apprehended immediately, what is in fact reiterated in every present moment, is the cause of first division, so "dis-obedience," or rather, the "Of," the preposition that makes disobedience the grounding condition of all that is to follow, launches the poem. Grammatical agency belongs to the one who "sings," but who is that? The poet who commands but is himself the child of sin and thus requires enlightenment? Or the muse who is commanded? Both are agents in the secondary sense, servants to something prior. It is the business of the sentence to launch the song, and this it does. Before the sentence can end, it must vest the song with grammatical agency; it is the song that "intends to soar." Intention is the bedrock of Milton's prosody. Denying death all morphological distinction and all original presence, conceding to death only the borrowed and perpetually deteriorating shape of that in which it takes up residence, the poet crafts a song that, line by line and sentence by sentence, defies dissolution. Spenser's is a very different project.

I have written elsewhere about the overdetermined and competing formal contracts—to pentameter and alexandrine, to a nine-line pattern of reiterated rhyme, to the divergent representational planes of epic persona and allegorical personification, to the triple and septenary formulas of fairy tale and biblical narrative, to the inherited figures of erotic praise and the evolving figures of Protestant politics, to the forward momentums of narrative and the lingering of exegesis—that make *The Faerie Queene* exceed all usual methods of authorial control. Five parts adrenaline and five parts inertia, the poem is chronically ahead of itself and chronically in arrears on its promises. It is fraught with redundancy, hiatus, and aggravated, crossbred, layered oppositions. Ungainliness is the soul of its poetic method; unfinished, it seems to us now, is what it was always destined to be. If Milton's syntax defies dissolution, Spenser's seems to woo it. These attributes are commonly observed and plausibly attributed to the distinctive generic affiliations of Milton's and Spenser's major poems: the relative dominance of Virgilian epic on the one hand and Ariostan romance on the other. I am arguing at present that something else—some opposition between poetic method and the perceived anatomy of death—is also at stake. And I would like in this context to consider two of Spenser's shorter poems.

2. Death and Generation

The undersongs in Spenser's wedding poems are those of a river and a wood. The river that governs the *Prothalamion* is a tidal river, obedient to the cycles of the moon and shadowed by temporality; it passes through a city whose "bricky towers" are obedient to the cycles of worldly pride and shadowed by pride's decay. The river may flood or may dry up altogether, but the poet of the *Prothalamion* bids "not yet": "Against the Brydale day, which is not long: / Sweete *Themmes* runne softly, till I end my Song." The woods that encircle that other song, *The Epithalamion*, are the woods of a rich estate, the source of wealth and title, obliging to merchants' daughters and to young men of the town, willing to second and sustain their public celebrations: "The while doe ye this song unto her sing, / The woods shall to you answer and your Eccho ring." But the posts and walls that are sprinkled with wine in honor of a colonial wedding will in three short years be overthrown and the colonist forced to flee. The woods are the same woods that Irenius, one of the interlocutors in Spenser's *View of the Present State of Ireland*, knows to be sheltering the remnants of an earlier and hostile population. The uneasiness that assumes melodic contours in the *Epithalamion*, as in its Thames-side sister, is in part a species of social and political foreboding. But the singer's darker intimations also go beyond the topical: bride and bridegroom turn to the act of generation under night's "broad wing."

The *Prothalamion* opposes a troubled mind to beneficent natural elements and derives from the social and political realm a crisis of soul. Like Redcrosse Knight in the sway of Despair, the speaker who makes his way toward the banks of the Thames at the beginning of the poem suffers more from failures of spirit, and from recognizing his failures of spirit, than from circumstance, distressing as circumstance may be. The blessings of a bountiful creation have been all but lost on him:

> Calme was the day, and through the trembling ayre,
> Sweete breathing *Zephyrus* did softly play
> A gentle spirit, that lightly did delay
> Hot *Titans* beams, which then did glyster fayre:
> When I whom sullein care,
> Through discontent of my long fruitlesse stay
> In Princes Court, and expectation vayne
> Of idle hopes, which still doe fly away,
> Like empty shadowes, did afflict my brayne,
> Walkt forth to ease my payne . . .

The very syntax bespeaks a mind in pursuit of shadows. "Calme was the day . . . When I . . . Walkt forth": well enough. The interruptive clauses in which Zephyr plays, a spirit delays, and beams glister admittedly digress, but "lightly," gratefully, in the manner of the breeze itself: this portion of the sentence can be parsed. But how shall we parse the clause (clauses?) that purport to explicate the "I"? "I whom sullein care ... did afflict?" This much would be plausible, but what then of "my brayne," which awkwardly competes with "whom" (meaning 'I') for the position of direct object of the verb? The preposition that introduces "idle hopes" appears to promise some tighter delineation of "expectation vayne," but the second phrase seems to reiterate rather than properly to modify the first. Sullen care appears to have derailed the sentence. While passing through the byways of idle hopes and empty shadows, the grammatical subject ("I") forgets the extent to which he has promised, by means of syntactical contract, to secure the dependent clause: "When I whom sullein care...." The force of grammatical agency passes willy nilly to the idle hopes and empty shadows; they afflict "my brayne"; the subjective binding force of "whom" is abandoned.

The speaker does in some sense rescue the sentence when he "[walks] forth," recovering the thread of action and, not so incidentally, the force of the containing clause. And he will, in the course of the poem, regain the shores of human kinship and studied hopefulness, but despair will retain its undertow. The poem's reiterated movement is "against:" "Against the Brydale day, which is not long." *Against* bears a temporal imprint of course: it may signify anticipation or temporal approach, as in *Hamlet*: "ever 'gainst that season comes / Wherein our Saviour's birth is celebrated, / This bird of dawning singeth all night long." The *Prothalamion* is actually a betrothal song, celebrating the double engagement of Katherine and Elizabeth Somerset, daughters of the Earl of Worcester, to their aristocratic bridegrooms some month or two before their wedding in the fall of 1596. The poet's song is sung before (*pro*) the bridal chamber (*thalamos*), in anticipation of (against) the bridal ceremony, which will not be long in coming (it is almost here).

Against may also signal a sort of exchange, a scale of reciprocity or return: "Against his great love, we have only obedience to offer" ("Against," *OED*, entry 14). In honor of the ceremony that binds the bride to bridegroom, and both to the larger community, the poet offers his song as a form of tribute and anticipatory payment for benefits received. The bridal day marks the public claim on private contract and private affection. The principals and their attendants are surrogates for a larger interest. The merest passerby is understood to have a stake in orderly alliance and sanctioned propagation. His song constitutes a formal gift or offering and in this guise it is recuperative. Like the more specific praise accorded to a patron of the wedding in stanza nine ("Great *Englands* glory and the Worlds wide wonder"), the bridal tribute restores a system of reciprocal obligation whose disruption has occasioned the poet's discontent. His song is offered *on account,* as antidote to disappointment and social unraveling.

But *against* is also and always oppositional. The song that celebrates the pleasures and the fruitful issue of a chaste bed imagines those blessings as "confounding" foes. "Fairness" is chronically partnered with foulness, as though beauty could not be known except as the product of contradistinction: even the silver river, the lifeline of the poem, seems "foule" next to the swans it bears. And swans themselves are "fowles": the fair/fowl pun bespeaks an endemic apprehension, as do the remarkable yokings of "Loves dislike" and "friendships faultie guile." Milton will later insist this mode of knowing is acquired: to know one thing by means of another, to know good by means of evil, is the epistemological fruit of the fall. Spenser paints in more ineffable gradations, but the over-againstness so chronic in this poem bears witness to a similar divide between the mortal and the transcendent. Wishing to attribute to the sister brides and their pair of bridegrooms a more-than-earthly brightness, he likens them to the double set of twins engendered on fair Leda by Jove: those twins are the children of rape; only by an act of violence can godhead be thought to enter the human directly.

Which may be why both temporal and topographical points of view are so elusive in the *Prothalamion.* The speaker describes himself in stanza one as walking along the banks of the Thames, yet in stanzas three and seven, and therefore in the stanzas that fall between them, he appears to be observing a bridal progression from the banks of the tributary Lee. He is both inside (stanzas eight to ten) and outside (stanzas preceding) the city of London. The particularity with which he binds perspective at the beginning of the poem, in the confession of sullen care, as later in the recital of birthplace and family ("London, my most kyndly Nurse," "An house of auncient fame") and in the lament for his patron Leicester, this grounding in personal history and aspiration gives way, albeit inconsistently, to overview.

The refrain is at once a bridge and a divide. The bridal day now "is," now "was," and its temporal oscillation is far more complex than the mere alternation of present and past. The "Brydale day" in stanza one is not, not yet, the day on which Katherine and Elizabeth Somerset will celebrate their betrothal to Henry Guildford and William Petre. Not yet tethered to individuated circumstance and expectation, the bridal day enters the poem obliquely, by way of an extended ornament: the riverbank and meads are adorned with flowers "fit" for the decking of "maydens bowres," which bowers bring the verses by way of association to "Brydale day." So too in stanza nine, where the refrain is grounded in a direct address to the Earl of Essex:

> Faire branch of Honor, flower of Chevalrie,
> That fillest *England* with thy triumphes fame,
> Joy have thou of thy noble victorie,
> And endlesse happinesse of thine owne name
> That promiseth the same:
> That through thy prowesse and victorious armes,
> Thy country may be freed from forraine harmes:
> And great *Elisaes* glorious name may ring
> Through al the world, fil'd with thy wide Alarmes,
> Which some brave muse may sing
> To ages following,
> Upon the Brydale day, which is not long:
>   Sweete *Themmes* runne softly till I end my Song.

The governing verb is "is," but it no longer signals the present tense, nor does this "Brydale day" primarily anticipate the one on which three prominent English families will seal an advantageous alliance. The bridal day imagined here bespeaks a much more sweeping futurity, a consummation not of young men and women but of the Elizabethan state.

How is it that "was" can enter the refrain at all? The *Prothalamion* is all before the fact (*pro*), all anticipatory. In the simplest sense, "was" signals the transition to historical narration. In stanza two, the poet begins his turn to the particular, the topical, wedding: the nymphs gather flowers "against" the bridal day that "was" not long, i.e., would not be long in coming; within the historical narration, this "was" is a species of futurity. And "was" obtains as well in stanzas three, four, five, and seven, all the stanzas that concern themselves with the actual, the bound-by-place-and-person wedding. The modulated refrain in stanza six ("Upon your Brydale day, which is not long: / Sweete *Themmes* run softlie, till I end my Song") can accommodate the present tense again not because it digresses from the Somerset betrothals to something more abstract but because it is more specific yet, beginning inside an interpolated "lay":

> Ye gentle Birdes, the worlds faire ornament,
> . . . .
> Joy may you have and gentle hearts content
> Of your loves couplement:
> . . . .
> Let endlesse Peace your steadfast hearts accord,
> And blessed Plentie wait upon your bord,
> And let your bed with pleasures chast abound,
> That fruitfull issue may to you afford,
> Which may your foes confound,
> And make your joyes redound,
> Upon your Brydale day, which is not long:
>   Sweet *Themmes* run softlie, till I end my Song.

In the present stanza, it is only the second line of the couplet that is sung by the poet; the first line is sung directly to the bird-brides by an attendant nymph.

I have been writing as though that other temporal marker, "not long," were unambiguous, but of course its ambiguity is the most resonant in the poem. Even in those syntactical configurations that bind "not long" most clearly to the realm of expectation—when the bridal day is most explicitly said to be, or to have been, nearly upon us—the phrase has a way of escaping its bonds, overshadowing imminence with brevity. Thus the justness of T. S. Eliot's adaptation in "The Fire Sermon" in *The Waste Land*:

> Sweet Thames, run softly till I end my song,
> Sweet Thames, run softly, for I speak not loud or long.

If ever an inversion decisively fulfilled an earlier poetic incarnation (and in eloquent illustration of the author's own theories about poetic tradition), this is it. Spenser's bridal day is fleeting. Even in the visionary ninth stanza of the *Prothalamion*, when national and political culmination are imagined as sung to "ages following," the culmination is "not long." That culmination is most unambiguously brief which is most sweepingly, least topically, invoked: in the first and final stanzas of Spenser's poem. Brevity is the one eternal verity. Like the river and the song, the bridal day is mortal: mortality is what it celebrates.

3. Death Again

> Ye learned sisters which have oftentimes
> Beene to me ayding, others to adorne:
> Whom ye thought worthy of your gracefull rymes,
> That even the greatest did not greatly scorne
> To heare theyr names sung in your simple layes,
> But joyed in theyr prayse:
> And when ye list your owne mishaps to mourne,
> Which death, or love, or fortunes wreck did rayse,
> Your string could soone to sadder tenor turne,
> And teach the woods and waters to lament
> Your dolefull dreriment.
> Now lay those sorrowfull complaints aside,
> And having all your heads with girland crownd,
> Helpe me mine owne loves prayses to resound,
> Ne let the same of any be envìde,
> So Orpheus did for his owne bride,
> So I unto my selfe alone will sing,
> The woods shall to me answer and my Eccho ring.

When, in the *Epithalamion*, the wedding song is sung by the bridegroom himself, the living terms of its refrain are "answer" and "echo." Its musical poles are song (including songs of "dolefull dreriment" and "th' unpleasant Quyre of Frogs") and silence; its rhetorical poles are prohibition and solicitation; its temporal poles are futurity and something yet more tenuous. This echoing refrain inhabits a temporality even more complex than that of the refrain in the *Prothalamion*. In some iterations, the song appears to be sanguine: "The woods shall to me answer and my Eccho ring." In others, more tentative and petitionary: "Be also present heere, / To helpe to decke her and to help to sing, / That all the woods may answer and your eccho ring." And in others poised upon a paradox of presence and omission:

Why stand ye still ye virgins in amaze,
Upon her so to gaze,
Whiles ye forget your former lay to sing,
To which the woods did answer and your eccho ring.

"Answer" is partnered more often than not in these verses by a modal auxiliary ("shall," "will," "may," or "should") conveying obligation or intent, hoped-
for or probable futurity. Sometimes "answer" enters the verses by way of
"that" ("That all the woods may answer"), which governs the subjunctive.
Three times "answer" is prefaced by the hortatory "let." In one very problematic case, in stanza twenty-three, the final line of the stanza seems to escape
the bonds of syntax altogether. The one condition in which the woods are
never made to answer nor their echo ring, not once in the course of twenty-
four stanzas, is the present indicative.

For two-thirds the length of his poem, in sixteen stanzas out of twenty-
four, the bridegroom promises or prompts an echoing "answer" as a positive
good. The groom "will" sing. The muses, the nymphs of Mulla, the hand-
maids of Venus, the minstrels and choristers, the young men of the town, the
very angels are enjoined to sing. The answering woods and ringing echo are
construed as a sustaining endorsement of the bride's beauty and her bridegroom's happiness. But with the bedding of the bride in stanza seventeen,
and for the duration of the poem, the force of the refrain is largely inverted:

Now it is night, ye damsels may be gon,
And leave my love alone,
And leave likewise your former lay to sing:
The woods no more shal answere, nor your echo ring.

Not only has the singer turned to silence and prohibition. He has also
turned from an imagined sympathy with the social and the natural worlds
to a place of oppositional and precarious "safety." In the language of a formal
spell or blessing, very like Puck's formal blessing of the bedchambers in that
other midsummer wedding poem, *A Midsummer Night's Dream*, the singer
now enjoins the woods to suppress the fearful sounds of screech owl, stork,
and raven. He peoples the world outside the bridal chamber with "false
treason" and "sad afray." He fears "housefyres" and "lightnings," "false whis-
pers" and "lamenting cryes." If the bedding of the bride betokens pleasure

and fecundity, it also betokens danger: the groom from his wedding chamber calls upon Juno to protect his love in childbed.

The *Epithalamion* is not a poem of despair. It casts the getting of children as a virtuous delight and a continuing re-enactment of creation, the bestowing of beneficent form: a "chast wombe informe[d] with timely seed." Children breed comfort, the poem affirms; posterity is an enlargement of spirit. But children are not an escape from mortality, quite the contrary. This is the brutal discovery that attends the Fall in *Paradise Lost*: our children "must be born to certain woe," says Eve, "devour'd / By Death at last." This is the brutal message behind the prayer of Spenser's bridegroom: the offspring for whom he prays will be, like us, mere "wretched earthly clods"; they will look for heaven's light from "dreadful darknesse." Children increase mortality's count. And, for the parent, children increase mortality's consequence; the fate of the self is no longer all.

Spenser's auto-epithalamion celebrates the work of generation and the union of flesh and celebrates perforce the flesh's strict entailment, which is death. The one is corollary to the other. The poet offers his *Epithalamion* as a wedding gift to the bride at the threshold where faith and darkness meet: "Be unto her a goodly ornament," he writes, "And for short time an endlesse moniment." Monument: enduring evidence or example, commemoration, portent, sepulchre. For: in tribute to, or (contrarily) enduring only as long as. Endless, short: a paradox. The gloss this time belongs to Wallace Stevens:

> Beauty is momentary in the mind—
> The fitful tracing of a portal;
> But in the flesh it is immortal.

Poetry's timeless, time-bound business: to trace both portal and mortality, to write against death, yes, but also into it.

Lyric Time

As with so many other aspects of the lyric, John Keats's odes and Walt Whitman's meditations provide almost inexhaustible opening gambits. Time, for instance, as a measure within and without the poem: that is, the conceit of the amount of time implied or covered within the "action" of the poem; the actual time the poem takes, say sonnet-time as opposed to fifty or eighty lines or the hundred-and-thirty-two lines required to cross the East River from Manhattan to Brooklyn; or timing time, the rhythm, the cadence, the metrical time, the length-of-line time across then down the page, pacing time. Then there is the time *after* the poem, relative to its displacement, density, and resonance, the reading and re-flective time, the breadth of time necessary to absorb the time of and with a lyric poem.

"Ode on a Grecian Urn," by nature—or should we say, by art—is circular in time; the reader turns it in the mind in order to see what the speaker sees. The action of the poem is, in effect, simultaneous, at-once with the condi-tion of the form of the urn, its "Attic shape." Although in fact a frieze, fro-zen in time, static in its circularity, the imagination brings the figures on the urn into life, animation, movement, though that movement goes "nowhere," is eternal, "For ever warm . . . for ever young." The urn is a "Cold Pastoral" be-cause it is locked inside its own eternity, in which what is depicted, the scene inscribed, will be always in a pose of potential life, overwrought. Cold time. The calf will never quite be sacrificed, the town will never not be empty, the lovers will never quite be kissed, "For ever panting . . . All breathing human passion far above, / That leaves a heart high sorrowful and cloy'd."

"To Autumn" *seems* also to promote stasis, stillness, except that the mind actively transforms. Yet it proceeds as might a painting if it were read, say, left to right, front to back, even up and down, processes that take time, create time as well as living in time. So T. S. Eliot writes in "Burnt Norton":

Only by form, the pattern,
Can words or music reach
The stillness, as a Chinese jar still
Moves perpetually in its stillness.

Same with an urn, moving perpetually in its stillness, as the mind perceives. The mortal, temporal ashes in the urn may be gone, but that fact only enhances the "eternality" of the urn's presence. The season autumn, as a contemplated object, has its stillness, too, but within itself a whole day passes, a whole agricultural workday, moving from the harvest to the store to the "stubble-plains" of "the soft-dying day." The cornucopia of its fullness, its harvest and storage, must be, in the nature of things, emptied in the end, no less than the archaic urn. The resonance of "To Autumn," however, unlike the urn ode, is that its time is about recurrence, return, and the living, time-bound seasons. The only season for the urn is a cold pastoral sort of spring—"Where are the songs of Spring?"—that will never change. And the only return is the turning of the shape of the urn. Different kinds of time, these two odes: one completely reiterative, the other completely cyclical.

At eighty lines, "Ode to a Nightingale" presents a little different take on time. It is much more of a participatory poem, the speaker directly centered in the scene—not, as in the "Urn" and "Autumn" a "disinterested" observer. (For Keats, "disinterested" is the opposite of sentimental or didactic.) The speaker has much on his mind, though his thinking time lasts but minutes, as long as it takes for evening to turn dark, which, in the duration of the poem, it does. "Shadows numberless" become "Darkling," as in "I cannot see what flowers are at my feet." Time of day becomes time of night, transitional, between waking and sleeping. The light itself is a late April and, perhaps, with revision, a mid-May ("mid-May's eldest child") light: which is to say, a falling light, at the edge of evening, when the spring air feels cleared of the business of the day. So the light is falling through the great trees on Hampstead Heath into the nearby lawn of Wentworth Place, where a nightingale has nested and is now finishing its last feeding and vespers and flying back and forth, singing, between places. Keats is listening, lost in thought, then in a deeper—as he thinks about it—meditative state. The bird, singing, flying, brings up all manner of concerns, those concerns in present time amplified, compared, and analogized in past time—the moment juxtaposed with mythic memory. Of all the odes, this one plays with narrative, story time. The speaker's heart aches, but his mind, too, is pained, numb, "as though of hemlock I had drunk," a deadly opiate. It is almost as if the speaker were more than "half in love with easeful Death," but were in fact close to death, while the nightingale, so alive at its natural tasks—singing, flying, building—is the sound of life calling to the speaker to stay—to stay away, to stay alive, to stay here, attentive, in the moonlight, like Endymion. The paradox seems to be that without the narcosis of the semi-sleep of the dark, the rich awareness of his situation—his intense indolence—would not be available to him.

No wonder he fantasizes flying with the bird: he who identifies with the "pale ... and spectre-thin ... and leaden-eyed." He wants to leave time, transcend it, since time is nothing but gravity and mortality, and all the pain and sorrow between the two. He has eighty lines of a carefully worked out stanzaic pattern of patience and self-reflection to come to terms, to reconcile, with the reality that his "vision" of this passing night has been a waking dream, and that like all such dreaming it may be predicated on time past— the moment locked in memory—but its energy is predictive of time future. We are doomed to dream our deaths as if they were life.

One hundred and forty-five years later, Philip Larkin borrows Keats's few-minutes-in-eighty-lines form to take a Whitsun weekend train from his workplace Hull, on the Humber, to holiday London, on the Thames. The dreaming now becomes daydreaming. And though the poetic form is nearly identical, the pacing and movement, the timing and time, develop very differently. "The Whitsun Weddings" is Larkin's homage, with wit, to Keats's intensely immobile predicament.

Even on The Flying Scotsman, the "fast" train between London and Edinburgh, the stopoff at Hull would mean up to a six-hour ride between London and Hull. Perhaps even slower going south. Larkin's problem, then, as to time, is not the momentary lapse of evening into darkness or birdsong within stillness or sunset shadow to moonlight. His problem is to travel some three hundred miles in eighty formally engineered lines, most of which are necessarily linked or enjambed, including the stanzas. (We are, after all, on a track.) The smug speaker ("At first I didn't notice what a noise / The weddings made ...") gradually becomes aware of what is going on around him, makes fun of the events, mulls them over, then has a change of heart ("this frail / Travelling coincidence"). From looking out the train windows to observing the wedding parties joining the train to seeing within himself and identifying with "how their lives would all contain this hour"—from the sequence of sights and insights, miles of towns "new and nondescript," and running landscapes both pastoral and industrial—Larkin "measures out" and times his train experience, making his great poem a masterpiece of motion and balance, realization, hard truth, and reconciliation. Larkin's tone, as always, is sardonic yet forgiving, since he himself is likewise always indicted. It is timing, however, here and in the best of his poems, that marks him out. The combination of quick strike and rumination, piercing commentary and compassion, judgment and identification that hold time to a slightly different standard, suspend it, then let it go.

Larkin, the gritty realist, is in truth a romantic, as Whitman, our fabulist, is in truth an all-embracing, all-forgiving realist, if by real we mean the whole of experience, not its parts. Whitman's famous ferry from Manhattan back to Brooklyn must have taken about twenty minutes. One hundred and thirty-two long lines, nine sections give him a good deal of room in which to muse, repeat, speculate, commiserate, observe, record, and travel in his mind between past and future, life and afterlife, here and now and when. Enough room that he is in our faces as we read his greatest of all our meditations, "Crossing Brooklyn Ferry."

It may seem improbable, but this extended meditation of Whitman's ferry ride occurs in less real time than the evaporating evening moments of Keats's nightingale ode. "Crossing" lives inside a single saturated instant of perception in which Whitman's hundred eyes take in the entire visual and emotional experience at once—those seconds that the sun is exactly "half an hour high" over the Hudson River as its December light cuts across the south end of Manhattan to reach the passengers and waters on and of the East River . . . "the fine centrifugal spokes of light round the shape of my head in the sunlit water." Whitman's point, of course, is that the Brooklyn Ferry is eternal—past, present, and future—and that we, its passengers, are, in the best sense, interchangeable with those who have traveled and those who will travel this well-worn water path. Whitman, too, is eternal, as the speaker and arbiter of his poem. His credential is his empathy with all he sees, all he embraces, all that matters, so long as these "parts" contribute to the whole, so long as they, "Great or small," "furnish" and fill the soul in its journey "toward eternity." But Whitman's all-encompassing vision—as it is often called—starts specifically here, on this ferry ride between particular, important places. It is "the float forever held in solution" that carries us between one island and the other, just as, metaphysically, we are borne from body to meta-body. The most moving moment in the poem, for me, however, involves Whitman's sense of time. Not simply his assertion that "time and distance avail not," that the future is no less alive than the present, the present no more alive than the past: but that he, Walt Whitman, of Brooklyn's "ample hills," lived too, that he was actually, truly alive once; that it is the poem, this ferry of a poem, that has brought him and his words into right now. Yet he speaks of himself in this guise in the autobiographical past tense, past time—"I too many and many a time cross'd the river of old," the old river that is still new, the old river that within thirty years of the poem would be crossed—in the same spot—by a wondrous bridge.

Whitman's ferry, it is worth noting, *crosses* against the grain of the flow of the river; it does not follow the arrow of the current, time's arrow. It crosses time, in longer and longer lines, the way great poetry is supposed to do. This horizontal/vertical tension is what ultimately holds time in the poem, and becomes both its subject and its object. "The impalpable sustenance of me from all things at all hours of the day": those palpable, external, objective forms we call buildings and boats and water and people, they are the bread of our being, the flesh of our word, which is carried forth, incarnate. Of time and against it.

ANN TOWNSEND

All the Instruments Agree:
Taking Time's Measure

This isn't the end. It simply
cannot be the end. It is a road.
You go ahead coatless, light-
soaked, more rutilant than
the road.

. . . .

If the most sidereal
drink is pain, the most soothing
clock is music. A poetry
of shine could come of this . . .

C. D. WRIGHT, "MORNING STAR"

I copy down these words on a train traveling at a high rate of speed away
from the town of Orte toward Venice, then pause for a moment. My teenaged daughter is alert and watching me from across the aisle. At fourteen,
she's changing with each day's passage, plunging forward in time as quickly as
this train. The landscape shuttles by, plains to terraced hills, sun to rain, our
five-hour journey punctuated by the stations through which we pass, by travelers who join us in our cabin and then depart. An enormous blue suitcase
blocks the aisle and thwarts the man pushing the food cart. His cart bumps
against the case each time he passes. He hefts it aside. It doesn't belong to us.
But, each time, he glares into our cabin.

At the Bologna station, two American students take the seats left by our
Italian traveling companions. They unfold their map, point to Sicily, their
destination. They are so friendly. Perhaps they feel disoriented from travel,
or grateful to have found some apparently familiar American faces. I hate to

tell them: this train's not running south to Sicily, but north. They freak out. The train speeds into a tunnel. They know three words of Italian—*ciao, bella, grazie*—but that's not what they're saying now. My daughter, studying her phrase book, looks up askance. The forty words she has learned balance on her tongue, ready. Meanwhile, the young women talk faster, they begin sentences with phrases like "back in Texas ..." or "if we were in Texas...." They pace around, sadly not in Texas.

Next to them, I feel ultra-competent. Of course this is an illusion. I want to maintain the illusion. So I draw a diagram on their map, advise them to catch the vaporetto in Venice, find a hotel. I know the water taxi's timetable. How strange, they say. Yes, I know, I know. But it makes me feel more at home. It's how I situate myself when I enter a new space. Now the two young women are fighting. One says to the other, "Get your nose out of that book and look at the scenery. For God's sake." The other: "I will be hating you very soon." In the end, they decide (simply by not deciding) to go to Venice.

What remains of that day on the train are moments both written and remembered: dislocation and reorientation, distance and recognition. We go to Venice. We get lost. We get found. When I feel at sea, I seek a horizon by which to steer. When I read a poem, I believe I situate myself in this adaptive way. To begin, I take cues from the map that grammar and syntax provide. I look for the localizing detail that characterizes each human voice. I learn where I am going, and at what speed, because the poem itself compels me to follow the map it establishes. In *Space and Place*, Yi-Fu Tuan observes that one of our most powerful human desires is to feel "oriented" in space and time. Narrative and narrative strategy (and most poems have at least the shadow of narrative) are concerned with pace and timing. With placement in space. With dramatic action, and the consequences which arise from our acts. Stories begin with what Tuan calls "untoward events." These shake up our spatial and emotional equilibrium. Suddenly, we're not in Texas anymore.

W. H. Auden's great elegy for W. B. Yeats begins by distinguishing how even the details of the weather help to locate us, particularly when something momentous occurs:

He disappeared in the dead of winter:
The brooks were frozen, the airports almost deserted,
And snow disfigured the public statues;

The mercury sank in the mouth of the dying day.
What instruments we have agree
The day of his death was a dark cold day.

The "instruments we have" for the measuring of time, pitch, and duration in poetry are not so different from those that measure the weather, if by weather we mean not only climate but also feeling. In this poem, "life" is ongoing and mostly oblivious to the poem's event: "the wolves ran on through the evergreen forests,/ The peasant river was untempted by the fashionable quays." The wolves and the river run on earth-time as opposed to literary time. Other people continue to live in their own particular stories. But not Yeats, for whom time has stopped: "it was his last afternoon as himself," the "current of his feeling failed; he became his admirers."

A poetic commonplace: one of the goals of lyric poetry is to "stop time." But this assumption avoids the difficult truth that nothing stops time, or even quite captures it. The slippery and vexed nature of this subject is expressed by St. Augustine's assertion that time "came out of the future, which did not exist yet, into the present, which had not duration, and went into the past, which had ceased to exist." It is easy to feel frustrated when we attempt to talk about time and poetry. Even the instruments we use to measure time are of human design, as arbitrary as their makers. Nonetheless. Each time we write, we make a mark. Whether we record an event, a dream, or an equation, the marks we make occur in space and time, they exist.

In his elegy for Yeats, Auden adds the weight of a larger *ars poetica*: poetry, he famously says, "makes nothing happen." Variously misunderstood, variously interpreted, this clause nonetheless helps to clarify how time operates in poetry. This line marks a turn in the poem, from straightforward mourning, with its limited scope ("A few thousand will think of this day/ As one thinks of a day when one did something slightly unusual"), to a larger claim for poetry's capacity to enlarge us. Poetry does not compel change in the political sphere, it does not cure or fix anything, it simply "survives/ In the valley of its making where executives/ Would never want to tamper. . . ." The closing section of the poem continues to divide the world's realms into walled-off compartments, where "the living nations wait,/ Each sequestered in its hate," where "the seas of pity lie/ Locked and frozen in each eye." But poets break through those boundaries simply by making poems that accompany us through our days:

Sing of human unsuccess
In a rapture of distress;

In the deserts of the heart
Let the healing fountain start,
In the prison of his days
Teach the free man how to praise.

How does this help locate us as readers or writers of poetry? We recognize
the power of the instruments we use to measure time, space, the weather.
It was a cold day. That's how we initially situate ourselves, but by the end,
we also know, despite every instrument at our disposal, we are governed by
forces beyond our ken.

Poets are not oracles (though some of us might believe otherwise), and
our poems are, like language itself, momentary, imprecise, and contingent.
Single-focus narratives with linear progress toward a sure answer have little
appeal for Auden. Contemporary public discourse overvalues the sound
byte, the quick take, the loudest voice at the table. Our public stories are
often shaped and limited by dichotomies of right and wrong. Poetry's task
is precisely the opposite. As elegist, Auden re-defines what elegy could accomplish. Beyond consolation and elevation, elegy is capacious enough to include critique: "You were silly," Auden says, "like us; your gift survived it all."

Back in Orte, the waiter in the train station restaurant motions to me.
He says, *"Buon giorno, sucera!"* He grins at me and wiggles his eyebrows.
I am in no mood to flirt. I frown. But no, I am mistaken. He isn't calling
me "sugar." He wishes to know the English word for "sucera." So I write
it: sugar. How to say it—he wants to know. I say it. He draws an ink box
around the word, reaches into the cooler, and hands me a Coke. "Sugar!"
he says. Poems ask us to read for nuance, to balance uncertainties. Even ri-
diculous uncertainties. A mark of genius, I read somewhere, is a mind capable of simultaneously holding two contradictory thoughts. Ezra Pound's
definition of image follows naturally from this: Image is "an emotional and
intellectual complex" rendered in an "instant of time." Figurative language
inevitably generates multiple readings because images embody the nuance
and multiplicity of momentary observation, here and then gone. Metaphors
slow us until we seem to live on poetry-time. When we read poetry we accommodate ourselves to the time pattern and pace that the poem initiates.

The particulars of poetic language act, in Yi-Fu Tuan's words, to "increase the burden of awareness" for a reader, rather than to provide final answers.

The English poet John Clare had a felicitous habit of wandering and writing throughout the course of a day, no goal or destination in mind. Traveling by foot, noting and recording the shifts and changes in the fields and woods around his native Helpstone, Clare left behind a record of daily life that is both particular and strange, where "crows crowd croaking over head,/ Hastening to the woods to bed." In *A New Theory for American Poetry*, Angus Fletcher argues that Clare's poems speak strongly to us because they expertly record action as it is lived in a particular place and time. We trust the wisdom that arises from the simple quotidian detail Clare sets down. Not only does a local landscape emerge out of these details, but so does a sense of the actual, or "time lived." Clare generates poetry out of the minutiae of bird's nests, tree boles, hedgerows, and we walk to the rhythm of his particular stride. His active, restless mind resides in these details; his poems continue to feel alive because they record the animals, plants, and acres that hum with a similar life. He locates himself by writing the scene, and in doing so, Fletcher says, he captures "a chastening and natural sense of the shortness of life, engaging us to wonder what we may be doing, being here at all, in the first place."

Clare's willingness to roam without a destination is consistent with a poetic intelligence based on diurnal knowledge. Diurnal knowledge, Fletcher says, is "the awareness of the daily, quotidian round of life . . . [which] connects us to the major traditional extensions of diurnal time, namely, the myth and fact of the changing seasons, often rendered as an undated yearly calendar." Clare finds his best self in the midst of this landscape, he rolls through these cycles, watching and recording as he goes. Transcendence or escape from these patterns is not possible for Clare. They embed themselves in his life.

In contrast to Clare's direct present tense meditations on time and place, poetry based on mythic stories must contend with an already established narrative pattern. In myth and fairy tale, transformative encounters jostle the presiding order. From the broken parts of the old order, in the aftermath, the words "once upon a time" cast a shaping net across the field of the story. But as Roland Barthes says in *Mythologies*, myth is also a conveyance for ideology. As such, the boundaries it institutes are static, conservative, and resistant to other outcomes. Is mythic time the closest thing we have to "stopped time"? No. Mythic time is not stopped time, but "never-time," or timelessness. It has remarkable scope. Its span is seemingly predetermined, already under way, and finished, all at once. Its very distance from us is what makes it feel true or universal rather than incidental or human.

Jorie Graham's "Self-Portrait as Apollo and Daphne" considers our impulse to shape and control time, and in the process refuses to let the script play out in the usual way. The "usual way" in a narrative of pursuit is that Apollo ought to capture Daphne. The myth differs from other, similar, stories because Daphne has no desire to be caught, and gives up her human form in order to avoid Apollo's touch. Daphne, in Graham's version, is a woman in a troubled and long-standing relationship, tired of cycling around the same arguments. "The truth is," the narrator says, "this had been going on for a long time during which they both wanted it to last." No way out in the current storyline, Daphne chooses to "go under, she would leave him the freedom// his autograph all over it, slipping, trying to notch it." Avoiding his gaze, his touch, avoiding possession, she steps out of the storyline and evades the ordinary inevitable outcome:

> she would not be the end towards which he was ceaselessly tending,
> she would not give shape to his hurry by being
> > its destination,
> it was wrong this progress, it was a quick iridescence
> on the back of some other thing, unimaginable, a flash on the wing of . . .

—on the wing of nothing. She refuses to play out the scene; she becomes instead

> part of the view not one of the actors [. . .]
> . . . .
> but the air the birds call in,
> the air their calls going unanswered marry in,
> . . . .
> and the air all round them neither full nor empty,
> but holding them, holding them, untouched, untransformed.

She turns into a tree. Graham focuses here on the gaps the tree branches enclose, the birds that occupy those gaps, diurnal life continuing, "the view" embedded with her presence.

Graham's poem doesn't revise myth or provide an alternate ending to the story. Its ending is always, and already, determined. What she provides instead is a delay, a pause in the syntax. She holds the plot's forward motion in abeyance in order to see the old story through a new lens. Where the story starts, and how it progresses, or fails to progress, is as important as how it ends, as Susan Stewart notes in *The Open Studio*:

> *In media res* "into the middle of things" is how Horace's famous rule to the young poet or maker is usually translated—to begin in the middle of the action, immersed in its density. . . . From this vantage, the poet can work forward or backward in time, establish causality after the fact, and bring consequence up against its instantiating moment. A mobility in time is made possible by beginning in this way, and beginnings of artworks acquire an independence from the contingency of real or experienced time, the time of existence and the time of history.

As pace and a sense of duration are embedded in the grammar of our sentences, as our lineation and stanzaic choices work to pitch these sentences into a faster or more leisurely pace, so too does the narrator's stance affect how we experience the time frame of the poem. Graham delays the ending by extending the duration of the moment, by detailing the transformation itself. The poem is limited in its scope by the nature of the story, and where it always ends. But her Daphne differs from other versions by the manner in which she "puts on" diurnal knowledge when she assumes the body of the tree. She slows down to recognize the quality of the air, the bird calls, the weight and pressure of the landscape itself.

In another poem that retells a mythic narrative, Louise Bogan's "Medusa," the constraints of mythic time influence Bogan's depiction of action and character, as well as her choice of syntax. The poem begins simply, by recounting in past tense, the surroundings as they appear just prior to the poem's climactic event, when Medusa looks at the narrator and turns her to stone. But first, the narrator must

> . . . come to the house, in a cave of trees,
> Facing a sheer sky.
> Everything moved,—a bell hung ready to strike,
> Sun and reflection wheeled by.

All is in readiness, yet nothing has happened. The first stanza anticipates the plot's leap forward. Still, the cyclical pattern of the seasons continues, the "sun and reflection wheeled by." In the second stanza, the scene congeals into still life "when the bare eyes were before me/ And the hissing hair,/ Held up at a window, seen through a door. . . ." The images stiffen into an almost sculptural stillness. Mythic retelling in this case mixes death, desire, and fate into a "dead scene forever now," image "fixed" in memory, part of the permanent record, iconic, traumatic:

> This is a dead scene forever now.
> Nothing will ever stir.
> The end will never brighten it more than this,
> Nor the rain blur.
>
> The water will always fall, and will not fall,
> And the tipped bell make no sound.
> The grass will always be growing for hay
> Deep on the ground.

The bell has halted in midswing, the day is balanced on its axis. The tense shift in the final three stanzas demonstrates a future already assured, and thus emptied of possibility. "Nothing will," "the end will," "the water will"—these phrases, and so many others, force the plot into a straight line, a dead end:

> And I shall stand here like a shadow
> Under the great balanced day,
> My eyes on the yellow dust, that was lifting in the wind,
> And does not drift away.

The narrator of the poem stands frozen "under the great balanced day." As Plath says, "fixed stars / Govern a life." For this poem, for many poems that rely on myth as a source, "the great balanced day" is a day of both perfect beauty and perfect death.

When a long-established cycle breaks, or seems to break, it is difficult to trust the change, to know if it is permanent or aberrant. Some beauty cannot to be trusted. So used to the seasons of racism, so used to the face of fear, the weather-watchers in Jean Toomer's "November Cotton Flower" aren't sure how to read what they witness. Is it a harbinger of things to come? In a season of doubt, Toomer writes of the sudden and startling appearance of a bloom on a cotton plant, the flower undeniably out of season:

Old folks were startled, and it soon assumed
Significance. Superstition saw
Something it had never seen before:
Brown eyes that loved without a trace of fear,
Beauty so sudden for that time of year.

The old folks who "were startled" rely on seasonal patterns simply in order to abide. What Toomer labels superstition might also be called diurnal knowledge. But this poem suggests a future where the world runs by different clocks, where brown eyes might love "without a trace of fear." Something new has arrived. Those who witness the sudden blossoming feel lost. They don't know whether to believe it. Toomer seeks transformation *inside* of diurnal knowledge. It's unsettling, he says, to see beauty where you don't expect to find it. May it last. In the time frame of this poem, Toomer suggests, it probably won't.

The forward passage of time emerges out of the grammar of the sentence, out of each choice the poet makes regarding cadence, line break, punctuation, or a poem's division into stanzas, what John Donne calls the poem's "pretty rooms." As we mouth the words, follow them with a finger, or declaim them aloud, however we receive them we do so through time and in time. Even as these instruments of time's measurement establish boundaries around experience, they may also be unsettled by the meaning of the poem itself. Adam Phillips, in *Equals*, wonders how long any of our claims can remain "true." Perhaps, he speculates, only in the moment we speak it can we be "held to our beliefs":

. . . to foist a consistency upon ourselves is to freeze time; to hold
something back by holding something over. . . . It seems to me right
that the truth is in the moment, and that what we can say about
what we believe is always of the moment. And that our beliefs, such
as they are, are only what we can say about them. . . . What we might
refer to as truths or beliefs are momentary bulletins from a continually evolving project.

This too "was Montaigne's concern," Angus Fletcher tells us. Wary of "re-penting earlier errors," Montaigne "perceived that early and late are fused in a cyclical movement of actual life which is so lacking in forward thrust that, instead of progression, we should speak of living as a state of "natural drunkenness." Julia Kristeva suggests that we should view a character not as a unified person but as a "series of events," or "insoluble problems." As she recognizes, we erect boundaries and rules to bring some order to chaos. In the process of creating a character, person, or voice, the author, Kristeva says, "thus gains a defense against the torment caused by the unknown, and . . . can replace grief with the intermittencies of a plot of his own devis-ing. . . ." Narrating "solves" anxiety, or at least temporarily holds it at bay, by giving it a limited scope and shape. Just as mapping out a route for train travel, or learning another word for a thing, can clarify a moment, so too can storytelling calm the "insoluble problems" of the self.

The stories, landscape, and diction of the rural South are essential to C. D. Wright's poetic sequence, *Deepstep Come Shining*. Firmly located in the landscape out of which the language arises, this collection passes on knowledge that is meteorological, geological, spatial, culinary, herbal, and erotic. Local knowledge enriches, it alarms and destabilizes, it helps to de-fines what feels "real." Further, being rooted in a place helps us distinguish the inherited knowledge that continues its forward motion inside each of us:

> There are enough signs. Of the lack of tenderness in the
> world. And yet. And yet. All you have to do is ask. Anyone
> here can extol the virtues of an onion. Where to get barbeque
> minced, pulled, or chopped. The hour of the day they have
> known the thorn of love.

The stories she embeds here are not "timeless" and do not seek to represent universal virtues. Rather, they rely on narrative present tense, recognize the "virtues of an onion" or the necessity of recording the fragile and ephemeral, whether it appears as folk wisdom, as a source of sustenance ("where to get barbeque") or as gift of a moment when, in Clare's words, the "crows crowd croaking over head."

However, the more we, Clare-like, strive to live in the diurnal moment, the more we are pained by our passage through time. "The fact is," Pascal says, "the present usually hurts." An entirely human desire to capture and hold past, present and future confounds us, leads us to rely on nostalgic re-telling, formulated plot, wishful thinking. According, again, to Pascal, "We are so unwise that we wander about in times that do not belong to us; and do not think of the only one that does; so vain that we dream of times that are not and blindly flee the only one that is.... Thus we never actually live, but hope to live, and since we are always planning how to be happy, it is inevitable that we should never be so." In the poem "Morning Star," from her collection *Tremble*, Wright captures the push and pull of this conflict within us: "It is a living/ season [...] / If the most sidereal/ drink is pain, the most soothing/ clock is music. A poetry/ of shine could come of this."

In Richard Wilbur's "The Reader," a woman returns once again to the books of her childhood. She takes pleasure in the reading itself, the way the page "turns now with a scuffing sound." But why read again? What does reading mean when you already know the ending ahead? She doesn't read to see what happens next—she already knows. Instead, her re-reading opens up the nuances of before-knowledge, as she watches, again, how characters are altered by time: "She sees their first and final selves at once,/ As a god might to whom all time is now." For the pleasure of living the moment all over again, even recognizing the consequences, she

> Still turns enchanted to the next bright page
> . . . .
> Caught in the flow of things wherever bound,
> The blind delight of being, ready still
> To enter life on life and see them through.

Not only does she enjoy the moment again, but out of that enjoyment grows an enlarged sensitivity to the manner in which time passes.

To see us all through—the subject of time is embedded in all of the essays in this collection, from the erotic's passionate engagement with the body and its changing face, to the pastoral's yearning gesture toward a nostalgic Eden, to elegy's direct ritual of mourning. To speak of time is to nod cautiously toward our own endings. In this regard, all the instruments agree. We're headed only one way. Time is, of course, always running, train, clock, line, poem, pulse, and heart.

About the Authors

DAVID BAKER is author or editor of ten previous books, including *Midwest Eclogue* (poems, W. W. Norton, 2005), *Treatise on Touch: Selected Poems* (Arc Publications, 2006), and *Heresy and the Ideal: On Contemporary Poetry* (criticism, University of Arkansas Press, 2000). He is Professor of English at Denison University where he holds the Thomas B. Fordham Chair of Literature and Writing. He also serves as Poetry Editor of the *Kenyon Review*.

LINDA GREGERSON is the author, most recently, of *Waterborne* (poems, Houghton Mifflin, 2002) and *Negative Capability: Contemporary American Poetry* (criticism, Michigan Poets on Poetry Series, 2001). Among her honors are an Academy Award in Literature from the American Academy of Arts and Letters and the Kingsley Tufts Poetry Award. She is the Frederick G. L. Huetwell Professor of English at the University of Michigan.

RICHARD JACKSON is the author of nine books of poetry, recently *Half Lives: Petrarchan Poems* (Autumn House Press, 2004), *Unauthorized Autobiography: New and Selected Poems* (Ashland Poetry Press, 2003), and *Heartwall* (University of Massachusetts Press, 2000), and two books of criticism. He has been awarded Guggenheim, Fulbright, and National Endowment for the Arts fellowships. Jackson teaches at University of Tennessee (Chattanooga) and in Vermont College's MFA Program in Writing.

ERIC PANKEY is the author, most recently, of *Reliquaries* (Ausable Press, 2005), *Oracle Figures* (Ausable Press, 2002), and *Cenotaph* (Alfred A. Knopf, 2000). His work has been supported by fellowships from the Ingram Merrill Foundation, the National Endowment for the Arts, and the John Simon Guggenheim Memorial Foundation. He is Professor of English and holds the Heritage Chair in Writing at George Mason University.

CARL PHILLIPS has published eight books of poetry, including *Riding Westward* (Farrar, Straus & Giroux, 2006) and *The Rest of Love* (FSG, 2004), as well as *Coin of the Realm: Essays on the Life and Art of Poetry* (Graywolf Press, 2004). His honors include the Kingsley Tufts Award, the Theodore Roethke Memorial Prize, and fellowships from the Guggenheim Foundation and the Library of Congress. He teaches at Washington University in St. Louis.

STANLEY PLUMLY has two books forthcoming from W. W. Norton: *Old Heart* (poems), September 2007, and *Posthumous Keats: A Meditation on Poetry Immortality*, January 2008. He is a Distinguished University Professor at the University of Maryland, College Park.

ANN TOWNSEND is the author of *The Coronary Garden* (Sarabande Books, 2005) and *Dime Store Erotics* (Silverfish Review Press, 1998). Among her honors are prizes and fellowships from the National Endowment for the Arts, the Ohio Arts Council, *The Nation* / Discovery Award, and the Pushcart Prize. She is Professor of English at Denison University, where she serves as Director of the Creative Writing Program.

Acknowledgments

Portions of this book first appeared in earlier versions in the following journals, to whose editors we extend our collective gratitude:

> *The Georgia Review* for the section "On the Sublime"
> *The Gettysburg Review* for Ann Townsend's "Meretricious Kisses"
> *The Kenyon Review* for Linda Gregerson's "Rhetorical Contract in the Erotic Poem"
> *Literary Imagination* for David Baker's "To Think of Time"
> *The Southern Review* for the section "On the Pastoral"
> *TriQuarterly* for Linda Gregerson's "Ode and Empire"
> *The Virginia Quarterly Review* for the section "On Meditation and Mediation" and David Baker's "Elegy and Eros"
> Linda Gregerson's "Mortal Time" is abbreviated from "Anatomizing Death," first published in *Imagining Death in Spencer and Milton*, eds. Bellamy, Cheney, Schoenfeldt (2003, Palgrave Macmillan).

The editors of this book are grateful to Denison University for its support of this project. We wish to extend our love and gratitude to those who have helped this project grow. The poet and critic Patricia Clark worked from the beginning with generosity and guiding intelligence as the organizer and moderator of each of our AWP panels. Judith Lyon first suggested that we convert our AWP lectures into essays and collect them in a book. Jeff Shotts and Fiona McCrae at Graywolf Press have been most gracious guides as this book has come to completion. To these good friends we extend our collective voice of thanks.

And to our daughter, Katherine Baker, our lasting love.

The text of *Radiant Lyre* has been set in Adobe Jenson Pro, a typeface designed by Robert Slimbach that captures the essence of Nicolas Jenson's roman and Ludovico degli Arrighi's italic typeface designs. Book design by Wendy Holdman. Composition by Prism Publishing Center. Manufactured by Friesens on acid-free paper.